TEXT WARS

TEXT WARS

Communication, Censorship, Freedom, and Responsibility

Edited by

HILDA DAVID
and
FRANCIS JARMAN

OXFORD
UNIVERSITY PRESS

OXFORD
UNIVERSITY PRESS

Oxford University Press is a department of the University of Oxford. It furthers the University's objective of excellence in research, scholarship, and education by publishing worldwide. Oxford is a registered trademark of Oxford University Press in the UK and in certain other countries.

Published in India by
Oxford University Press
22 Workspace, 2nd Floor, 1/22 Asaf Ali Road, New Delhi 110002, India

First edition published in 2021

ISBN-13 (print edition): 978-0-19-949907-6
ISBN-10 (print edition): 0-19-949907-1

ISBN-13 (eBook): 978-0-19-099260-6
ISBN-10 (eBook): 0-19-099260-3

Typeset in Minion Pro 10.5/13
by The Graphics Solution, New Delhi 110 092
Printed in India by Rakmo Press Pvt Ltd

CONTENTS

ACKNOWLEDGEMENTS

Christoph Werner. 'Freedom of Suppression'. An earlier version appeared in the author's *Lifting the Iron Curtain: Tales of a Bygone Country* (Hamburg: Tredition, 2019).

Bhikhu Parekh. 'The Rushdie Affair and the British Press: Some Salutary Lessons'. We are grateful to Lord Parekh and to the Equality and Human Rights Commission (EHRC) for permission to reprint this essay.

Aruni Kashyap. 'At Age Eleven, My Friend Tells Me Not to Wear Polyester Shirts' and 'My Aunt Talks about Being Raped by Soldiers' were first published in the March 2018 print edition of the poetry journal *Juked 15*.

M. Mohankumar. 'Much Ado about a Bridge' was first published in issue 29 (2017) of *Kavya Bharati*, the poetry journal of the Study Centre for Indian Literature in English and Translation (SCILET) at The American College, Madurai.

Githa Hariharan. 'The Spark in Their Words: The Texts Lived by Basava and Kalburgi' first appeared on the Indian Cultural Forum website, available at: https://indianculturalforum.in/2018/04/20/the-spark-in-their-words/ (accessed 9 July 2020).

Sashi Kumar. 'Where *Is* the Mind without Fear?' This is a slightly abridged version of the lecture given by Mr Kumar on 14 September 2017 in the Paul Linder Love Endowment Lecture Series at the Study Centre for Indian Literature in English and Translation (SCILET) at The American College, Madurai, Tamil Nadu. We are grateful for the permission to print Sashi Kumar's lecture.

Introduction

HILDA DAVID

Ideas are a battlefield, and texts are weapons in those battles. 'Text' is understood here in the broadest sense, as an object that can be 'read' to transmit information, so not only novels, films, paintings, and advertisements are texts, but also shopping lists and even clothes. The text constitutes a coherent set of signs that provides a message, the contents of which are more significant than the medium through which they are conveyed.

The contents that concern us in this book—tolerance and intolerance, repression, subversion, cultural identity, especially with reference to India—are more important, and more controversial, than those to be found in shopping lists, although they impinge upon the everyday, too, in areas such as food (see Chapter 17, 'Caste on the Plate') and dress. And we may not ignore the processes completely, since fast, large-scale communication has now become easier, faster, and almost universally accessible, magnifying the problems and dangers that were always there.

The present volume contains many different text types. It is our intention to show the *range* of possible responses to the phenomena, whether visceral, journalistic, or analytical. Some of the contributions are direct and passionate, and of obvious, almost brutal, relevance; others are subtle and reflective, inviting the reader to 'think again'.

The four words in the subtitle of the book all denote complex and challenging issues. *Communication* is now everywhere, all-present, and inescapable, but has technology outstripped our intellectual and emotional resources for using it? Ironically, the globalization of communication has not made communication easier. This is because the default position for most members of a culture still remains taking matters at face value, that is, attaching to them their own, comfortingly familiar, cultural meanings, and failing to understand that behind words and actions may lie motivations and intellectual systems to which they have had little or no access.

Given the potential for misunderstanding, have we been able to develop adequate mechanisms for regulating communication without encroaching on people's *freedom* to choose? The ideas conveyed shape us, how we see ourselves, and how we wish our social environment to be, and are therefore empowering. However, from the earliest times those in power have understood this, and have sought to control our access to knowledge and impose their own agenda. Governments and institutions find themselves locked in conflict with the creativity and conscience of artists, writers, and thinkers, and resort to *censorship*. Social pressure may also be brought to bear to limit or even crush controversial expressions of individuality.

Yet, however tempting it may be, it would be wrong to reduce the debate about freedom of expression to a straightforward binary of good vs bad, liberty vs repression. Total freedom, unfettered by *responsibility*, brings with it its own dangers. Ideas and knowledge create power, and 'power without responsibility' (to quote Prime Minister Stanley Baldwin, commenting colourfully in 1931 on the influence of the press magnates on British politics) is 'the prerogative of the harlot throughout the ages' (Jenkins [1987] 2012, 110).

The four terms used in the subtitle therefore exist in a state of precarious tension with each other.

The present collection, to which many different hands have contributed, provides an introduction to these problems and conflicts. It is divided into three parts, with the second and third sections being devoted exclusively to India.

The reason for beginning with 'non-Indian' material is quite simple: it is because India's current problems are far from being unique. The challenges and forms of repression currently in evidence are only too familiar, in time and space, and it might be helpful to be reminded of them in a broader context before turning to the narrower one.

Yet, there is more to it than that. To claim that India somehow represents a special case comes perilously close to the very mindset that we are warning against here. That mindset is Hindutva, an extreme, absolutist form of Hindu nationalism, currently on the upsurge, that has been described as being 'almost in a classical sense, Fascist in its ideology, Fascist in its class support, Fascist in its methods, and Fascist in its programme' (Patnaik 1993, 69). A collection of texts *only* about India carries with it the risk of falling into precisely that trap, and of encouraging something not unlike the Japanese *nihonjinron*, the 'myth of Japanese uniqueness' (Dale 1986), those (often ridiculous) writings and theories that have so bedevilled the self-understanding of members of another great Asian nation.

None of this is to deny that there are certain questions and problems that are characteristically and typically Indian, and this is borne out in the 'ethnographic density' of some of the texts. Nor is it, of course, to deny, treacherously and unpatriotically, the importance of modern India, or the startling magnificence of the earlier cultures of the subcontinent.[1]

India's own *nihonjinron* are easy to find—for instance, the mythoscience, or 'Modi-fication of science', that has thrived since the Bharatiya Janata Party (BJP) came to power in 2014 (Doniger 2018, 173, 181). A few recent examples from the Indian press should suffice to show what is meant.

In January 2018, at a meeting of the Central Advisory Board of Education (CABE), Satyapal Singh, Minister of State for Human Resource Development (and a former Mumbai police commissioner), insisted that Indian mantras had codified the laws of motion long before they were framed by Isaac Newton.

[1] It is not surprising that a volume by A.L. Basham devoted to India in a classic series titled Great Civilisations, which included *The Splendour That Was Egypt*, *The Glory That Was Greece*, and *The Grandeur That Was Rome*, had the title *The Wonder That Was India* (1954).

Darwin's theory of evolution was also 'scientifically wrong', in Singh's opinion. 'Since the man [*sic*] is seen on earth, he has always been a man,' after all, none of our ancestors had ever mentioned seeing an ape turn into a man, had they?

At the 2019 Indian Science Congress, G. Nageshwar Rao, vice chancellor of Andhra University, claimed that Ravana, in the religious epic Ramayana, had 24 types of aircrafts and a network of landing strips in what is now Sri Lanka. And another scientist, K.J. Krishnan, said that Newton and Einstein were both wrong and that gravitational waves should be renamed 'Narendra Modi Waves' (*BBC News* 2019).

Even more grotesque claims than these are discussed by Wendy Doniger in her witty account of the subversion of science under Narendra Modi, but she also reminds us that many genuine scientific advances were made in early India and are documented in the shastras. 'These [...], however, are not the texts cited by the theocrats, who insist on locating ancient Indian science firmly in religion, which is to say, in the Vedas' (2018, 181).

Unsurprisingly, there have been calls from predictable quarters for the educational curricula to be changed, to bring them in line with these 'revelations'; indeed, for Indian schools to change their whole approach to educating the young. For example, at the January 2018 CABE meeting, the Madhya Pradesh Minister of School Education, Kunwar Vijay Shah, proposed the replacement of 'yes, sir' and 'yes, ma'am' in schools with 'Jai Hind!', and asked for 'national flag hoisting and (the) national anthem (to) be made compulsory in all the schools'. Another minister present at the meeting, Mahesh Sharma, said that 'value- and culture-based education was the need of the hour' (Pandey 2018).

But whose values? And whose culture?

If the revisionists succeed, India will be redefined by having its institutions forced into line with what can best be described as a crude nationalist agenda. When the Nazis undertook something similar in Germany after their political takeover in 1933, this process of synchronization became known as the *Gleichschaltung*. The *Gleichschaltung* of India is already underway.

The first section begins with an overview essay, in which Francis Jarman maps out the territory and, in particular, the difficult balance that needs to be found between (potentially irresponsible) freedom and (potentially oppressive) control. After a survey of censorship in the past, he considers what options are open to writers or intellectuals who find themselves stifled by repression, though he also asks whether artistic freedom must necessarily be an absolute. He analyses the 'five defences' of art advanced by Anthony Julius (2002), before trying to bring the two extreme positions (freedom vs control) closer together by approaching artistic freedom from a slightly different standpoint.

The contributions that follow illustrate, expand upon, or complement the points made in Jarman's essay. First, there are two case studies.

CHRISTOPH WERNER, who grew up in communist East Germany, describes in personal terms what it was like to live under a system that was remorselessly repressive, yet also stupid.

It is not only thuggish regimes that can apply overwhelming pressure—this can also come from the media and the outraged local community. BHIKHU PAREKH's account of the British response to Salman Rushdie's controversial novel *The Satanic Verses* (1988) illustrates how a difficult situation was exacerbated by its inadequate treatment in the British press.

JOACHIM GRIESBAUM addresses the trickiest problem of freedom and control in the modern world: that of the internet. If the current anarchic freedom is not to become a trap, great improvements in information literacy need to be made.

The remaining contributions in this section cover three important, but often overlooked, aspects of the topic.

JERRY PINTO describes a major constraint on the creative writer—the internal censor. It has been termed 'the scissors in your head' or, in legal parlance, the 'chilling effect' (Fellion and Inglis 2017, 18–19), and refers to the inhibition resulting from the fear or threat of a possible sanction.

JÜRGEN BENEKE reminds us of the misunderstandings that can arise in interactions between members of different cultures, how the challenges inherent in such communication are more subtle than most people realize, and how intellectual laziness and sloppy thinking (as well as intolerance) govern our dealings with the Other. Although Beneke's remit is to investigate communication problems between, say, Americans and Japanese people, the Other can also be someone of a different generation, gender, social class, or ethnic group. His findings, therefore, have massive relevance for our dealings with the *intra*-cultural, too (especially in a nation as diverse as India)—dealings that are made more difficult by prejudice and discursive falsification.

Finally, Jane Dryhurst Beckerman introduces us to the life-enhancing work of a conservative writer and social commentator, John Betjeman. 'Radical' and 'progressive' are often assumed, wrongly, to be epithets applicable only to left-wing causes. But shouldn't *all* good writing challenge us out of our complacency and fixed thinking, making us more alive? Constructive subversion can come from the right as well as the left.

The second section contains poems and a cartoon strip that address the present condition of India.

Sanjukta Gupta references/reworks a famous poem by Tagore (*Gitanjali* 35) to warn of the bitter crisis into which the country may now be plunging.

Each of the four sonnets by Peer Khan deals with a different, disturbing aspect of modern India, including the recent 'motorbike murders' (see Chapter 15, 'The Spark in Their Words'). His use of the taut sonnet form gives the poems a compelling directness.

The cartoon strip by Manjula Padmanabhan offers an ironic take on the role of censorship in India.

Aruni Kashyap's work is a reminder of the many who are exposed to violence and injustice, and whose voices are seldom heard.

R. Raj Rao's poems reflect the lives of gays in India—lives spent in the shadow of intolerance, hatred, and persecution.

On a gentler note, M. Mohankumar's poem 'Much Ado about a Bridge' reveals how Indian officialdom often works (or rather, doesn't).

India is becoming a battleground for a war that, in the interest of civilization and decency, must not be lost. The contributions in the third part of the book begin with a passionate opening statement by Nayantara Sahgal, who describes the grim situation that led her to return her Sahitya Akademi Award: an 'unmaking of India' that goes against all that India has stood for and striven for since Independence.

Githa Hariharan draws a connection between two inspirational Lingayats: the poet and reformer, Basava, from almost 900 years ago, whose legacy has sadly been appropriated by conservative elements supportive of the new right wing in India, and the academic, writer, and Basava-expert, M.M. Kalburgi, who was gunned down in 2015 at his own front door by thugs who sped away on a motorcycle.

In a powerful, sometimes personal, account, the Tamil writer and scholar PERUMAL MURUGAN explains how traditional 'values' have relentlessly crushed freedom of expression in India.

The mechanisms of repression indeed reach deep into everyday life. DIPTI NAGPAUL-D'SOUZA recounts how the documentation of culinary practices in India has discriminated against those of the Dalits.

We reprint the text of a petition, signed by 160 Indian filmmakers and others from the Indian film industry, protesting against the denial of screening permission for a number of films by the Ministry of Information and Broadcasting.

In a salutory warning against overly simple explanations for genuine problems, KINGSHUK NAG argues that though the press and media in India may be increasingly unfree this can hardly be blamed on Narendra Modi.

The playwright RAMU RAMANATHAN shows how Mumbai, the city that he both loves and hates, is woven into his plays. He considers the interaction of creative practitioners and performers, their public and their environment, and their often difficult relationship with the authorities.

PREMILA PAUL asserts the vital importance of memory narratives, if the blunders of modern Indian history are not to be repeated in the future.

HILDA DAVID's 'Stories' is just that, a collection of short pieces about people (especially playwrights) who have a story to tell, but stories that may be hindered, delayed, opposed, or remain ambiguous.

SASHI KUMAR's lecture at a South Indian university is challenging and disturbing, yet not without hope. 'Where *is* the mind without fear?' he asks, referring to the famous poem by Tagore. The answer to that question could be: among such young people as those who heard the lecture, who will surely not allow their country and its traditions of secularism and tolerance to be destroyed.

Our thanks are due to the contributors, but also to many others who gave their help or support, including Professor R.P. Nair, director of SCILET, for allowing us to use Sashi Kumar's inspirational Paul Linder Love Endowment Lecture; Prashant Paul, for transcribing the video recording; Ananya Bhatia and Namita Gokhale, for their help in the early stages of the project; Suhail Mathur as our literary agent, The Book Bakers; and Darshana Sarkar at Oxford University Press. Special thanks go to Premila Paul, Jerry Pinto, Ramu Ramanathan, and R. Raj Rao.

If we have missed anyone, we sincerely beg their forgiveness. Similarly, although we have made every effort to acknowledge the sources of contributions and quotations, if we have overlooked something or got it badly wrong, we will do our best to put it right in future editions of the book.

The individual contributions represent the views of their authors, of course, which are not necessarily shared by the editors, the other contributors, or the publishers.

PART ONE

1

Drawing Lines

FRANCIS JARMAN

> Art, like morality, consists of drawing the line somewhere.
>
> —G.K. Chesterton, 1928

Whether they are writers, musicians, visual artists, or performers, society needs its artists: to entertain, to enlighten, and to show the endless possibilities open to us if we call upon all our reserves of creativity and imagination. Artists also need society: for existential support, for source material and inspiration, and for encouragement. Yet, the relationship between them has been difficult and controversial for more than two thousand years.

Can artists survive without the oxygen of freedom, and how is that freedom to be defined? And the corollary question: can an open society survive without creative artists? Wherever political totalitarianism or religious extremism takes hold, artists are singled out to be terrorized, crushed, and eliminated. That is the first topic of this essay (I), followed by the question of how artists respond to oppression (II).

The next section covers more difficult ground (III). We might argue that the freedom of artists should be protected. Does that mean, though, that there should be no constraints whatsoever imposed on creative art? Does that mean that the aesthetic be permitted to operate on a different, and superior, plane to the political, and without ethical restrictions?

If artistic activities are seen as being qualitatively different from non-artistic ones, need the privilege of freedom be extended to every Tom, Dick, or Harry? Should it be extended, for instance, to journeymen such as pamphleteers and journalists, for whose right to free expression other, non-aesthetic, arguments would have to be found? Yet, how confident can we be in keeping these categories separate, in distinguishing between, say, the makers of art films and the makers of (non-artistic) documentaries? Do we know what distinguishes 'great' art from the more mundane? Do we know what an 'artist' is? Or 'art'?

These questions are highly contentious. The concluding part of this essay (IV) offers a slightly different take on 'artistic freedom'.

I

Why should certain works be forbidden? There are three main reasons (or excuses), which overlap with each other considerably.

First, they should be forbidden because of their potentially bad moral influence on the masses, the electorate, the simple-minded, women, servants, children, the general public, specific population groups, indeed, any vulnerable people in need of protection from corruption—this is (or claims to be) the *moral argument*.

Up to the mid-twentieth century, 'dirty' passages in European and American books were often translated into Latin, presumably because the educated were believed to be less easily corrupted than the uneducated. As late as 1961, R.H. van Gulik's *Sexual Life in Ancient China*, a detailed and learned study of its subject that could hardly be mistaken for 'light reading', let alone pornography, contained page after page of text in Latin. Simple folk (the kind without a Classical education) had to be protected from descriptions of sexual activity!

At the 1960 trial of D.H. Lawrence's *Lady Chatterley's Lover*[1] (strictly speaking, the trial of its would-be publisher, Penguin Books

[1] A fine example, incidentally, of the 'Barbra Streisand effect', in which attempted suppression only serves to draw greater attention to what is intended to be suppressed.

Limited), the prosecuting counsel, Mr Mervyn Griffith-Jones, invited the members of the jury to consider whether they would approve of their young sons or daughters reading the book. 'Is it a book that you would have lying around in your own house?' And, in a vivid illustration of the arrogance to which this defence of censorship so often tends, he asked, 'Is it a book that you would even wish *your wife* or *your servants* to read?' (Hyde 1990, 62, my emphases). The jury was comprised of both men and women, and, far from being sophisticated upper-class types, 'five of [them] apparently had difficulty in reading the [juryman's] oath' (Sutherland [1982] 1983, 23); it is unlikely that any of them had servants.

Who then is this vulnerable, corruptible reader so needing of protection? The defending counsel at the trial, Gerald Gardiner, QC, put that question in his opening remarks:

> In a case like this one is permitted to reflect that nobody suggests that the Director of Public Prosecutions becomes depraved or corrupted; counsel read the book, they do not become depraved or corrupted; witnesses read the book, they do not become depraved or corrupted; nobody suggests the judge or the jury become depraved or corrupted. *It is always somebody else; it is never ourselves*. (Quoted in Hyde 1990, 82, my emphasis)

Second, they should be forbidden because of the directly dissident influence of the works or ideas in question (previously docile populations could be led to question official wisdom, or even to rebel)—this is the *explicit political argument*.

Over the centuries political troublemakers have been subjected to persecution by nervous governments. Thomas Paine, for instance, whose publications encouraged and supported first the American Revolution and then that of the French, was pursued by government agents and imprisoned (in France, where he escaped the guillotine by fluke). He finally died, execrated and scarcely mourned, in distant America. Karl Marx was harassed by the police and moved from country to country. He frequently hid behind pseudonyms and spent the last thirty years of his life in British exile.

Finally, they should be forbidden because their very existence is evidence of a free and open society. Just by being there, they constitute a potential threat to one of the chief weapons of social control. This is because many regimes in history have felt the need to shape and direct society, restricting access to knowledge (and therefore the power to act) to a privileged group—this is the *implicit political argument*.

In 213 BC, the Chinese ruler Qin Shi Huang ordered the burning of *all* books, except for scientific works, official historical records, and books by seventy approved scholars. A more recent Chinese tyrant, Mao Zedong, instigator of the so-called 'Cultural Revolution', revelled in the comparisons made between his own persecutions and those of Qin Shi Huang:

> He buried 460 scholars alive; we have buried forty-six thousand scholars alive. ... You [intellectuals] revile us for being Qin Shi Huangs. You are wrong. We have surpassed Qin Shi Huang a hundredfold. (Quoted in Gracie 2012)

The Church in the European Middle Ages kept its sacred texts and rituals inaccessible by forbidding the use of the vernacular, thus maintaining its monopoly of knowledge (and power) and preventing access to ideas that were not in keeping with organized mediaeval Christianity. Everyone had to be protected from exposure to dangerous, unorthodox knowledge—if need be with murderous ruthlessness, as portrayed in Umberto Eco's famous novel, *The Name of the Rose* (1980).

Critics of the Church risked being burnt at the stake. This happened to the reformer Jan Hus at the Council of Constance in 1415, despite the fact that he was given a promise of safe conduct. The man who had inspired Hus, John Wycliffe, whose translation of the Bible into English shook the foundations of late mediaeval England and sowed the seeds of the Reformation, only escaped burning by dying first.[2]

The final defeat of the Moors in Spain confronted the Church with a huge problem: how to cope with the physical evidence of a sophisticated and literate *non-Christian* culture? Its response was to burn vast numbers of books in Arabic. In Granada in 1499, Archbishop Ximenez de Cisneros ordered all Korans, commentaries, and theological works to be destroyed. The only books that escaped were 300 philosophical and medical texts, and some books that were dropped by the soldiers on their way to the bonfires. Estimates of the number of books burnt have ranged from 5,000 to a million.

[2] His body was later exhumed, and burnt posthumously.

> When the mountainous pile of religious books was complete, Ximenez gave order to apply torches to it, and in a few moments the gigantic bonfire blazed, and crackled, and lit up the crowded Bibarrambla with its glow. (Walter Starkie quoted in Bosmajian 2006, 64)

It is in this context that the German writer Heinrich Heine made one of the characters in his play *Almansor* (1823) say, 'Wherever they burn books, there, in the end, they will also burn people' (Heine [1823] 2013, 11, my translation). He was indeed right about the Church, in Spain and elsewhere—it burned not only books but heretics too.

Heine would still be right, more than a century later, when in 1933 the Nazis organized public burnings of works by authors—Jews, liberals, radicals, pacifists, and 'progressives'—whom they disapproved of. Thousands of books by (among others) Karl Marx, Heinrich Mann, Erich Kästner, Sigmund Freud, and Erich Maria Remarque were denounced and thrown into the fire by students. No definitive list of the burnt books can be made since the students were given freedom to add their own choices. Writings by other writers (such as Carl Zuckmayer, Thomas Mann, and Heinrich Heine) are also known to have been cast into the flames. This, in a country that had once had the world's finest system of higher education.

On 10 May 1933 in Berlin, Kästner was secretly witness to the public burning of his own books on the Opera Square. A policeman recognized him but said nothing—after all, only a few months earlier the police had been cracking down on the Nazis as public enemies (Stern 2001, 120). The new Propaganda Minister, Dr Joseph Goebbels, declaimed: 'You do well in this midnight hour to commit to the flames the evil spirit of the past! [...] From the ruins the phoenix of a new spirit will rise victorious!' (*Wikipedia*: 'Bücherverbrennung', my translation). A few years later, the Nazis shot or gassed, and then buried or incinerated millions of human beings.

The explanations outlined here seldom come singly, and the context within which an act of censorship takes place may be complex and opaque.

Thus, in the year AD 8, the poet Ovid was banished from Rome and forced to spend the last ten years of his life in Tomis on the gloomy Black Sea coast of what is now Romania. Was this his punishment for writing the cynical *Ars Amatoria* (The Art of Love) and the witty

Metamorphoses, at a time when the strait-laced policy of the emperor was to encourage traditional virtues?

Perhaps, though this could be an anachronistic exaggeration of the importance of a mere poet. Ovid blamed his exile on two things—in his own words, *carmen et error* ('a poem and an error', Ovid 2003, 207). The poem would have been one of those mentioned earlier, but what was the mistake about which he 'must be silent' (2003, 208)? Had he been drawn into the jockeying for power, and for the imperial succession, within the ruling family? Had he witnessed, and gossiped about, or even participated in scandalous behaviour in circles close to the emperor, behaviour that exposed the official policy on morality as hypocritical? Such a reading might be supported by another event of that year: the charging of the emperor's granddaughter Julia with adultery, and her subsequent exile to a remote island.

Even in open, liberal societies, the need may be felt to bring artists to heel, making an example of them and reminding their admirers that there are boundaries that must be adhered to.

In 1967, at the height of the 'Swinging Sixties' in Britain, the system suddenly came crashing down on one of the rock groups adored by young people: the Rolling Stones. A heavy-handed 'drugs bust' at Redlands, the Sussex home of guitarist Keith Richards, yielded a small quantity of 'substances'; there were prison sentences for Richards and Mick Jagger, and a plethora of lurid details in the press. Shock! Horror! Men wearing makeup! A fey hanger-on of the group body-searched by a policewoman because he was mistakenly believed to be a woman! And what had Jagger and his girlfriend Marianne Faithfull, naked and wrapped up in a rug, been doing with a chocolate bar? Much of this was later revealed to be hysterical nonsense.

On 1 July 1967, unexpected support for the pop stars came from an editorial in the arch-conservative *Times* by the formidable William Rees-Mogg: 'Who breaks a butterfly on a wheel?' (a misquotation from a poem by Alexander Pope). Rees-Mogg suggested that the actions of the authorities had been taken for political reasons and were out of proportion.

> If we are going to make any [legal] case a symbol of the conflict between the sound traditional values of Britain and the new hedonism, then we must be sure that the sound traditional values include those of tolerance

> and equity. It should be the particular quality of British justice to ensure that Mr. Jagger is treated exactly the same as anyone else, no better and no worse. There must remain a suspicion in this case that Mr. Jagger received a more severe sentence than would have been thought proper for any purely anonymous young man. (Rees-Mogg 1967)

If anything, Rees-Mogg was understating the case. Elements of the establishment had been angered by the provocations of 'sex, drugs and rock 'n' roll' and in hitting back they had chosen the highest profile targets they could find (George Harrison of the Beatles had also been at the party, but left before the police arrived).

An interesting twist to this theory came years later, when Marianne Faithfull, in an interview with Bella Todd of *Time Out* magazine, speculated that the frenzied persecution of the Rolling Stones might have been aimed at drawing attention away from a far greater scandal, the systematic sexual abuse of children by rich and powerful public figures:

> We came along at the perfect time, the hippies and the drugs. Because what was really going on was Rocks Lane.[3] … We covered all that up for them. We were silly little hippies having a lovely time. We were nothing. (Todd 2016)

Having mentioned the rich and powerful, we might now ask *who* it is then, in a controlled society, who will tell us what is good for us? In earlier days, it was certainly not the artists, poets, and writers. There are *no* poets in Plato's *Republic* (Book X), where Socrates is made to say that

> we must give poetry entry into our city as far only as hymns to the gods and encomiums of the good are concerned. But if you receive the honeyed Muse in lyric or epic [poetry], be sure that pleasure and pain will be kings in your city, instead of law and whatever reasoned argument the community shall approve in each case to be best. […] There is an ancient feud between philosophy and poetry. (Plato 1956, 407)

[3] Rocks Lane was the scene of alleged child abuse by establishment figures in the 1970s and 1980s.

No wonder Karl Popper, in *The Open Society and Its Enemies* (1945), attacked Plato as one of the great enemies of free society. Ironically, Socrates was himself executed for allegedly corrupting the young.

Who knows best what is good for us? There are eight main candidates, with some overlap between the categories:

1. Our rulers: princes, ministers, and politicians
2. Our spiritual leaders: priests, gurus, imams, rabbis, and other 'holy men' (only rarely are they women)
3. Our secular wise men and women: philosophers, professors, media commentators, and other professional experts
4. Our law-enforcers: judges, public prosecutors, censors, and policemen
5. The guardians of our health: doctors, nurses, and psychiatrists
6. The guardians of our children: teachers, educationalists, and social workers
7. Self-appointed authorities: public-spirited citizens, busybodies, vigilantes, organizers, and moral campaigners
8. Finally, our creative artists

We shall come to the self-appointed authorities (7) and the creative artists (8) in just a moment.

Points 1 to 6 are what might be called *institutional* censorship, which has taken different forms from country to country, and even from genre to genre. For example, until 26 September 1968, theatre censorship in Britain was exercised by the Lord Chamberlain, a senior officer of the royal household, a hoary tradition left over from the days when the monarchy was sensitive to vulgar criticism.

The playwright David Mercer told me in a private conversation in 1970 how, before the abolition of this function, whenever a new play of his was in rehearsal, he and the director had to secure permission from the Lord Chamberlain for the play to be publicly performed. This procedure inevitably involved some polite haggling over the number of vulgarities to be allowed. Mercer would include a few extra, and wholly unnecessary, swear words or obscenities in the text, so that he could then agree to such offers as: 'If you'll be so kind as to take out three of the uses of "bloody" in your play, Mr Mercer, we'll perhaps see a way to let you keep the two uses of "bugger". And the word "knickers".'[4]

Since the 1960s, as institutional censorship in many countries has waned in the face of 'permissiveness'—once one of the most emotionally loaded and resonant words in the English language; it has increasingly been the 'self-appointed authorities', whether religious fanatics or moralistic busybodies, who have been most prominent in protests and demonstrations, bans, boycotts, and attempts to lay down the law on what is proper and decent.

In Britain, one such public-spirited citizen (to her admirers, at least) was the schoolmistress Mary Whitehouse (1910–2001). Whitehouse launched the Clean Up TV Campaign (1964) and the National Viewers' and Listeners' Association (1965), and was greatly concerned about the spread of 'filthy language' in the media, including words such as 'fuck' and 'cunt'. Although common in Britain in vulgar everyday speech, the 'F-word' and the 'C-word' were taboo in formal discourse and polite conversation, were excluded from the *Oxford English Dictionary* until 1972, and are still banned from many newspapers, usually being rendered as 'f***' and 'c***'.[5]

The date of the first use of the 'F-word' on British television is uncertain. Although there seem to have been earlier instances of the word being spoken, incomprehensibly in drunkenness or *sotto voce* as an expletive, the 'honour' is traditionally awarded to the theatre critic Kenneth Tynan:

> On 13 November 1965, Tynan participated in a live TV debate, broadcast as part of the BBC's late-night satirical show *BBC-3*. He was asked

[4] Knickers? It is remarkable what the moralistically minded have sometimes considered to be a potential source of moral corruption, such as the Iranian censors who demanded cuts to a TV documentary about water buffalo because '[showing] buffaloes walking out of the water from behind is provocative' (*BBC News* 2018).

[5] Many, but not all, newspapers have an outright ban. When United States (US) President Trump's Communications Director, Anthony Scaramucci, lambasted a colleague as 'a fucking paranoid schizophrenic', *The Observer* reprinted the F-word without asterisks in a front-page article (Smith and Gambino 2017).

> whether he would allow a play to be staged in which sexual intercourse was represented on the stage, and replied: 'Well, I think so, certainly. I doubt if there are any rational people to whom the word "fuck" would be particularly diabolical, revolting or totally forbidden. I think that anything which can be printed or said can also be seen.' No recording survives of the programme, but [the satirical magazine] *Private Eye* always maintained that Tynan's stammer made it the first three-syllable four-letter word. (*Wikipedia*: 'Kenneth Tynan')

The consequence was widespread indignation. Mary Whitehouse wrote to the Queen, calling for Tynan to have 'his bottom spanked' (evidence that she had a sense of humour?).

When Whitehouse complained that there had been 44 uses of 'bloody' in one 25-minute TV programme (an episode of the comedy series *Till Death Us Do Part*), declaring that this was 'the end of civilisation as we know it', she was widely mocked. The most elegant riposte came from Alan Bennett, whose 1977 play *The Old Country* contained the following reflection by one of the characters:

> VERONICA: I saw somebody peeing in Jermyn Street the other day. I thought, 'Is this the end of civilisation as we know it? Or is it simply somebody peeing in Jermyn Street?' (Bennett 1978, 33)

Ironically, 'bloody' had already been at the centre of a storm (in a teacup) many years before, when George Bernard Shaw, a more serious-minded challenger of bourgeois sensibilities than Tynan, inserted the word into his play *Pygmalion*, which, after its premiere in Vienna in a German translation (1913), was brought to London:

> The press swarmed about the theatre and … all London knew that Eliza was scripted to cry out: 'Not bloody likely!' The *Daily Sketch* speculated on the 'forbidden word … Will Mrs. Patrick Campbell[6] speak it? Has the censor stepped in, or will the word spread? If he does not forbid it then anything might happen!' When Campbell did pronounce the 'incarnadine adverb' (as the *Daily Mail* fastidiously put it), the audience laughed for a full 75 seconds. Appalled by the shallow response, Shaw stormed off. (Ellis 2004)

Preachers and politicians made a fuss, but not the theatre audience, the critics, or the general public. 'Bloody' failed to bring about the

[6] The actress playing Eliza.

end of Western civilization—although that was almost achieved by the First World War, which broke out a few months later.

If there has been non-institutional censorship, through social pressure, from the right, there is now increasing pressure from the left, in the form of 'political correctness' (PC). The spread of this postmodernist ultra-relativism means that it is now unacceptable to refer to anyone who is in any way different or disadvantaged in a manner that might be construed as prejudiced, hurtful, or demeaning. Ludicrous euphemisms abound, and any kind of handicap or inferiority is transformed into a 'challenge'.

PC is easy to mock but hard to caricature, because it caricatures itself: it is only a short step from the now omnipresent 'physically challenged' (disabled) to 'mentally challenged' (retarded) or 'vertically challenged' (short). Even the term 'political correctness' itself has become non-PC, 'co-opted by the white power elite as a tool for attacking multiculturalism, [it] is no longer "politically correct"' (Beard and Cerf 1992, 87). Political correctness is part of the mindset of the current 'snowflake' generation of young middle-class adults in the West, who, growing up sheltered and indulged, are emotionally fragile, self-centred, and poor at handling challenges to their world view (*Wikipedia*: 'Generation Snowflake').

The whole PC phenomenon would be laughable, were it not for the detrimental effect it has had on higher education in North America and Western Europe. There are reports of university departments caving in to their snowflake students' demands for 'safe spaces' where they won't be exposed to certain topics or ideas; agreeing not to invite controversial speakers to campus; or helping to rewrite history by reducing the role of 'DWEMS' ('Dead White European Males') in the curriculum, and erasing memorials to historical oppressors and colonialists.

II

How can an artist or intellectual respond to overwhelming social or political pressure? With outright defiance, naturally, though that is a strategy that often ends in tears.[7]

[7] Some of the following points were first raised in my essay 'Writing as Resistance?' (Jarman 2014–15).

Stephen Dedalus, the protagonist of James Joyce's semi-autobiographical *A Portrait of the Artist as a Young Man* (1916), advised 'silence, exile, and cunning' in the face of the overwhelming stranglehold that the Roman Catholic Church had over Irish society:

> You have asked me what I would do and what I would not do. I will tell you what I will do and what I will not do. I will not serve that in which I no longer believe, whether it call itself my home, my fatherland, or my church: and I will try to express myself in some mode of life or art as freely as I can and as wholly as I can, using for my defence the only arms I allow myself to use—silence, exile, and cunning. ([1916] 2000, 268–9)

Joyce himself chose *exile*—the writer had already fled abroad. He couldn't write *in* Ireland, but in exile, which 'had become both an artistic and a personal necessity' (Goldberg 1962, 13), he didn't write substantially about anything *other* than Ireland.

Many Irish writers—including G.B. Shaw, Sean O'Casey, Samuel Beckett, and Edna O'Brien—found it easier to live *outside* Ireland, which Stephen Dedalus ('with cold violence') called the 'old sow that eats her farrow' (Joyce [1916] 2000, 220). In her autobiography (2012), O'Brien describes how, on a visit to Ireland, she found herself at a lively public meeting, in an atmosphere of 'physical oppression', defending her personal life and her work. The chairman of the meeting had already pointed out, in his opening remarks, 'that it was a rare thing for Ireland to talk to an Irish writer in public before he, or she, was dead or embittered' (2012 [2013], 143).

For D.H. Lawrence, the need to leave his native England was probably both artistic and personal. Lawrence belonged to that tiny group of people who, in a time of conflict and war, were suspected of being a spy by *both* sides. Lawrence eloped with his future wife Frieda Weekley, the German-born spouse of his former professor, and went to the garrison town of Metz, which was then in Germany. While they were there, Lawrence was briefly held under arrest on suspicion of being a British spy, and only released after the intercession of Frieda's influential father, Baron von Richthofen.

Following the outbreak of the war with Germany, the peculiar writer with a German wife and a suspicious penchant for foreign travel was subjected to petty bullying and humiliation by the British authorities. This culminated in his persecution under the Defence of the Realm Act. What happened is described in fictionalized form in Lawrence's novel *Kangaroo* (1923). Looking back, his protagonist Richard Somers, now in Australia,

> faced out all his memories like a nightmare in the night, and cut clear. He felt broken off from his fellow-men. He felt broken off from the England he had belonged to. The ties were gone. He was loose like a single timber of some wrecked ship, drifting over the face of the earth. Without a people, without a land. So be it. He was broken apart, apart he would remain. (Lawrence [1923] 2016, 116)

Lawrence left Britain and spent most of the rest of his life travelling. In a letter to J. Middleton Murry (2 February 1923) he wrote, 'It has been a savage enough pilgrimage these last four years' (Lawrence 1996, 251). While his exile was voluntary, he already had a dubious reputation—*The Rainbow* (1915) had been successfully prosecuted for obscenity—and Britain had become for him an uncomfortable place in which to write and publish; there were health considerations, too.

Apart from that of Ovid, described earlier, the most famous exile of a great writer is probably Dante's, and like Ovid's it was not self-chosen. The poet became caught up in the politics of his native city, Florence, and spent the rest of his life in exile, dying in Ravenna, where his body lies buried—the imposing, much-photographed tomb in Santa Croce, Florence, is empty.

If the beautiful lines in *Paradiso*, XVII, 55–60, are to be believed, Dante felt the pain of exile very deeply.

> You shall leave everything you love most dearly:
> this is the arrow that the bow of exile
> shoots first. You are to know the bitter taste
> of others' bread, how salt it is, and know
> how hard a path it is for one who goes
> descending and ascending others' stairs.
>
> (1986, 55–60)

Yet Dante's greatest work was written in exile, and he may even have been energized by the bitterness of his situation. If he had remained in Florence, embroiled in civic infighting, would he have been able to find the distance and the balance to produce the *Divine Comedy*?

In the years before and during the Second World War, many German artists and intellectuals fled from Nazi-controlled Europe and went into exile, often in the United States of America (USA). Most had no real choice—as Jews or left-wing opponents of the Nazis, their lives would have been in danger if they had stayed. But many prominent Germans, including the composer Richard Strauss and the playwright Gerhart Hauptmann, *did* stay, some for better reasons than others. Strauss, for instance, was regarded by the Nazis as too important to be allowed to leave, and he had to cooperate with them in order to protect his Jewish daughter-in-law and his half-Jewish grandchildren.

The novelist Thomas Mann and his wife were in Switzerland when the Nazis came to power in 1933. Their children called them from Munich on the telephone, advising them not to return—their father had made his contempt for the Nazis very obvious in his public statements—but 'Mann at first did not understand the implications of their cryptic message about the "unfavourable weather" in Munich, and replied that it was extremely pleasant where he was' (White 1965, 8).

Mann was possibly too famous to be dealt with thuggishly, and the Nazis might have attempted to rein him in (as they did Strauss) with a mixture of flattery and threats (his wife Katia had a Jewish family background). But as Mann wrote to his fellow-author Hermann Hesse on 26 July of that year,

> I've had a struggle and now it's over. True, there are still times when I ask myself: Why? Other people manage to live in Germany—[Gerhart] Hauptmann, Ricarda Huch, Hans Carossa,[8] for instance. But the temptation is short-lived. I couldn't do it. I'd suffocate and waste away. And it is impossible for purely human reasons as well, because of my family. (Quoted in Heilbut 1996, 526–7)

Shortly after the war began, the Manns flew from Sweden to Britain. It is conceivable that the Nazis may have tried to kill him on the way:

> Having heard that Luftwaffe pilots had been flying close enough [to the passenger planes] to examine the passengers, Katia demanded that

[8] Distinguished German writers of that time.

> Thomas exchange window seats with her. A few days later, the brother-in-law of the publisher Benjamin Huebsch was shot through the same window. [Mann's daughter] Erika was convinced 'that they got the wrong man and were really gunning for T.M.'. (Heilbut 1996, 568)

Mann chose to spend the war years in American exile, from where he made political broadcasts to Germany.

After the war ended, Thomas Mann expressed the view, in one of the German newspapers newly licensed by the American military government, that it had not been a small number of criminals who were responsible for the Nazi horror, but the German 'elite', hundreds of thousands strong. His remarks challenged those writers and intellectuals who had stayed behind, and one of them, Frank Thiess, responded to the criticism arguing that their 'inner emigration' had built an 'inscape' untouched by Hitler, adding that he had gathered more intense experience by staying than he would have done by watching the German tragedy from the 'dress circle and first-row seats abroad'.

Mann, unrelenting, wrote that books printed in Germany between 1933 and 1945, that is, books that were acceptable to the Nazis, were 'less than worthless, and […] not good to handle. An odour of blood and shame sticks to them' (Demetz [1970] 1972, 47–8). Mann's return to Germany in 1949 was a failure and the country's greatest writer spent the last years of his life in Switzerland.

Thomas Mann's son Klaus was also a novelist. *Mephisto* (1936) is a savage account of an actor, Hendrik Höfgen, who (metaphorically) sells his soul to the Nazis when he decides not to go into exile but to stay and work with the regime. (It is also a thinly-disguised portrait of the author's former brother-in-law, the famous actor Gustaf Gründgens, who chose to stay in Germany just as Klaus Mann had chosen to leave.)

Höfgen is a complicated character and many different elements play a role in his Mephistophelian choice, including greed, vanity, professional ambition, and cowardice. Others stay in Germany for less complex reasons.

> Joachim, the fat character actor, simply said, 'I am and will always remain a German artist and patriot no matter who rules my country. I would rather live in Berlin than anywhere else in the world and I have not the

> smallest desire to become an expatriate. In any case, I couldn't earn as much money anywhere else.'
>
> [... He] would have emigrated and become a fanatical anti-fascist if only he had received a tempting enough offer from Hollywood. ([1936] 1995, 204)

That last dig may have been a reference to Marlene Dietrich, who had moved to the USA in 1930 under contract to Paramount. She resisted lucrative offers to return to Germany, and, like Thomas Mann, acquired American citizenship and worked for the Allies during the Second World War.

In that other totalitarian colossus of the mid-twentieth century, the Soviet Union, exile was normally at the behest of the state.

During the 'Khrushchev thaw', Soviet visual artists briefly turned away from mind-numbing socialist realism and towards modern and abstract art ('Formalism'). The leadership reacted with fury. Attending an exhibition called 'Thirty Years of Moscow Art' in December 1962, Khrushchev bellowed at the artists—and threatened them with exile.

> Are you pederasts or normal people? I'll be perfectly straightforward with you: we won't spend a kopek on your art. Just give me a list of those of you who want to go abroad, to the so-called 'free world'. We'll give you foreign passports tomorrow, and you can get out. Your prospects here are nil. What is hung here is simply anti-Soviet. It's amoral. Art should ennoble the individual and arouse him to action. And what have you set out here? Who painted this picture? I want to talk to him. What's the good of a picture like this? To cover urinals with? (Sjeklocha and Mead 1967, 94)

If the offer had been meant seriously, some Soviet artists might even have accepted it. But exile cuts both ways—for those who feel rooted in their culture and language, it is not an escape but a punishment. Both Boris Pasternak (in 1958) and Alexandr Solzhenitsyn (in 1970) declined to travel to Stockholm to receive the Nobel Prizes for Literature that they had been awarded after learning that if they did so they would be denied re-entry to the Soviet Union.

Pasternak had been attacked at the plenum of the Central Committee of the Young Communist League by its leader, Semichastny (who was reading notes given to him by Khrushchev), in a speech that was broadcast live on television and the radio. Pasternak, Semichastny declared, was a 'mangy sheep' who 'had spat in the people's face' and was worse than a pig, because a pig 'never makes a mess where it eats or sleeps'.

> Why shouldn't this internal emigrant breathe the capitalist air which he so yearned for and which he spoke of in his book? I am sure our society would welcome that. Let him become a real emigrant and go to his capitalist paradise. I am sure that neither society nor the government would hinder him in any way—on the contrary, they would consider that his departure from our midst would clear the air. (Quoted in Finn and Couvée [2014] 2015, 180)

The unhappy Pasternak renounced the prize. Confused and emotional, he wrote to Khrushchev:

> I learn that the government 'would not put any obstacles in the way of my departure from the USSR'.
>
> For me [leaving] is impossible. I am tied to Russia by birth, by my life and work.
>
> I cannot conceive of my destiny separate from Russia, or outside it. Whatever my mistakes or failings, I could not imagine that I should find myself at the centre of such a political campaign as has been worked up round my name in the West.
>
> Once aware of this, I informed the Swedish Academy of my voluntary renunciation of the Nobel Prize.
>
> Departure beyond the borders of my country would for me be tantamount to death and I therefore request you not to take this extreme measure against me. (Quoted in Finn and Couvée [2014] 2015, 182–3)

Solzhenitsyn by comparison toughed it out. He accepted the prize, but refused to travel to accept it. In 1974, two years after the expulsion of the poet Joseph Brodsky, himself later a Nobel laureate, Solzhenitsyn was forcibly expelled from the country and deprived of his citizenship (*Wikipedia*: 'Alexandr Solzhenitsyn').

To survive as a writer in the Soviet Union without compromising your integrity it was necessary to be *cunning*. Under the vilest conditions of repression, literature flourished 'underground', where the *samizdat* (self-published) network ensured that copies of forbidden texts, including major works by Pasternak, Solzhenitsyn, and Brodsky, were produced and circulated, at great personal risk to all involved. As the writer and activist Vladimir Bukovsky explained, 'I write it myself, I edit it myself, I censor it myself, I publish it myself, I distribute it myself, I sit in jail for it myself' (Komaromi n.d.). The term *samizdat* was coined in opposition to *gosizdat* ('state-published'); there were also *tamizdat* publications, published outside the Soviet Union and smuggled in, and *magnitizdat*, or bootleg tape-recordings (Ramm 2017).

The writers were playing a game of cat and mouse with the authorities: if they were caught, the consequences could be horrific. For writers living in a comfortable liberal democracy, an unexpected knock on the door probably heralds a visit from the neighbour or the postman, and not beatings, torture, and death. It is sobering how much Soviet writers were prepared to risk and how important their work was to them. As the poet Osip Mandelstam said,

> Why do you complain? Poetry is respected only in this country—[because] people are killed for it. There's no place where more people are killed for it. (Mandelstam [1970] 1999, 161)

Mandelstam himself died, probably of cold and hunger, in a Siberian transit camp in 1938.

Writers sometimes hide behind pen names.[9] Women writers may conceal their gender behind a masculine or ambiguous-sounding name to secure wider acceptance: famous examples include Anne, Charlotte, and Emily Brontë, who published as Acton, Ellis, and Currer Bell respectively; Amantine Dupin (better known as George Sand); Mary Anne Evans (George Eliot); and Karen Blixen (who sometimes wrote as Isak Dinesen).

A pen name may be used because of the sensational nature of the published work, as when a still unknown Victorian author wrote the sexual memoir *My Secret Life* under the name Walter; the French writer Anne Desclos, rising to a challenge by her lover Jean Paulhan that no woman could write an erotic novel, published the sadomasochistic *Story of O* (1954) under the pseudonym Pauline Réage (*Wikipedia*:

[9] This can also be for harmless reasons, as when an author is active in different genres or has different writing personalities—the most spectacular example being the Portuguese poet Fernando Pessoa (1888–1935), who used more than seventy 'heteronyms'.

'Anne Desclos'); or when the journalist Joe Klein published his controversial *Primary Colors* (1996), which seemed to offer insider details of Bill Clinton's first presidential campaign, as Anonymous.

But a pen name can also be a necessity, if public knowledge of the writer's identity might endanger his or her life. The identity of Martin Marprelate, the author of virulent anti-episcopal tracts that enraged the government in late sixteenth-century England, was so well disguised that it has never been discovered.

More recently, Ibn Warraq has been used as a pen name by an energetic critic of Islam, the author of works such as *Why I Am Not a Muslim* (1995), *Leaving Islam: Apostates Speak Out* (2003), and *Why the West Is Best: A Muslim Apostate's Defense of Liberal Democracy* (2011), from which it should be apparent that he has turned his back on Islam. And—as he told a panel meeting at the 60th Session of the United Nations Commission on Human Rights in 2004—'It is clear, quite clear, that under Islamic law an apostate must be put to death. There is no dispute on this ruling among Classical Muslim or modern scholars' (Warraq [2004] 2010, 322).

Ibn Warraq has described his reasons for using a pen name:

> I [...] should like to continue my research and to travel in Islamic lands, hardly thinkable for the author of *Why I Am Not a Muslim*.[10] And can one any longer doubt the danger of criticising Islam in the West after the Rushdie affair and the assassination of Theo van Gogh? Are Western intellectuals prepared to pay for the security of Muslim dissidents? Most of us cannot afford the luxury of private security guards and must take our own precautions, adopting pseudonyms being the simplest. ([2009] 2010, 34–5)

Another controversial scholar of Islam sheltering behind a pen name is Christoph Luxenberg, who in 2000 published a sensational work of Koran revisionism. A few years later, in 2004,

> [when] a Muslim radical murdered the Dutch director Theo van Gogh for a film criticising Islam, Christoph Luxenberg saw his name ripple through Internet forums 1,000 times and immediately knew why.

[10] The choice of title was perhaps a conscious echo of the philosopher Bertrand Russell's *Why I Am Not a Christian* (1957).

> 'The safety of experts on Islam is topical again,' he said—in a surprisingly detached tone for the author of a critique of the Koran who fears it could one day spark similar anger.
>
> Van Gogh, murdered last week for a film slamming Muslim treatment of women, set out to be provocative. But such is the apprehension among critics of Islam that even an obscure German professor of ancient Semitic languages keeps a very low profile.
>
> 'Christoph Luxenberg' is a pseudonym. The professor hides his work from his own students—even those who recommend it to him, not knowing he is its author. He gives interviews by phone and offers little hint of who he really is or where he lives.
>
> This has served Luxenberg well over the past four years, when his book *The Syro-Aramaic Reading of the Koran* was only available in dense academic German. But he doesn't know what to expect when an English translation appears next year.
>
> 'I fear a strong reaction in the Islamic world,' he told Reuters late on Wednesday by telephone. 'My Muslim friends tell me that many people will jump on this book.' […]
>
> [Although] he originally thought he could publish under his own name, Muslim friends warned him not to. He said van Gogh's murder 'confirms how right they were'. (Heneghan 2004)

A different kind of cunning was employed by the novelist E.M. Forster. Throughout his life, Forster was attracted to men, but lived in a time and place where this was illegal and dangerous. He had to find ways to express himself as a writer in a homophobic society. His travels in Europe, and to Egypt and India, can hardly be described as an exile, though Italy opened his eyes to the exciting alternatives that life could offer: 'The beautiful country where they say "yes". […] Where things happen' (quoted in Furbank [1977] 1978, 96), and Egypt and India provided him with comparatively safe opportunities to indulge his sexuality.

In his writing, however, Forster had to be careful. He made several of his protagonists girls, since he couldn't write about the emotional lives of men, especially his own, in the way that he probably wished. This doesn't necessarily mean that, say, Lucy Honeychurch in *A Room with a View* (1908), his most charming heroine, is just a boy *en travesti* (Gramsden 1962, 34).

> It is not so important that Lucy is [Forster] sexually, although she could be him in the guise of a girl; what matters is that her *situation* is his.

> [Trapped in a stifling relationship with his mother, he] had become coerced, imprisoned in a way of life which is usually the lot of women; yet, because it was an unusual one, if he had re-created it in a novel it would have seemed implausible. (And he would have been more recognisably autobiographical.) But the world is full of girls who live wretchedly at home until they can escape through marriage; the fact of Lucy's femaleness did not mean that her experiences were so very different from her creator's. (Beauman 1993, 102–3)

Other gay writers have also chosen to manipulate their female characters for personal emotional purposes. For example, Thomas Mann's biographer, Anthony Heilbut (1996), asserts that, whereas Mann's brother, the novelist Heinrich Mann, 'frequently chose a female persona […] Thomas rarely treated women except as surrogates for his own homoerotic tendencies' (1996, 112). In Thomas's *Joseph in Egypt* (1936), the mad infatuation of Mut, Potiphar's wife, with Joseph 'is often cited as Mann's rare depiction of heterosexual lust. [But in] his diaries he admits that she's his stand-in, and that he based her passions on his own for Paul Ehrenburg' (Heilbut 1996, 541–2).

The deception may even be posthumous: when Michelangelo's grand-nephew decided, in 1623, that he would publish his famous grand-uncle's poems, he made a number of changes. 'Out of prudence […] he altered this or that masculine gender' and 'softened this or that expression especially in the "Cavalieri" poems' (Tusiani [1960] 1961, 13). The handsome young Tommaso dei Cavalieri was probably the love of Michelangelo's life, and the dedicatee of thirty of his sonnets and other poems (half a century before Shakespeare addressed most of *his* sonnets to an unnamed young man), but for the sake of the great artist's reputation the 'he' had to become a 'she'.

Silence may be the harshest choice. We have seen how, during the Nazi tyranny, many eminent German writers ducked their heads under the parapet and survived—the 'inner emigration'—even though some, like Erich Kästner, were well known as opponents of Nazi ideology. Kästner was permitted to live quietly in Germany, but not to write. His popularity (he was the author of *Emil and the Detectives* [1928], one of the finest of all children's novels) may have saved him.

Yet Kästner's 'silence' was not absolute. He was allowed to continue writing for the theatre and the film industry, though under pseudonyms, and in 1942 he was granted a special exemption (as 'Berthold

Bürger') to write the script for Goebbels' prestigious film project, *Münchhausen*. Kästner's own account of his reasons for staying in Germany, and of what he did during this time, is not wholly convincing (*Wikipedia*: 'Erich Kästner'), and he later 'took refuge in affluence and alcohol' (Stern 2001, 133).

Forster employed silence as well as cunning. The manuscript of his only explicitly homoerotic novel, *Maurice* (first drafted in 1913–14), was hidden away for years, with only trusted friends being allowed to read it. By the time that the social and legal environment in Britain had changed to such an extent that it could at last be published, it no longer seemed relevant. Around 1960, Forster wrote on the cover of the manuscript: 'Publishable—but worth it?' (Page 1987, 118). It was published posthumously in 1971.

The problem of publication—and thereby of self-exposure—was one faced by many gay writers. Their sexual preference was 'the Love that dare not speak its name', a phrase from a poem by Oscar Wilde's lover Lord Alfred Douglas. Asked about it at his trial in 1895, Wilde, rashly spurning caution, spoke up defiantly:

> 'The Love that dare not speak its name' […] is beautiful, it is fine, it is the noblest form of affection. There is nothing unnatural about it. It is intellectual, and it repeatedly exists between an elder and a younger man, when the elder man has intellect, and the younger man has all the joy, hope and glamour of life before him. That it should be so the world does not understand. The world mocks at it and sometimes puts one in the pillory for it. (Linder n.d., 'Testimony of Oscar Wilde')

Wilde got a prison sentence, a fate far crueller than merely being mocked or put in the pillory of media scorn. Gay writers everywhere took note.

While he was in Egypt, Forster had met the poet Cavafy (Konstantinos Kavafis, 1863–1933). In his Introduction to a collection of Cavafy translations (1961), W.H. Auden, himself both gay and a poet, announced, 'Cavafy was a homosexual, and his erotic poems make no attempt to conceal the fact' (Cavafy 1961, ix). This was true, but ingenuous, because no concealment was necessary. Cavafy's poetry appeared during his lifetime only in pamphlets, booklets, and handouts for friends and admirers; the first substantial publication came two years after his death. The poet had made his life in Alexandria safer by sheltering in silence, at the price of obscurity.

If Cavafy chose silence, the novelist Salman Rushdie (Chapter 3, 'The Rushdie Affair and the British Press') seems to have embraced a perverse and peculiar kind of exile. On some level of consciousness, he must surely have known that *The Satanic Verses* (1988) would be found offensive by Muslims; maybe also that, although well-educated believers might rumple their noses in distaste (and secretly enjoy the novel's wit), the less sophisticated—encouraged by their mullahs and imams—would rush out onto the streets, ripping up or burning a book that they hadn't read (and probably couldn't anyway) and baying for its author's blood.

Rushdie endured years of hiding, watched over by bodyguards. His exile made a loud statement about freedom of expression, but to little avail: Islamist terror and political expediency were louder. As he noted, with bitterness, nothing hurt so much in the 'dark decade' after the Khomeini fatwā as the way that India, the country that had been his 'primary source of artistic inspiration', rejected him, denying him an entry visa.

> India was the first country to ban *The Satanic Verses*—which was proscribed without following India's own stipulated due process in such matters, banned before it entered the country by a weak Congress government led by Rajiv Gandhi, in a desperate, unsuccessful bid for Muslim votes. (Rushdie [2002] 2003, 196)

There are even situations where all three responses to oppression may come into play.

When a group of army officers (the so-called 'Colonels') seized power in Greece in 1967 and imposed press censorship, the conservative newspaper proprietor Helen Vlachos chose to close down her publications rather than be seen collaborating with the dictators.[11] Her silence, she later said, was her loudest voice (*Wikipedia*: 'Helen

[11] I remember reading a pithy comment that she supposedly made—'Imagine you are a restaurant owner, and the government says, "From now on you will serve only turds." Clearly, your restaurant has to close.' However, I haven't been able to confirm the source.

Vlachos'). But in private, and in interviews that she gave to the international press, she was outspoken. She infuriated the principal members of the junta, describing them as 'ignorant and mediocre', except for one, Brigadier Pattakos, who, though he was mediocre too, stood out from the rest because he behaved like a clown. She said that she was more afraid of her dentist than she was of the Greek strongman, Papadopoulos (Vlachos 1970, 47).

There may have been calculation in her courage: she must have known that the Colonels would handle her more carefully than they did students or communists, because of the respect that she enjoyed internationally and because, as a well-known conservative, she was popular with the Greek middle classes, whose support (or at least acquiescence) the Colonels relied on.

Held under house arrest, she employed her cunning to escape, slipping out of her apartment, past the guard, and hiding in an empty bachelor flat 'where furtive comings and goings were the natural thing, though the lady visitors were not usually of my age and type' (Vlachos 1970, 144). In the meantime, her husband was making 'familiar noises' to reassure the guard in the corridor outside: calling the dogs, running a bath, and tottering dangerously about the apartment in his wife's high-heeled slippers so as to produce the accustomed *tap-tap* sound.

Vlachos needed to dye her hair black. The day before her flight, when she moved into a hotel near the airport, there was a near disaster. The people at the reception noticed that her fake passport wasn't in order. She had to go immediately to a government department, where with remarkable *sang-froid* she filled in reams of forms with details of her fake identity. Eventually she was able to leave Greece—and go into exile.

Living in a relaxed and democratic political environment, it is only too easy to write about the terrible dangers and choices faced by those trying to survive, and keep their integrity, under much more difficult conditions. It is hard to know how you yourself would behave in such a situation.

I went to Greece twice when I was a student, once just before the Colonels seized power, once afterwards, and on my second visit I noticed the difference. Almost on my first day, I was roughed up in the street in Athens by soldiers for no reason I could think of other than my hippy-ish appearance. No one intervened to help me.

A few days later, on a ferry to the islands, I noticed a man squatting in a corner of the passenger lounge listening to music on a cassette recorder. Going closer, I was struck by how marvellous the music was. I asked if he could play it louder, and he said no. He asked me to move away, please, and not draw attention to him, because the music he was playing was by Mikis Theodorakis. He would be arrested, and I might be arrested too.

Why was that? Because on 1 June 1967, the Colonels had published Army Decree No. 13, which banned playing and even *listening* to the music of Theodorakis (*Wikipedia*: 'Mikis Theodorakis'). The composer himself was arrested, jailed, banished to a remote mountain village, and then held in a military prison. Finally, in 1970, and suffering from tuberculosis, he was expelled from Greece.

My encounter with the gentleman on the ferry reminds me of a song by Alexandr Galich, the most famous of the subversive *magnitizdat* singer–songwriters in the Soviet Union:

> Untruth roams from field to field,
> Sharing notes with neighbouring untruths,
> But that which is sung softly, booms,
> What's read in whispers, thunders.
>
> (Quoted in Ramm 2017)

III

Is it enough to say, 'Hands off—it's art!'?

Art is a process, with an end product (or the intention to produce one). Some forms of art involve a performance, where the end product is ephemeral rather than a physically tangible object, though the performance may gain some permanence by being recorded. Forms such as theatre, concerts of music, ballet, or public readings of literature entail a complex interaction between the original work, its performers, and a receptive audience.

The 'art work' is generally deemed to have some kind of significance—to be beautiful, spiritually uplifting, delightful to the senses, pleasing to the intelligence, challenging, or emotionally moving—some quality that raises it above the everyday. Special claims are therefore made for art, and for the persons and activities of artists. At least since the Romantic Movement, artists have come to be seen less as gifted craftsmen (or talented amateurs) and more as spiritual guides, capable of leading us to enlightenment, inspiring us, enriching our souls, and teaching us how to see. As Shelley declared in 'A Defence of Poetry' (1821):

> Poets are the hierophants of an unapprehended inspiration; the mirrors of the gigantic shadows which futurity casts upon the present; the words which express what they understand not; the trumpets which sing to battle and feel not what they inspire; the influence which is moved not, but moves. Poets are the unacknowledged legislators of the world. (1840, 57)

Or, as the philosopher–novelist Iris Murdoch more prosaically put it, 'The way we grasp the world changes, and the artist knows first, like the animals whose behaviour foretells an earthquake' ([1992] 2003, 4).

Art, in the view of many, and not only of the artists themselves, therefore needs to be 'ring-fenced' and indulged, like religion, science, pets, and small children. In return for this privileged status, creative artists should deliver something that people consider to be of value and worthy of respect. Their efforts have in all periods been subject to popular scorn or expert criticism, with or without good cause, but never so much as in modern times. Here are a few examples from the world of the visual arts.

In 2001, the Turner Prize, Britain's premier art award, was awarded to Martin Creed for *Work 227: The Lights Going On and Off*, which consisted of an empty room in which … the lights went on and off (Delaney 2010).

In the previous year, one of the works shortlisted for the Turner Prize had been Tracey Emin's *My Bed*:

> The piece was made by Emin in 1998 when she was living in a council flat in Waterloo. It shows her real bed at the time in all its embarrassing glory, with used condoms, dirty underwear and empty bottles of alcohol strewn across the crumpled stained sheets. (Ellis-Petersen 2015)

A well-known exhibit at the Tate Modern is Carl Andre's *Equivalent VIII*, which consists of 120 firebricks in a plain, rectangular arrangement (*Wikipedia*: 'Carl Andre').

Doug Fishbone's *30,000 Bananas* was installed in front of the National Gallery in London in 2004: a pile of 30,000 bananas, alluding (according to the artist) to 'Inca legends' and to 'Nazi references of structural and institutionalised violence and greed'. ('I could have done that!')

There was a fundamental lack of agreement about the worth of these efforts, with reactions ranging from adulation to mockery, a lack of consensus best explained as a result of the shaking of people's trust in their ability to evaluate art, which has been eroded by four different developments.

First, it has come under pressure from above, from *critical theory*. Today, any and every work, however firmly established in the canon, may be deconstructed, revealing its subtext and its personal or political agenda, and exposing the idol's feet of clay; or, at the very least, be re-located, unflatteringly, within a context of oppression or commercialization.

At its worst, critical theory often seems sterile, when it sneers and cheapens, projecting negativity. *Ways of Seeing* (1972), based on John Berger's influential television series, reproduces multiple tiny images of Leonardo's famous cartoon of *The Virgin and Child with St. Anne and St. John the Baptist*, rather than a full- or even half-page image, to emphasize how the picture is now mass-marketed. The cartoon hangs in a chapel-like room of its own, so is an example of 'bogus religiosity'. 'It has acquired a new kind of impressiveness. [...] It has become impressive, mysterious, because of its market value' (23). To this I would say (albeit subjectively): *no*, there is more to Leonardo's picture than that! I have seen reproductions of the cartoon countless times, but every time that I see the original work, in the National Gallery in London, it takes my breath away. To score a political point, Berger and his collaborators have let their prejudices get the better of them.

Second, art is also under attack from below, from crude, populist *relativism* and *political correctness*, both of which undermine our confidence to differentiate, critique, and (if necessary) flatly reject: 'I say that the Beatles are as good as Mozart!'; 'The storytellers of the So-and-So tribe in New Guinea are as great as any DWEMS such as Shakespeare or Dante!'; 'Who says that your opinion is worth more than mine?'; and so on. But if everything is of equal value, *nothing* is of value. And then anything, by anyone, can be art.

Third, art has been made vulnerable and seemingly irrelevant by *the artists themselves*, who in music, literature, and the graphic arts have, in search of the new, fractured traditional forms and espoused the experimental without always carrying wider public taste with them.

Finally, the status of art has been called into question by 'democratic' changes in its *forms of production* that sidestep canonical rules and criteria (collages, found poetry, computer-generated literature, and so on) and often make patrons and 'gate-keepers' unnecessary (self-publishing, blogging).

It hardly came as a surprise when a representative of the American Society for Aesthetics lamented in 1993 that the central question of aesthetics—What is art?—had become 'increasingly intractable', so that the viability of the field as a philosophic discipline was in jeopardy (see Torres and Kamhi 2000, 13–14). If philosophers themselves shrink from defining the concept, then the terms 'art' and 'artist' are truly up for grabs. It also does not help when critics such as Roberta Smith resort to absurdly circular propositions such as 'If an artist says it's art, it's art' (Torres and Kamhi 2000, 11).

Avant-garde artists, poets, and musicians have (no pun intended) painted themselves into a corner where hardly anyone except other avant-gardists likes or claims to understand what they are doing. Their energies are devoted less to communicating with the society they live in, and more to *épater le bourgeois*, that is, to freaking out the middle classes (the social milieu from which they themselves often come). They are widely regarded as weird and useless. An old cartoon in *Punch* magazine (21 July 1982) shows a lady at a smart party introducing her husband to the other guests. He is dressed as a rabbit and is holding his drink in one hand and a pineapple in the other. His wife explains: 'Gregory's an artist—he doesn't have to *mean* anything, he just is.'[12]

As the traditional hierarchies of subjects and techniques are increasingly ignored, Andy Warhol's 1968 prediction that in the future everyone would be famous for fifteen minutes (Guinn and Perry 2005, 4) may be coming true. In 1973, the German artist Joseph Beuys announced, 'Every human being is an artist' (*Wikipedia*: 'Joseph

[12] Echoing the lines from Archibald MacLeish's poem *Ars Poetica* ([1926] 1985) that 'A poem should not mean / But be'.

Beuys—Sculptor'). But it is not just a matter of happily letting everyone 'do their own thing', or that 'anything goes'. The problem is that the particular 'anything' produced by the supposed artist—Carl Andre's famous firebricks, mentioned earlier, or Warhol's *Brillo Box* (1964), indistinguishable from (though far more expensive than) the Brillo Boxes available from supermarkets—can be lauded and admired, and can add to its creator's wealth and fame, yet still be of questionable worth.

Much of this is harmless, but there are areas in which art can actually offend, attracting a repressive reaction: it can offend against the established rules of art itself, against the beliefs and values of its audience (the most important kind of transgressive art), and against the laws of the state (the areas often overlap).

The first of these is not especially relevant to our present purposes. New directions in the arts have usually earned the disapproval of the artistic establishment. Picasso is a case in point. In an after-dinner speech in 1949 at the Royal Academy, its then President Sir Alfred Munnings, 'the respected sporting painter', 'declared that if he saw Picasso walking down the street, he'd kick him up the backside' (M. Brown 2017), while it was the view of the novelist Evelyn Waugh, expressed in a letter to *The Times* (19 December 1945), that 'Señor Picasso's paintings cannot be intelligently discussed in the terms used of the civilised masters' (Taylor 2014, 60).

Picasso was disliked by some, but not universally; besides, critical approval was not long in coming. Moreover, his works could hardly be taken as examples of offensiveness of the second or third kind. Staying with the visual arts, the same could *not* be said of the following, however.

In 1961, Piero Manzoni filled 90 tin cans each with 30g of his own excrement and called it *Merda d'artista* (artist's shit). The cans were to be sold at the current price of gold. The Tate bought one in 2000, reportedly for £22,300 of British public money (Milner 2002); one was sold at a Sotheby's auction in 2007 for €124,000, while a year later a can fetched £97,250; one was sold for £182,500 at Christies's in 2015; and in 2016 another fetched €275,000 (including auction fees) in Milan, setting a new world record.

Manzoni, who died soon afterwards, seems to have been cocking a snook at his father and at the art world, and if that is true it was a good joke and he made his point. But the art world has not recognized that it was taken for a fool, and has not moved on. As the disgusting items continue to be bought and sold, the art world remains firmly stuck (so to speak) in the shit.[13]

Manzoni's 'achievements' were easily trumped by those of the Austrian artist Günter Brus (sensitive readers please skip the following quotation).

> [Brus's] aggressively presented actionism intentionally disregarded conventions and taboos with the intent of shocking the viewer. Sentenced to 6 months in prison after the *Kunst und Revolution* event at the University of Vienna in 1968, he fled to Berlin with his family and returned to Austria in 1976. Brus urinated into a glass then proceeded to cover his body in his own excrement, and ended the piece by drinking his own urine. During the performance Brus also sang the Austrian National Anthem while masturbating. Brus ended the piece by vomiting and was subsequently arrested. Through this piece and his other performance works, Brus hoped to reveal the still fascist essence of the nation. (*Wikipedia*: 'Günter Brus')

Far from being laughed into obscurity, Brus received a series of prizes, and a museum was opened in his honour in Austria.

An additional feature of his performance works was Brus attacking himself with a razor-blade. Should actual physical cruelty (even self-directed), as opposed to its mimetic representation, have any place in art? 'Snuff films', the most extreme example, are fortunately almost universally condemned as unacceptable—although real images of killing, torture, and mutilation abound on the internet.

Even the dead are not left in peace. In 2015, the Polish artist Artur Żmijewski exhibited his video *Game of Tag*, filmed in 1999 inside the Nazi death-camp Stutthof. It shows men and women running around, laughing, playing a naked game of tag, inside a gas chamber. In response to complaints, the Krakow Art Museum said that it should be shown 'because it was a matter of freedom of expression', while

[13] There remains some doubt about whether the cans really do contain human excrement. They are of steel 'and thus cannot be x-rayed or scanned to determine the contents, and opening a can would cause it to lose its value; thus, the true contents of *Artist's Shit* are unknown' (*Wikipedia*: 'Artist's Shit').

Mr Żmijewski himself declared that, while the people in the video were having fun, 'they are also very serious. They know where they are—in the gas chamber of a former Nazi extermination camp' (*BBC News* 2017).

They may have known where they were, but did they know *why* they were doing what is shown in the video? And whether the effect intended by the artist, whatever that may have been, was achieved? And how it weighed against the offence that they caused to the memory of the victims, and to the sensibilities of their living family members?

A frequently recurring question is whether artists should be permitted to abuse *animals*—a more helpless target than human beings—to create an effect or an audience reaction, and, sadly, there seems to be no consensus on this, whether among the avant-garde or in law. In 1971, the British comedian Spike Milligan therefore felt obliged to take the law (and a rock) into his own hands when an American 'environmental and ecological artist' named Newton Harrison announced that he would electrocute sixty catfish as part of an 'exhibition' at the Hayward Gallery in London (*Harrison Studio* 'Portable Fish Farm').

In 2005, the international press reported on some strange goings-on in Denmark, when the art museum Trapholt

> found itself in hot water over goldfish in a food blender. The artist, Marco Evaristti, said he wanted people 'to do battle with their conscience', so visitors were given the option of pressing the 'on' button. Consequently, some fish got liquidised, landing the gallery in both the courts and the headlines (the judge ruled in favour of the gallery, not the fish). [...] The director of Trapholt art museum was adamant that 'an artist has the right to create works that defy our concept of what is right and wrong'. (Hankins 2005)

At the risk of stating the obvious, the author of the article reminds art students that 'cutting off a chicken's head might get you noticed, but it doesn't mean you're any good'. She also quotes the Swiss sculptor Alberto Giacometti as saying that if he discovered a cat trapped behind a Rembrandt painting and in danger of suffocating, he would destroy the canvas to save the cat. ('Even if the painting belonged to Giacometti?' one might ask.)

Let me end this freak show with my favourite example, that of the student at a prestigious European art school who submitted as his term project a pile of his own excrement, tastefully presented under a cheese glass. His examiners were put in a quandary. It would be uncool to reject the 'work of art', but if the press found out about it the college would become a laughing stock. One of the professors came up with a face-saving solution. The merits or otherwise of the turd need not be discussed (thank goodness!) because the student's submission could be rejected on formal grounds—the work was not the fruit of a whole term's labours, but had taken 48 hours at the most to produce (personal communication to the author).

It is not only in the visual arts, of course, that 'works' of this kind prompt the question whether we are now in the fairy-tale realm of the Emperor's New Clothes, with artists behaving like spoilt toddlers, smearing the playpen and shouting to attract attention to themselves.

Against the background of such behaviour, how can the right to total artistic freedom be justified? In *Transgressions: The Offences of Art* (2002), Anthony Julius outlines the 'five defences of art'.

(*a*) The 'First Amendment defence' is simply freedom of speech, such as should be available to all in a free society.

But should the right to free speech also be extended to those who for amusement shout 'Fire!' in a crowded theatre, or those recommending the pleasures of cannibalism, rape, or paedophilia? If a society is to function successfully, the idea of freedom of speech (or of expression, or behaviour) that is divorced from its social consequences is untenable. Although it is not easy to make clear-cut connections between, say, pornography and rape, or between descriptions of extreme violence and 'copy-cat' acts of viciousness, no one today would support Oscar Wilde's sweeping claim that '[no] book or work of art ever produces any effect on conduct at all' (quoted in Fellion and Inglis 2017, 151).

The counter-culture of the 1960s and early 1970s was famous for its advocacy of freedom, in particular the right to free love and to the unrestricted use of drugs. 'Let it all hang out!' The hedonistic lifestyles of rock musicians seemed to offer young people a model in this regard, and much media attention was paid to their thoughts and views on life. But the libertarianism often masked selfishness and irresponsibility. A cartoon in *Private Eye* (1968) neatly skewered these pretensions. It shows a thick-lipped rock star (with some resemblance to Mick Jagger) accompanied by a scantily-dressed female admirer. He is telling her: 'Get your knickers off baby, I wish to follow the dictates of my conscience' (Ingrams 1971, 196). In hindsight, it was foolish to build up popular musicians such as the Rolling Stones—already well on their way to becoming members of the international jet set—into social revolutionaries or political martyrs, and to take their loudly expressed opinions so seriously.

(*b*) The 'aesthetic alibi' states that art is a privileged area in which the otherwise unsayable may be said, as in the days when a court jester was the only person allowed to mock the prince, thereby fulfilling a necessary social function.

But if the 'unsayable' needs to be said, surely it will be for some urgent reason not necessarily connected with aesthetics? (Beyond the circles of artists and critics, questions of aesthetics are seldom held to be a matter of urgency.) And why should it be the 'aesthetes', the creative artists, who have to step up to the plate to do it?

Julius rightly points out that there is a 'certain tension' between these first two arguments, one of which asserts the broad rights of everyone, the other, rights granted to a limited and privileged group (Julius 2002, 26).

(*c*) The 'estrangement defence' argues that art has a serious civilizatory duty to perform, namely, to alienate and to problematize. As Kafka wrote (rather hyperbolically) to his friend Oskar Pollak in 1904:

> Altogether, I think we ought to read only books that bite and sting us. If the book we are reading doesn't shake us awake like a blow to the skull, why bother reading it in the first place. [...] A book must be the axe for the frozen sea within us. That is what I believe. (Quoted in Pawel [1984] 1992, 158)

Where writers boldly go, theorists will eventually follow. The Russian Formalist critic Victor Shklovsky (1917) introduced the term 'defamiliarization' (Russian, *ostranenie*), for the 'making strange' that is at the root of all art. And in the theatre, there is Bertolt Brecht's *Verfremdungseffekt* (variously translated as the Alienation, Distancing, or Estrangement Effect).

There is a lot to be said for this argument, which rests on the idea that society can only advance and renew itself through confronting and resolving challenges, by having its orthodoxies questioned, and (when necessary) by being given a good shaking. That challenge can come from gadflies of the right as well as from radicals of the left (see Chapter 7, 'John Betjeman, the Subversive Conservative'). Boundaries are meaningless if they are never approached and occasionally breached, if only momentarily; and the breaching may even serve to restore belief in that boundary, and lead to its being strengthened rather than allowing a destructive flood of wickedness and amorality to pour through the opening.

But is an ability to provoke debate, controversy, and reflection be reason enough to legitimize something as a 'work of art', to be ring-fenced and protected, without consideration of its other features and its possible consequences? If 'loudness' and originality are all that is needed, where does that leave 'quieter' work, produced within a long-term tradition and following established rules and patterns? Work that claims the right to respect on the basis of technical quality or outstanding beauty, rather than on its ability to shock? Art that mediates rather than alienates?

I have argued (Jarman 2014–15) that, living as we do in an age that feverishly questions and challenges, constantly subverts and deconstructs, we tend to forget that there was a time when great art could be produced to eulogize kings or prelates, because they were powerful, or to praise a flower, or a woman, simply for being beautiful. Artists didn't explicitly adopt critical poses or stances in their work, but got on with creating their paintings, poems, or plays. The subversive was often present, but the grand attitudes that we have come to expect from artists, their self-dramatization, their yearning for acknowledgement, their existential *Angst*, their alienation from society, and scorn for its values: none of these things were of much interest, except maybe to the artists' families, lovers, and closest friends. Creative artists weren't supposed to take *themselves* seriously; only their work.

Yet, while it might not be the only kind of art that is worthwhile (whatever Kafka might say), it is nevertheless transgressive art, the art that shocks and enrages, that concerns us here. And there is plenty of room for debate.

The narcissism (or playpen infantilism) of many modern artists has already been referred to. The broader question also needs to be raised of who it is that decides that we *need* to be shocked, and in which ways. What gives *them* the right to interfere in *our* lives?

Accepting the estrangement defence provides a glib answer to those questions. We should accept that artists are different from the rest of us, and that the onus is on *us* to understand *them*. By this account, artists are sensitive and progressive, Shelley's 'unacknowledged legislators', revolutionary geniuses constantly pushing the envelope of human perception. And since they are members almost of another species, a privileged elite, it logically follows that they should be allowed to operate outside of society's norms and rules—in the name of 'art'.

(*d*) The 'canonic defence' claims that art exists within a tradition and can therefore only be evaluated within that context.

Thus, today's orthodoxy was once iconoclastic, and today's iconoclasm may become the orthodoxy of a coming generation. The passing 'shock' is part of a necessary process, and the development must be allowed to take its course. Julius points out how the act of naming the new British art prize after Turner (an artist once considered shocking and revolutionary, but now a revered 'classic') was itself a deployment of the canonic defence (2002, 45).

Underlying this argument, however, is a questionable attitude to progress in art. Is the new *inevitably* an improvement on the old? Are the arts on an unrelenting upward trajectory, driven by pioneers and experimenters, as if they were the cultural section of the Whig Interpretation of History?

In the second part of *Human, All-Too-Human: A Book for Free Spirits* (1879–80), Nietzsche expressed his doubts about the frenzied modern obsession with the new:

> Three-fourths of Homer is convention, and the same is the case with all the Greek artists, who had no reason for falling into the modern craze for originality. They had no fear of convention, for after all convention was a link between them and their public. Conventions are the artistic means *acquired* for the understanding of the hearer; the common speech, learnt with much toil, whereby the artist can really communicate his ideas. [...] What the artist devises beyond convention he offers of his own free will and takes a risk, his success at best resulting in the setting-up of a new convention. As a rule originality is marvelled at, sometimes even worshipped, but seldom understood. A stubborn avoidance of convention

means a desire not to be understood. What, then, is the object of the modern craze for originality? ([1879–80] 1913, 256)

We need to ask who is in charge: who determines and guards the direction that this progressive development will take? If it isn't the general public (so uninformed, so easily swayed by media fads and gimmicks, advertising, and peer pressure), doesn't that mean (again) that a 'priesthood' is needed, an elite who consider itself qualified to define the canon, and to issue dispensations that allow artists to break social rules (or the law) in the name of art?

Finally, there is (*e*) the 'formalist defence': that art is a separate mode of existence, to be taken on its own terms.

This defence is naturally more easily applied to, say, a piece of music or an abstract painting than to literature or figurative art, which normally invite us to look for a narrative—for associations and meaning. To deny that there are disturbing elements of content in, for instance, Nabokov's novel *Lolita* (paedophilia) or in the films of Leni Riefenstahl (Fascism), or even to dismiss these content elements as irrelevant or of secondary significance, preferring to see only wit, beauty, or technical brilliance, is a serious humanitarian failure. If done under the pressure to be 'progressive' or fashionable, it is an act of extreme bad faith.

These five defences may, singly or in combination, be raised as protection against the heavy hand of social control and censorship, yet do not *necessarily* guarantee it. Even the (perhaps) most appealing of arguments, the estrangement defence, can hardly be extended to cover a work of art that might have attracted the wrath of the censor for some technical, personal, or political reason but which isn't genuinely challenging, which doesn't 'bite and sting us', which isn't 'an axe for the frozen sea within us'.

Every case must be looked at on its own merits and in its context. And as far as the libertarian side of the debate is concerned, there will probably never be agreement that the need of the artist for free, unfettered expression should *always* and *under any circumstances* be given precedence over the needs and values of society.

On the other hand, with respect to the statist side of the debate, there should, in an open, liberal society, be consensus that there be as little censorship of art or interference with artists as possible. The history of such interference has been neither edifying nor consistent, and if they are not to cause harm, the mechanisms for such intrusions by the state should be kept to a minimum, and intelligently fine-tuned.

The two strong positions on art and freedom (that is, no control versus complete control) exclude each other, and neither of them is unwaveringly supportable at least in the kind of society that would be pleasant for most people to live in.

The '*all* art must be free' position collapses in the face of the unspeakable horrors that humans are capable of. 'It should [...] be possible to acknowledge', Julius writes, 'that there are some limits that we need', just as there are 'others that we need breached. (2002, 188).

The 'art must be subject to control' position has been shown to be vulnerable to abuse when the controls are exercised by those with a ruthless agenda or left to capricious buffoons.

No attempt will be made here to square the circle, but instead I would like to try to bring the positions slightly closer together by focusing on the idea of '(artistic) freedom' from a different viewpoint than the usual (stridently libertarian) one.

IV

Two points need to be made.

The first is that freedom cannot be an absolute. For practical reasons, freedom can never mean total, unrestricted freedom for every individual, because people's actions would encroach upon and restrict the freedom of others. In effect, this is the Golden Rule of 'Do as you would be done by', which has been asserted on numerous occasions in human history, in religious teaching, in philosophy, and in political discourse.

Thus, Article 4 of the *Declaration of the Rights of Man and of the Citizen* approved by the National Assembly of France on 26 August 1789, stipulated:

> Liberty consists in the freedom to do everything which injures no one else; hence the exercise of the natural rights of each man has no limits except those which assure to the other members of the society the enjoyment of the same rights. These limits can only be determined by law.

In *On Liberty* (1859), John Stuart Mill declared: 'The liberty of the individual must be thus far limited; he must not make himself a nuisance to other people' ([1859] 2002, 59). In the same year, Abraham Lincoln wrote: 'Those who deny freedom to others, deserve it not for themselves; and, under a just God, can not long retain it' ('Letter to Henry L. Pierce'). And Nelson Mandela (1994) insisted that 'to be free is not merely to cast off one's chains, but to live in a way that respects and enhances the freedom of others' ([1994] 1995, 751).

The second point, so easily forgotten in an era of human rights declarations, is that in historical practice freedom has never been an inalienable privilege, but a hard-earned condition. It is less a question of 'being free' than of 'doing freedom'. Freedom evolved over many centuries, in contexts of oppression, struggle, responsibility, and commitment. Freedom that is taken for granted and passively accepted will soon be lost—it must be appreciated and, if necessary, defended.

The most famous formulation of this idea is in the funeral speech (c. 431–430 BC) that Thucydides puts into the mouth of the Athenian leader Pericles. The Peloponnesian War has begun and the city already has many dead to be mourned. Pericles praises the democratic constitution of Athens and the freedom and tolerance of its people, their respect for the law, and their love both of beauty and of the things of the mind; he tells the assembled citizens:

> This, then, is the kind of city for which these men, who could not bear the thought of losing her, nobly fought and nobly died. […] They gave her their lives, to her and to all of us, and for their own selves they won praises that never grow old, the most splendid of sepulchres—not the sepulchre in which their bodies are laid, but where their glory remains eternal in men's minds, always there on the right occasion to stir others to speech or to action. For famous men have the whole earth as their memorial: it is not only the inscriptions on their graves in their own country that mark them out; no, in foreign lands also, not in any visible form but in people's hearts, their memory abides and grows. It is for you to try to be like them. Make up your minds that *happiness depends on being free, and freedom depends on being courageous.* (1954, 120–1; my emphasis)

More than two thousand years later, the motto 'Freedom is not free' was inscribed on the Korean War Veterans Memorial in Washington, DC.

Athenian democracy was far from perfect—freedom didn't extend to women or slaves—and it would be naïve to pretend that either of these wars was solely about freedom. But the general point holds good. As Mill wrote, in February 1862, in the context of another great conflict:

> War is an ugly thing but not the ugliest of things; the decayed and degraded state of moral and patriotic feelings which thinks that nothing is worth war is much worse. [...] A man who has nothing which he is willing to fight for, nothing which he cares about more than he does about his personal safety, is a miserable creature who has no chance of being free, unless made and kept so by the exertions of better men than himself. (Mill 1862)

If freedom needs to be spoken up for, who better to do it than artists? It would be a noble task for them to be Shelley's 'legislators of the world', but to achieve it by reconnecting with their own society, in that middle ground between programmatic political art and avant-garde posturing, and winning acknowledgement through earning (rather than just demanding) the right to be heard and respected.

Morality, art, law, and governance all require lines to be drawn. These have to be drawn carefully, in full understanding of why they need to be there. In most cases, it will not be for all eternity. It also needs to be recognized that whoever oversteps such a line, when the time comes, should know why they are doing it.

2

Freedom of Suppression

CHRISTOPH WERNER*

My bell was ringing as if a very determined thumb was pressing the button. The November day was dark. A slight cold rain fell, with gusts of wind pushing against the old windowpanes of my student digs, making them rattle. I had just settled down in my clammy study to work on my examination paper about Graham Greene's latest book, *A Burnt-Out Case*, and was losing myself in the characters of Querry, Dr Colin, and Rycker. My brother in West Germany had promised to send me as much secondary literature regarding Greene as he could lay his hands on. He had smuggled *A Burnt-Out Case* into the German Democratic Republic (GDR), then commonly known in West Germany as 'The Zone', when he had last visited me. The frontier was still sort of open, the erection of the Berlin Wall one year ahead of us.

* An earlier version of the present essay appeared in *Lifting the Iron Curtain: Tales of a Bygone Country* (2019), a collection of reminiscences about life in East Germany.

Since I was impatiently waiting for the mail service to deliver the promised books and journals, I jumped up and ran to the door to get the parcel from the postman. But alas, it was not the postman who had rung. Instead, two tall gentlemen in the uniforms of customs officers were looming over me and asking if they could come in. I was so surprised that it didn't occur to me to inquire what they wanted. And anyway, being a well-trained GDR citizen and a German at that, I respected uniforms as a matter of course.

When they had settled down on my bed and my only spare chair, one of them, obviously the ranking officer, started to inform me that a parcel with books and journals from Hanover (in West Germany) had been impounded by their customs comrades because it contained printed material from the class enemy. I ventured to answer that I was expecting books by and about the British author Graham Greene who was well-known for his critical attitude toward Western imperialism, and who particularly disliked the Americans, as could be seen from his book, *The Quiet American*. And, moreover, this book had been favourably reviewed in the 'Organ of the Central Committee of the Socialist Unity Party' (that is, the *Sozialistische Einheitspartei Deutschlands* [SED], in other words the Communist Party), *Neues Deutschland*. I soon suspected the two comrades to be officers from the district branch of the Ministry of State Security (or Stasi), so to put them in a good mood I used the full title of the *Neues Deutschland* newspaper and let it be known by my remark and the tone in which it was voiced that I was an avid and faithful reader of the Party's most important instrument of popular enlightenment and propaganda.

But they were not to be distracted. They insisted that the propaganda of the class enemy came disguised in many forms so that, under the cover of a certain anti-Americanism, an author such as Greene could easily get into the minds of unsuspecting and, particularly, young people. Had he not maintained that society can only be changed by first making the individual happy? Now I was flabbergasted. Educated *Stasi*-people? Who even knew about Graham Greene? And was it not, the other visitor chimed in, the socialist revolution, the fundamental changes in our country, that was the precondition for making the individual happy? And not, as my author wanted to make us believe, the other way round? And what about the representation of our Soviet friends in *The Third Man*?

I asked, well, what about it? 'There you are!' said the man, 'You didn't even notice in what a disparaging way the Soviet military policeman in the Vienna International Patrol is described?' He took a slip of paper from his jacket pocket and read from it: 'When they arrested Anna in the early hours of the morning, she was still in bed. The Russian, not giving Anna an opportunity of letting him in, put his shoulder to the door and tore out the bolt. They got in and told Anna to get dressed. The writer goes on to say that the Russian watched Anna dressing while the Englishman left the room. The Frenchman watched the reflection of the girl dressing in the mirror of the wardrobe. The American, of course, would never leave a girl unprotected with a Russian soldier and so stayed in the room but with his back chivalrously turned.'

He looked up from his notes and said, in a harsh voice, that I ought to be able to see (if I wanted to, that is) that the Soviet soldier, a soldier of the glorious Red Army, which had borne the main burden of the fight against the Nazis, was being shown here as inferior, and as prone to raping women.

And that is why they could not allow such literature in our country, he added.

They knew, the ranking officer said, that I had in my possession a number of books by Greene, and that they tolerated it because I was a student of English literature. But if I needed reviews, interpretations, and so on, I was asked to turn to GDR or Soviet sources.

Later, I learned that the institute where I was studying English had been paid an unannounced visit by two men who wanted to speak to my professor. The secretary, with whom I was on very good terms, me being young and interested and she being rather frustrated in her marriage, told me that she had heard my name through the closed door to the professorial study. So they had obviously been academically briefed by the professor who, by the way, sat in the East German Parliament, the Volkskammer, for the SED, representing—or what she understood by the term—a constituency in the district of Halle, my university town.

The well-disposed reader may now wonder why the Ministry of Truth (read: Ministry of State Security) bothered so much with a simple and well-meaning student. There are, I believe, a number of reasons, most of which I only became aware of later when I read my *Stasi* files after the fall of the Berlin Wall.

First of all, my studies of English and German were intended to produce a school teacher for the Extended Secondary School, or Gymnasium as it is called today. And well-qualified English teachers were rare, the older generation from before the war having been pensioned off for the most part, and Nazi teachers having been removed after 1945. There were not enough applicants for teacher training. So they tried to keep me on board and at the same time make me good. Also, the border to West Germany was still open at that time and one could easily leave the country via Berlin. In July 1961 alone, the month before the building of the Wall, 30,000 people left East Germany.

Second, my father was a Lutheran minister, and at the time I am referring to, the state had just begun to ease up on the church, so they possibly feared that he might cause trouble via the church authorities.

Third, they wanted to keep an eye on me—as I learned from my files much later—because I had once made fun of the gymnastics we had to do during lecture breaks, comparing that somewhat alien activity to the physical jerks so heartbreakingly described by George Orwell in *1984*. That book had also been spirited across the border from West Germany by my brother. The 'Unofficial *Stasi* Informant' (Inoffizieller Mitarbeiter or IM) in my student group had categorized my remarks as hostile-negative. (But that, as I said, I only learnt from my files.) Also, I was at that time not a member of the communist youth organization FDJ (Freie Deutsche Jugend, or 'Free German Youth') as all of my fellow students were, and therefore required special attention.

The fourth reason that I think might have contributed to the Sword and Shield of the Party (as the *Stasi* liked to see themselves) keeping tabs on me was a correspondence I had been in with a friend in Rostock on the Baltic coast. He had been studying medicine there and had taken part in an illegal leaflet campaign in which the bigoted information policy of the communists had been criticized. My friend was thrown out of the university and fled to West Germany via the 'green frontier', thereby risking his freedom. The secret police undertook a search of his flat and found my letters, in which I had referred to Party functionaries unflatteringly as 'bonzes'. They alarmed the district attorney of Rostock, who then ordered a search of my digs.

Now that was interesting. Two men on a motorcycle—they hadn't even thought me important enough to justify the use of a car—stopped in front of the old house and asked for admission. They then produced a warrant from the district attorney and began a search of my study. They took away some folders with typed sheets and notes connected with my examination paper, and copies of my letters to my friend in Rostock.

Nothing official came of the house search except that my then girlfriend, who shared the flat with me and hadn't been present during this procedure, threw her hands up and said that, for heaven's sake, she hadn't dusted the (sparse) furniture that day, and what *would* the men now think of her? Her relationship to the state was a very trusting one, and I later heard that she had joined the SED.

With regard to trying to get printed material, books, newspapers, and journals from West Germany or other capitalist countries, I read much later about the following incident.

Hermann Kant, president from 1978 to 1990 of the East German Writers' Union, who was a *Stasi* informant with the code name 'Martin', complained to his *Stasi* controller about the ignorance of the GDR customs administration. The Dutch Minister for Trade had sent a copy of the novel *Billiards at Half-Past Nine* (German: *Billard um halb zehn*) by Heinrich Böll (who later won the Nobel Prize for literature) to a well-known political figure in the GDR. The book was confiscated and a notification sent to both the sender and the addressee that the book was of an anti-democratic character and could therefore not be allowed in (the book wasn't returned to the sender, though).

All this despite the fact that an East German publishing house planned to publish the book in the following year in the GDR! Just imagine the stink that the Minister in the Netherlands raised when he went to the press with this story. Kant's controller promised he would inform his superiors of the need to educate and enlighten their otherwise-so-dedicated warriors.

It may well be that this fresh approach had already borne fruit in my case, and that they had taken the trouble to inform themselves about the matter in question. Of course this would not go so far as to let all kinds of books through, but at least they had tried to convince the person for whom the book was intended, which was of course a futile endeavour.

Anyway, I succeeded in finishing my paper on Greene, though not without my professor proposing some major alterations. To her mind there was too much talk of damnation, redemption, hell, and so on, too much of the murky territory of shifting boundaries typically inhabited by Greene's characters, in short, too much Greeneland. She suggested that I insert a sizeable amount of Marxist terminology—ideological highlights, she called them—which I duly did. So there was then quite a lot in it about the class struggle, albeit this was hidden under the surface of the text, which discussed socialism brightening the horizon, which Greene not so much made explicit but allowed the reader to sense in the subtext, and so on. She also hinted that she would prefer a conclusion along the lines that Greene (at least for a time) had been a comrade-in-arms of the socialist countries in their fight against Western colonialism. This didn't contribute much to a better understanding of Greene, but it did get me a good mark.

Luckily, the paper went astray when the institute moved to other premises, so I didn't need to feel ashamed about it for too long afterwards. And there was always the consolation that to further their careers most people worked like that.

As for reading Western journals, I remember what a Professor of Political Economy by the interesting name of Rippel (ripple) once told me, 'between you and me and the lamp-post'. Since his main area of work at the university was the economics of capitalism, from time to time, he couldn't help but need to use the odd Western source for his work—in this case it was the West German *Spiegel* magazine. They had a so-called poison cabinet at their institute where such documents were held under lock and key, and only made accessible to the director and the Party secretary. When Rippel needed a certain article, the Party secretary would fetch the journal, open it at the specified place and let Rippel read it, carefully ensuring that he didn't befoul his socialist consciousness by wandering off onto other pages.

After having finished my studies, I worked for two years—that was mandatory—as a school teacher. Very soon, I got into trouble with the school inspector, who sat in on one of the weekly meetings of the staff. This was in the year 1962, when the Berlin Wall and the 1,400 km fortified frontier had not been in place for long.

The healthy and useful separation from West Germany was still a much-discussed topic, and was also a subject in lessons. As the English master, I was allowed to read the British communist paper, the *Daily Worker* (some years later renamed the *Morning Star*), and to use it for teaching purposes in my classes. At that time (and virtually from the start), the *Daily Worker* had failed to use the designation 'anti-fascist barrier', preferred by the GDR authorities and particularly recommended for schools, and would refer to the Wall as: 'the Wall'. Fool and eager beaver that I was, I quoted the *Daily Worker*'s arguments, which praised the Wall as an effective means of stabilizing the East German economy, and I called the Wall 'the Wall', as I thought that I should use authentic English.

Just a few days before that, I had talked in another one of my lessons about English nursery rhymes, citing among them the sweet: 'Humpty Dumpty sat on a wall, Humpty Dumpty had a great fall; all the king's horses and all the king's men couldn't put Humpty together again'.

The son of the school inspector led a wretched life in my class. He could hardly follow my enlightened teaching and got bad marks, so he didn't much like me (just as I didn't like him, for that matter). But in this case, he had successfully managed to learn the nursery rhyme by heart (as I had told the class to) and he quoted it to his father.

In the staff meeting I was then severely called to order by the inspector. He demanded to know through what thought process I had allowed, willingly or not, a comparison to be made between our anti-fascist bulwark (that was the word he used, having obviously consulted a dictionary for the word *Bollwerk*) and a capitalist nursery rhyme, thus belittling the historic fortification of our frontier in Berlin? I remained mute and looked so contrite that the headmaster intervened, referring to my youth and inexperience as a teacher, and promised to look after me better in the future. So I was spared the procedure known as 'extensive self-criticism' (which was regarded as the first step to betterment).

Here, chronology demands that I mention the fate of the East German author Erich Loest, who at that same time was serving a seven-year sentence in Bautzen II, a *Stasi* penitentiary known for its particularly strict discipline. The rogue writer had taken part in discussions on the need for de-Stalinization in the GDR and, even worse, had pleaded for the removal of Walter Ulbricht from his post as the First Secretary of the Central Committee of the Socialist Unity Party. He was consequently brought to trial and, with others, convicted of having taken part in a 'counter-revolutionary grouping'. The most eager of the debaters had actually been an informant. While I was sitting in the staff meeting I had of course remembered the article in the *Neues Deutschland* newspaper on Christmas Eve, 1958, informing its readers, us students included, that Loest and others had formed a subversive group and been punished accordingly. That didn't really encourage political criticism of any kind, and therefore I was glad to get away with my Humpty Dumpty/Wall pun.

It is interesting how highly the communists regarded the influence of literature on the minds of their people—and how much they overrated it. I suspect that they never lost sight of Stalin's words that 'writers are the engineers of the human soul'. They obviously still believed that, just as an engineer can put a well-functioning machine together, so a writer could make the human soul function in a predetermined and desired way.

Erich Loest, incidentally, found two of his own books in the prison libraries: a collection of love stories, in the remand prison of the city of Halle, popularly known as 'The Red Ox', and one of his novels, in the Bautzen II penitentiary. The *Stasi* had clearly not been thorough enough in mucking out these libraries, and had not done a good job of rewriting the past by making Loest an unperson. In his autobiography, the writer said that this took them another year. I will add that he could regard himself lucky, as one of the Soviet writers present at the meeting in which Stalin exuded his wise words in 1932 was later put in a Gulag prison-camp and finally shot dead in 1938. He obviously hadn't done enough soul engineering.

Later, when I was a lecturer in the English department of a technical college, I had another stroke of good fortune in connection with the affair of the pugnacious poet, writer, and singer Wolf Biermann. He had angered the GDR authorities too much and was duly stripped of his GDR citizenship in 1976. This happened while he was on an officially authorized tour in West Germany, and it provoked protests from prominent GDR writers and intellectuals.

Many persons and institutions were now approached by the authorities to sign resolutions supporting Wolf Biermann's expulsion, even though his was a little-known name among us ordinary folk. I for one had never heard of him before I read his name in *Neues Deutschland*. But that did not matter, we were told by the Party secretary of our department; we were told to simply trust the Party and sign the resolution to be published in *Neues Deutschland*. It was my luck that I fell ill and had to stay at home for a few days, so the resolution went ahead and was printed without my name being on it. I was thus spared a moral decision in which I am not sure how I would have responded.

To be fair, I have to add the following. Before the GDR collapsed in 1989–90, I left the country by means of an exit permit, for which my family and I had been waiting for three years (and for which we were punished by being made to lose our jobs). In my new job at a provincial university in West Germany I also had the choice occasionally of speaking up or keeping my mouth shut in order to avoid the risk of losing my temporary employment. This reveals what I suspect is one of the commonest traits of human character, or at least of *my* character, which can be fittingly summed up in the words of Bertolt Brecht: First the grub, *then* the morals.

Talking about newspapers, I ought to mention two occurrences that shed light on the close, no, intimate relationship between the print media (indeed *all* media in East Germany) and the Party.

The first happened a few years after Erich Honecker had become First (later General) Secretary of the SED, Chairman of the National Defence Council, and Chairman of the State Council (virtually the President of the country)—he had, with the help of his Soviet boss Leonid (the 'son of a lion') Brezhnev, forced his predecessor Walter Ulbricht to step down from all these posts. I met a young man on the staircase in front of our flat. He was my neighbour in the newly built city of Halle-Neustadt, about 20 years old, and working in the printing shop of the district of Halle SED newspaper *Freiheit* (meaning 'liberty'). He was very excited and told me that he had to rush to his place of work as something very grave had happened there.

Just as the first copies of the newspaper were about to be sent out to the subscribers and kiosks that day, a wide-awake colleague had by chance held the front page against the morning sun outside the shop and discovered a frightful coincidence. A photo of Erich Honecker showed a black bar across his forehead!

How had this come about? The black bar shone through from another photo on the back of the front page, and was actually scaffolding which was still in place around a new building in Halle-Neustadt, much praised for its size and its low-rent flats. A dark-coloured, wooden board of this scaffolding shone through the paper, giving the General Secretary of the Central Committee of the Socialist Unity

Party a *Brett vorm Kopf* (or 'board across his head'), which is a not very nice way of saying that someone is a blockhead.

Newspaper readers, the young man admitted, do not usually hold newspapers against the sun when reading them, but what if it should happen? He had therefore been called, on his day off, to hurry to his place of work to help pulp the 50,000-odd copies already printed. And so he rushed off, though not without telling me of the damage this mistake could have done had the class enemy got wind of it!

How the above-mentioned intimate relationship between the Party and the media, in this case *Neues Deutschland*, can have far-reaching and unexpected consequences is shown by my second example. One day, I believe it was in the early 1980s, the paper announced in a short article that the monthly payments for old-age pensioners, which were notoriously low, were to be increased, I don't remember by what percentage. At that time, I had an acquaintance who had an acquaintance who knew somebody in the GDR government. And thus I learned that neither the government nor the Party had planned to increase the pensions, nor could the country afford this increase economically. But since the newspaper was the Organ of the Central Committee of the Party and thus could never err, and also since people had long been waiting for such an increase, the pensions were indeed grudgingly raised by a modest amount, thus adding to the national debt. The editor responsible for this fake but rectified news was said to have been banished to the Letters to the Editor department, an outcome that could have been much worse. As if to make amends, the newspaper in its edition of 12 March 1984 contained no fewer than 43 (!) photos of General Secretary Erich Honecker visiting the Leipzig Trade Fair.

A reporter on East German radio, Radio DDR, kept his job, however, even though he mistakenly thought he could crack a joke by saying in the morning radio programme: 'As there are no bananas to be had at the moment, cheer up and eat an extra egg.'

Should you be wondering why people in East Germany were so stubbornly reluctant to believe in the cause of socialism, it may have been because they got 90 per cent of their direct information from West German radio and TV. (This was discovered by the Stasi itself, but of course never made public.)

Beyond the reach of the Stasi were the editors of the West German magazine *Tempo*, who came up with the following prank:

On 19 March 1988 a number of people in East Berlin and the GDR found in their mailboxes or on their doorsteps as well as in railway stations, phone booths, and other public places copies of *Neues Deutschland* that were actually complete fakes. The Hamburg magazine had produced 6,000 copies of the newspaper that looked exactly like the real thing, and contained the most outrageous news.

For example, that *glasnost* ('transparency'), Gorbachev's new political course in the Soviet Union, was to be introduced in the GDR, that 5,000 political prisoners had been set free, that dissidents who had fled East Germany were asked to return and promised a hearty welcome, that the most stubborn and obtuse members of the Political Bureau, the real centre of power in the country, had been fired, and, to crown it all: that the Stasi had been abolished.

From now on people would be able to buy the *Playboy* magazine (sporting the German title *Spielmann,* literally 'Playman'), and travel agencies would offer flights to Los Angeles, Rome, and Madrid, taking off from either Schönefeld (in East Berlin) or Tegel (in West Berlin), whichever the passengers preferred.

Neues Deutschland, the real one, waited almost ten days before it published a lame denial, saying that 'a primitive fake of *Neues Deutschland*, produced in West Germany, had been disseminated', and that this would not help improve relations between the two countries. Of course, nothing was said about the contents of the fake publication.

This was no doubt one of the few times when people read the newspaper with any real interest. Nothing is known about the number of people in the GDR who were taken in by the deception. Probably not very many as the announced measures and news items sounded too good to be believable. One-and-a-half years later, though, every promise had come true.

It is one of the great ironies of recent history that the SED in October/November 1989, after they had gotten rid of Erich Honecker and replaced him with Egon Krenz as the new General Secretary, Chairman of the National Defence Council, and Chairman of the State Council, initiated their own downfall. Thousands of demonstrators in the streets of Berlin and other major cities in East Germany, notably Leipzig, had finally lost their fear. They forced the Party and the government (which were virtually identical) to start those very reforms that had been so mischievously reported in the fake edition of *Neues Deutschland*. But it was too late. Frantically shoring up their Stalinistic regime, they had simply clung to power for too long.

I was, as I said, in West Germany at the time, and I watched the famous press conference of Günter Schabowski on TV. Ever since then I have been very fond of the German word *unverzüglich*. To an English native speaker, this word, with its eerie umlaut (ü), may look and sound sinister—and it is also hard for the English tongue to pronounce (try it!)—but to me it has a very sweet ring to it. In fact, the word is rather old-fashioned and literary, and tends not to be used much in everyday German. But Günter Schabowski, member of the Political Bureau, being an educated man, did indeed use it.

When Schabowski was asked, in the above-mentioned press conference on 9 November 1989, when the new travel regulations announced by the government were actually to come into force, he was caught off balance. He fumbled with his papers, stuttered, and finally said that people were free to travel to the West 'unverzüglich', that is, right away, immediately. He did this forgetting or overlooking the fact that his boss, Egon Krenz, had fixed an embargo on that item until 4 o'clock the following morning.

As a consequence, the frontier guards, first at the check points in Berlin and later along the entire western frontier of the GDR, were taken by surprise and virtually overwhelmed by the crowds eager to take advantage of the new freedom. Left helpless, and in the absence of orders from their superior officers, the guards opened the barriers and let the people through. So, when the SED at long last moved towards replacing freedom of suppression with freedom of expression—of which the Schabowski press conference was a sure indication—they inadvertently brought their own regime crashing to the ground.

3

The Rushdie Affair and the British Press

Some Salutary Lessons*

BHIKHU PAREKH

The author of *The Satanic Verses* is as complex and fascinating as his book. As a Muslim growing up in the cosmopolitan, but predominantly Hindu, city of Bombay, Rushdie is a child of two different cultures and is one of the very few Indians to write about the two communities with almost equal affection and understanding. As an Indian who was educated and spent a large part of his life in England, he acquired a second cultural home and added two more dimensions to his plural identity, those of an immigrant and an anglicized Indian. Unlike *Midnight's Children*, in which he explored his roots in Bombay and sought to capture its changing identity in the context of the changes

* Bhikhu Parekh's magisterial analysis of the reactions to *The Satanic Verses* was published in 1990, soon after the events it describes, and has never been bettered.

in his own, and unlike *Shame*, an inferior work in which he wrote about Pakistan, *The Satanic Verses* is a meta-novel, exploring the very process of self-exploration, and intimating a distinct view, almost a theory of the nature of the self. It depicts the way the self, which is inescapably embedded in a specific language, pattern of relationship, and natural and social environment, undergoes changes in response to its changing environment, holds on to the past while contemplating the future gestated in the womb of the present, and constantly reconstitutes itself. As Rushdie (1989) once put it:

> I did not want to write a kind of sociologically based fiction about how terrible it is today for black people in England. I wanted to write a novel which at its most fundamental level is about metamorphosis—the nature of it, the process by which it happens, its effect on the metamorphosed self and on the world around it, and its link with the act of travelling. Not least because the pressures exerted by migration are one of the classic contemporary locations of metamorphosis—what I call 'translation': a carrying across of the self into another place and another language.
>
> I am fascinated by how the classic roots of the self in language, society and place are disrupted by the act of migration: you suddenly find yourself in a new culture with different rules, and a new language, and for a while you flounder. The self is forced to find different principles on which to invent itself. That's what I was really trying to write about.

An immigrant cannot write about his experiences as an immigrant so long as he remains one. In order to write about them, he needs to transcend, and look at, them from the outside, and hence must cease being a mere immigrant. If he is nothing but an immigrant, he is overwhelmed by his experiences and lacks the distance and detachment needed to write about them. If he ceases to be an immigrant altogether and 'goes native', he is too distant and detached from them and possesses too non-emotive a memory of them to write about them with passion and intensity. An immigrant can meaningfully write about his life only from within the space created by his dual outsider/insider identity. He must feel settled enough to abstract himself from his experience of immigration, see it in the round, and enjoy the confidence needed to face its tensions and turmoil with equanimity. Yet he must remain sufficiently unsettled to feel the experience of migration in his bones and retain a chastened sense of exile. *The Satanic Verses* therefore called for a much greater degree of internal integration in its author than his earlier works, and engaged the whole of his personality. As Rushdie put it in an interview with Gerald Marzorati (1989):

> In writing *The Satanic Verses* I think I was writing for the first time from the whole of myself. The English part, the Indian part. The part of me that loves London, and the part that longs for Bombay.
>
> But most of the time, people will ask me—will ask anyone like me—are you Indian? Pakistani? English?
>
> What is being expressed is a discomfort with a plural identity. And what I am saying to you—and saying in the novel—is that we have got to come to terms with this. We are increasingly becoming a world of migrants, made up of bits and fragments from here, there. We are here. And we have never really left anywhere we have been.

Even as a scientific method of inquiry must be adequate to, and capable of, grasping the true nature of its subject matter, a literary technique must correspond to the reality it seeks to explore. Since at least the First World War, magic realism, which combines surrealism with heightened language, has appealed to many writers as the only mode in which to depict a reality that continually overtakes the imagination and refuses to conform to conventional canons of rationality or even intelligibility. The interplay between the extraordinary and the mundane that occurs in so much Latin American fiction or in Günter Grass's *Tin Drum* is not merely a literary technique, but a reflection of the world, in which the fantastic is often part of the everyday life. Not surprisingly, Rushdie uses the hallucinatory devices of magic realism to capture the immigrant's experiences of the world, and his novel abounds in strange and impossible events. A girl subsists on a diet of butterflies; two men falling from an aeroplane miraculously survive, one sprouting an angelic halo, the other horns and a tail; they undergo bizarre experiences, and much of the novel is full of dreams occurring within dreams. Such events, described in an appropriately melodramatic and racy prose, taking liberties with ordinary rules of grammar, spelling, and propriety, are intended to give the reader some idea of just how fantastic life has become. Anxious to break down the conventional dualism of good and evil (the 'ethic of impurity' as he once called it), Rushdie deliberately mixes up the sacred and the profane, fact and fiction, the holy and the obscene, and frequently uses the four letter word, both simply and in different, at times somewhat distasteful, combinations.

I

Rushdie devotes two chapters in the novel to one Prophet Mahound who, on the basis of divine revelations, founded a new monotheistic religion in the hedonistic city of Jahilia.[1] The names, descriptions, remarks, and experiences of their central characters, the themes explored, and the sequence of events leave little doubt that he had Islam and its founder in mind.[2] When it was published in September 1988, British Muslims protested. They did not seem much concerned about its critical discussion of Islam to which most of them had long been accustomed, but felt strongly about its treatment of Muhammad, his disciples, and his wives, a sensitive subject for Muslims for centuries. They resented that he had been called an impostor who made up his revelations as he went along, made deals with the Archangel, and treated religion as a kind of business. They were deeply offended that he had been called 'a smart bastard' and a debauchee who, after his wife's death, slept with so many women that his beard turned 'half-white' in a year. They resented too that his three revered colleagues were called 'those goons—those fucking clowns', the 'trinity of scum'. Like any great religious text, the Koran is full of rules and injunctions about forms of worship, helping the poor, concern for those in need, moral purity, self-discipline, and surrender to the will of God. The Muslims bitterly complained that *The Satanic Verses* had mockingly reduced it to a book of 'spouting' rules about how to 'fart', 'fuck' and 'clean one's behind'. They also felt distressed by the brothel scene in the book in which twelve prostitutes increased their earnings by taking the names of, and pretending to be, Mahound's wives. In short,

[1] For a further discussion, see Parekh (1989a).

[2] Rushdie himself admitted this; see Appignanesi and Maitland (1989, 28).

they felt outraged and distressed by what they took to be the book's mocking tone, its 'obscene' and 'abominably foul language', and the 'outrageous liberties' it had taken with their religion.

In retrospect, what strikes one about the Muslim protests since October is not so much their intolerance as their timidity, not their feeling of rage but their sense of hurt, not their anger but their distress. Muslim leaders did not translate the offensive passages into Urdu or Arabic for fear of provoking violent reactions among their followers. They quietly pursued the matter with the publishers, Members of Parliament, the Attorney-General, and the Prime Minister. Many of them did not at this stage ask for a ban on the book, and were content to plead for the insertion of a statement that it was a work of fiction and did not, despite the appearance to the contrary, provide an accurate history of Islam. Neither its author nor its publishers seem to have taken them seriously enough to engage in a dialogue with them. According to Muslim leaders, the publishers either did not reply to their letters and telegrams or did so without any sense of urgency and seriousness. As for Rushdie himself, he tended to dismiss the protesters as illiterate fanatics who had neither read nor understood the book and were only bent on suppressing a critical scrutiny of their cherished dogmas.

The British press was just as dismissive. Neither the quality nor the quantity papers published the offending passages, invited Muslim spokesmen to state their case, or themselves made an attempt to read the book with their eyes. Instead they mocked the Muslims, accused them of 'intolerance', and wondered if a tolerant society should tolerate the intolerant. Although Muslims were intensely frustrated and angry, and although isolated individuals spoke of violence, no Muslims, to my knowledge, threatened Rushdie's or his wife's life or even threw a stone at him or his house, something any one of the thousands of hotheads could have easily done at a time when he was unguarded and vulnerable.

When their noisy but peaceful protests and their fairly large but mostly unreported demonstrations got nowhere, a small group of Muslims burned a copy of *The Satanic Verses* in Bolton on 2 December 1988. That too aroused no national interest. Evidently a London solicitor advised them that they stood a better chance of attracting attention if they burned a copy after duly alerting the national media. They did that in Bradford on 14 January 1989, and secured instant national publicity. Rather than stimulate a reasoned discussion of their grievance as they had naively hoped, the book-burning incident led to a torrent of denunciation. Muslims were called 'barbarians', 'uncivilized', 'fanatics', and compared to the Nazis. Many a writer, some of impeccable liberal credentials, openly wondered how Britain could 'civilize' them and protect their innocent progeny against their parent's 'medieval fundamentalism'. Hardly anyone appreciated that the burning of *The Satanic Verses* was more an act of impatience than of intolerance, and that it bore no resemblance to the Nazi burning of libraries and persecution of intellectuals. No one cared to point out either that only a few months earlier, several Labour Party Members of Parliament had burnt a copy of the new immigration rules outside the House of Commons without raising so much as a murmur of protest.

Muslim protests in Britain were now beginning to attract international attention. Some Muslim leaders unwisely tried to internationalize the issue by making representations to Muslim heads of state. In response to these and other factors the late Ayatollah Khomeini made his notorious intervention and pronounced a death sentence on Rushdie on 14 February 1989. His fatwā marked a turning point in the development of Muslim consciousness. Tolerant, and even a little timid until then, the British Muslims suddenly experienced a sense of power. They had managed to extract a statement of regret from Rushdie; they now commanded media attention; they were courted by the British Government; and they had succeeded in shifting national attention from themselves to *The Satanic Verses*. The sense of power, combined with a mean desire for revenge at having been ignored for so long, generated a new mood of aggressive intolerance. Those who knew better lacked the courage and good sense to warn their community against the enormity of the contemplated act. The orthodox had the field all to themselves and took full advantage of it to whip up powerful feelings of hatred and vengeance. The national press exacerbated the situation. It sent out correspondents to Muslim areas, especially to Bradford, where they interviewed leaders and even young and confused Muslim boys and girls with leading questions, and created the overwhelming impression that the entire Muslim community was seething with a bloodthirsty spirit of vengeance. Unintentionally, the press united the Muslim community, created a new orthodoxy, and made every Muslim who wished no harm to Rushdie feel 'inauthentic' and not a 'true Muslim'. Even some of my sensible Muslim students fell into this tragic trap.

In their new mood, the Muslim leaders escalated their demands. Hitherto most of them had been content to insist that the book should carry the religious equivalent of the health warning on our cigarette packets. They now demanded that the book be banned, not be issued in paperback edition, and be withdrawn from public libraries, and that the existing law of blasphemy which protected the Anglican church be extended to other religions as well. A few pursued their case for separate Muslim schools with increased vigour, and some even pressed for the recognition of the Muslim civil law.

II

The British press's reaction to the Muslim reaction, which it had done much to engineer, albeit unintentionally, followed a sad and predictable pattern.[3] A death threat to any human being, especially a prodigiously gifted and courageous writer, is naturally a traumatic experience for any society, especially one so peaceful as Britain. The fact that some of their fellow citizens placed their religious loyalty above the basic obligations of citizenship set a dangerous precedent. The further fact that they should take orders from an external authority was reminiscent of Pope Pius V's call for the murder of 'that wicked woman', Queen Elizabeth I, in the sixteenth century, and was obviously unacceptable to a nation whose history as an independent sovereign state began with the rejection of an extra-territorial authority. Not surprisingly, almost the entire British press got emotionally unhinged and lost its balance.

The liberal papers dutifully published some of the offending passages from *The Satanic Verses*, but neither interpreted nor set them in a context. *The Guardian* (16 February 1989) led the way by reproducing half a dozen passages first published in the Muslim magazine, *Impact*, as long ago as 10 November 1988, but without explanatory comment. Some newspapers invited Muslim spokesmen to state their

[3] See Parekh (1989b).

case, but neither their regular columnist nor their editorial writers sought to engage in a dialogue with them. Most concentrated not on the book, the source of the controversy, but on the Muslim threat to Rushdie's life.

Anthony Burgess (*The Independent*, 16 February 1989) compared Muslims to Nazis who 'shame' Britain 'through the vindictive agency of bonfires'. Since they wanted a 'theocratic state' and did not like a secular society, they should 'fly to the arms of the Ayatollah or some self-righteous guardian of strict morality'. Their protest was mindless, 'unjustified by argument, thought or anything more intellectual than the throwing of stones [*sic*] or the striking of matches'. Even the otherwise sane and perceptive Peter Jenkins (*The Independent*, 1 March 1989) thundered against the 'Bradford auto-da-fé', that 'barbaric act of intolerance', and congratulated Mrs Thatcher for standing up, like a good Christian, for a writer who had been rude to her. He speculated on why the Ayatollah had waited so long before issuing his fatwā and retailed a fanciful story. Evidently the Iranian radicals, anxious to use the Bradford burning incident in their struggle against their liberal rivals, 'one fine morning' pushed a draft of the fatwā before the Imam. Jenkins conceded that the story could not be authenticated, but that did not stop him from claiming a 'ring of truth about it'. After all it enabled him to father the fatwā on Bradford Muslims and trace the root of the trouble to people under British control.

Hugo Young (*The Guardian*, 21 February 1989), one of our finest columnists, who never once lost his balance throughout the controversy, wisely concentrated on condemning the Ayatollah's death threat, and the failure of British Muslims to treat it with the contempt it deserved. Even he, however, did not explain why the otherwise law-abiding Muslims felt so strongly about the book, whether the right to free speech could ever be absolute, and whether a creative writer was not subject to at least moral, as opposed to legal, constraints.

All the newspapers, including the liberal, debated whether British society had an obligation to tolerate the intolerant and whether multiculturalism was not a dangerous doctrine. An otherwise perceptive editorial in *The Independent* (18 February 1989) thundered against the evils of something called fundamentalism. A *Guardian* editorial asked Muslims to recognize that they were living in a secular society and that they must change their ways of thought and life. Several newspapers wondered if Britain had not made a 'mistake' in 'letting in' too many Muslims. Even Roy Jenkins, father of the Race Relations Act, 1976, lamented that 'we might have been more cautious about allowing the creation in the 1950s [*sic*] of a substantial Muslim community here'. He went further and reached the most bizarre conclusion that the Muslim behaviour had strengthened his 'reluctance to have Turkey in the European community' (*The Independent*, 4 March 1989). Apparently all Muslims, like the proverbial Chinese, looked the same to him, and one threatened misdeed by a section of them was enough to damn the lot.

It was depressing to note how the legitimate rage against the Ayatollah's murderous impertinence and outrageous Muslim support for it escalated step by even sillier step to a wholly mindless anger first against all Bradford Muslims, then against all British Muslims, then against all Muslims, and ultimately against Islam itself. There is quite a pile of disturbing raw material in this metamorphosis which anyone concerned about the moral health of Britain will one day have to analyse. Some 'liberal' commentators, a few of them with a leftist past, such as Fay Weldon, became instant experts on the Koran. They attacked its alleged inhumanity and 'bloodthirsty' conception of Allah, unfavourably compared them to the Bible and its 'loving' God, and gave us most valuable insights into the psychology of the mediaeval crusaders. The neutral observers were left wondering on which side of the debate lay 'fundamentalism', 'mediaevalism' and 'intolerance'. The history of the last one thousand years with its crusades, the white man's—and latterly woman's—burden, and the 'civilizing' empire, was tragicomically re-enacted before our eyes, and its white and brown *dramatis personae* parroted well-worn lines of their banal roles in all too familiar accents.

The conservative press fully shared these rather ugly feelings and was less inhibited about expressing them. Some conservative writers even used the occasion to settle their old scores with liberals in general and liberal intellectuals in particular. The best example of this was provided by Peregrine Worsthorne in his signed editorial in *The Sunday Telegraph* (19 February 1989), considered important enough to be reproduced in *The Daily Telegraph*. Working himself up into a fine state of anti-liberal triumphalism, he produced quite a catalogue of indictments against liberal intellectuals. They were all hypocrites as they had protested against bigotry and fundamentalism only when one of them was its victim. They were all lacking in judgement because they had failed to grasp the obvious point the conservatives had been making for years, namely that the multi-cultural society they had glorified and foisted on Britain was a dangerous and unwise experiment. They were also guilty of blatant inconsistency in accepting restrictions on free speech in racial but not in religious matters. Worsthorne went so far as to advocate restricting free speech in religious matters so as to teach liberal intellectuals a measure of self-discipline and humility. He claimed to hear menacing anti-Jewish and anti-Christian voices from 'the pulpits [*sic*] of many British mosques', and prophesied that in the future more violence would come from the Muslims than from the National Front. The comparison itself was suggestive.

While attacking the Muslims, some sections of the conservative press attacked Rushdie as well. Unlike the liberal press, which solidly stood by him, some conservative commentators criticized his 'poor judgement', 'provocative' utterances, and 'bad manners' in mocking people's sacred beliefs. Hugh Trevor-Roper even thought that if a Muslim thug should 'waylay him [Rushdie and not, of course, Trevor-Roper] in a dark street and improve his manners, society would benefit and literature would not suffer'. The attacker could justifiably plead 'gross provocation' and Trevor-Roper 'would not shed a tear' (*The Independent*, 10 June 1989). Some conservative papers were far more interested in Britain's lucrative trade with Muslim countries than in free speech, and attacked Rushdie for jeopardizing it. Almost all of them took perverse delight in the fact that he was forced to flee his own people and seek the protection of the state he had lambasted in their name. They saw in this a conclusive refutation of his politics, his lack of integrity, a vindication of the liberal society's resilience and greatness, and, of course, the forgiveness of Christian Britain and its generous Prime Minister. They rubbed all this in with unctuous self-righteousness and turned a most painful episode into an occasion for national self-congratulation.

III

In light of some Muslim leaders' charge that the publication of *The Satanic Verses* was part of a 'Zionist conspiracy', the Jewish participation in the debate makes fascinating reading. As one would expect from a sophisticated and politically diverse community, the Jewish commentators covered a wide spectrum, demonstrating how ill-founded the charge was. Let us take four fairly typical comments.

Barbara Amiel (*The Times*, 24 February 1989) commented on the difficulty liberal Britain faced in living with Muslims 'whose entire moral ethos is illiberal and for whom tolerance is anathema'. Britain was a 'Christian' liberal democracy and the immigrants must accept its central values, which she left unspecified. She attacked the race relations legislation, including the 'Committee for Racial Equality' (meaning the Commission of Racial Equality), and condemned the alleged official and unofficial reluctance to discuss the high Afro-Caribbean crime rate. 'Speaking as a Jew, (if the Jews had been responsible for such a crime rate) I would want that figure to be released, and I would want the Rabbi to discuss it in synagogue.' She saw nothing wrong in American immigration officers some decades ago giving arbitrary and easily pronounceable names and surnames to newly arrived East European immigrants; that was necessary to create a united and 'recognisable American nation'. She opposed both the extension of the blasphemy law and the creation of state-funded Muslim schools.

Lord Jakobovits, in his capacity as the Chief Rabbi, wrote a long letter to *The Times* (4 March 1989). While condemning the threat against Rushdie's life, he contended that 'the book should not have been published'. In a civilized society, all, including creative writers, had an obligation to respect and 'generate respect' for other people's religious beliefs and to do nothing that ridiculed or denigrated them. Rushdie had 'abused' freedom of speech. Free speech was not an absolute value, which is why we had laws against blasphemy, pornography, libel, incitement to racial hatred, subversion, and breaches of national security. There should be similar laws prohibiting the publication of anything likely 'to inflame, through obscene defamation, the feelings or beliefs of any section of society, or be liable to provoke public disorder and violence'. Lord Jakobovits was against extending the law of blasphemy, not only because the definition of blasphemy varied from religion to religion, but more importantly because in a 'predominantly Christian' society 'majority faith' was entitled to privileged treatment. The basic objective behind its extension could be better, and more effectively, secured by legally redefining the limits of socially tolerable conduct.

Melanie Phillips, 'writing as a Jew' (*The Guardian*, 3 March 1989), was also balanced and sensible. She criticized the strong assimilationist and homogenizing thrust at the heart of British society, showed how the Jews had suffered as a result, and pleaded for cultural pluralism. Each ethnic community had a right to preserve its distinct heritage, and British society was the richer for that. Like the Catholics and Jews, the Muslims were therefore entitled to have their own schools, subject to certain obvious guarantees. She was one of the first to show why the blasphemy law and the law against racial discrimination were qualitatively different, and to argue that the latter was fully defensible while the former was not.

Gerald Kaufman (*The Independent*, 1 March 1989) was one of the first to expose the racism informing much of the national debate on the Rushdie affair. The liberals were prepared, he said, to fight against racial discrimination and stand up for Muslims so long as they conformed to liberal notions of acceptable conduct and did not get above themselves. Muslims were worth fighting for so long as they remained passive objects, but resented and rebuked the moment they began to act as self-determining subjects asserting their legitimate rights as British citizens. Kaufman lamented the ease with which the press and the public had slipped into the racist stereotyping of Muslims, and made a forceful plea for better inter-cultural understanding, cultural pluralism, and the Muslims' right to preserve their identity by all available means.

IV

The Muslim response to British society's reactions to their protests was extremely poor. Their leaders did not know how to handle the media and speak in idioms intelligible to their white fellow citizens. They responded to the Ayatollah's fatwā with incomprehensible immaturity and indecent haste. They never presented their case with care and in terms of principles British society itself avowed. Nor did they produce well-argued pamphlets or articles. And when some were invited to write by the liberal press, the quality of some of their offerings was pretty poor. Shabbir Akhtar (*The Guardian*, 27 February 1989), a talented thinker, began well with a strong attack on the hubris underlying the dominant mood of 'our light and their darkness', but soon lost his way. He insisted that *The Satanic Verses* was a bad book, but did not say why, and averred that it was only praised because of its anti-Muslim thrust, a considerable exaggeration. 'Anyone who fails to be offended by Rushdie's book *ipso facto* ceases to be a Muslim', he solemnly declared without noticing how much such a fundamentalist and narrow-minded view was bound to alienate those he was seeking to persuade. He insisted that blasphemy was never to be tolerated because it invariably led to secularism. All nations, he went on, were 'fanatical' about something, be it football, sex, or religion; and of the various forms of fanaticism, that 'on behalf of God' was the best and the noblest. He neither defended nor pursued the consequences of this strange assertion. Akhtar wondered how Muslims should live in a secular society and suggested the naive alternatives of *hijrah* (immigration) and *jehad* (holy war), between which he predictably could not make up his mind. In his subsequent writings he took a much more sophisticated line. However, his defence of 'fundamentalism', which he rarely defined, and his attack on Rushdie's alleged apostasy rested on weak grounds and persuaded few.[4]

Yaqub Zaki, a Briton converted to Islam and a professor at Harvard, wrote a disappointing article in *The Times* (28 February 1989). He was convinced that Rushdie's book was 'obscene and overflows with blasphemies', but did not mention, let alone discuss, them. He fell into the trap of talking about blasphemy, but never explained how this essentially Christian concept applied to Islam. Unlike Jesus who is semi-divine, Muhammad is entirely human. He is neither a Son nor an incarnation of God but a prophet, and therefore attacks on him have a very different religious meaning from those on Jesus or Rama. Zaki emphasized Rushdie's alleged apostasy, a specifically Islamic concept that made little sense to, and carried no conviction with, non-Muslims. He did not explain either why Rushdie was not at liberty to give up his religion. If Rushdie was never a believer or later ceased to be one, his book could not be an act of apostasy.

While not a Muslim himself, Edward Said is an Arab and known for his pro-Muslim sympathies. As one would expect, he was erudite

[4] Shabbir Akhtar's *Be Careful with Muhammed! The Salman Rushdie Affair* (1989) is a perceptive and well-argued book, but it too reasons within a narrow and uncritical framework.

and perceptive, but ambiguous (*The Observer*, 25 February 1989). He insisted on Rushdie's right to write as he pleased, and was against both banning the book and threatening its author with violence. Said, however, subtly distanced himself from the book and wondered if it was intellectually fair and politically wise. Rushdie came 'from the community of Islam', and had written the book 'both in and for the West'. As such he was expected to offer a 'sympathetic' account of Islam, especially when the West so much misunderstood and reduced it to terrorism and fundamentalism. Sadly, the book portrayed Islam both 'irreverently and blasphemously' [*sic*]. Said formulated the Muslim agony thus:

> Why must a Muslim, who could be defending and sympathetically interpreting us, now represent us so roughly, so expertly and so disrespectfully to an audience already primed to excoriate our tradition, reality, history, religion, language and origins? Why, in other words, must a member of our culture join the legions of orientalists in orientalising Islam so radically and so unfairly?

The book, like its author, was situated 'in history', and should not have ignored the political reality of the contemporary world, in which Islam felt under siege and needed a critical, but sympathetic, interpretation. Said's article, which begged a number of questions, conveyed the impression that while Rushdie was right to write the book, he should have been more balanced and judicious.

V

Like the Muslim response, that of the non-Muslim intellectuals of Asian origin was also rather disappointing. Their ranks included many talented men and women who were knowledgeable about Islam and could have mediated between the Muslims and British society at large. As far as I know, none of them initially felt concerned enough to write about the subject in either the ethnic or the national press. Some of them only woke up in the aftermath of the Ayatollah's fatwā[5] and their intervention took the form of an advertisement in *The Guardian*

[5] I was one of them and regret not having been able to read the runes aright in time.

(25 February 1989). Despite some of its commendable sentiments, it showed how little the intellectuals understood their fellow Asians. The fact that the entire ethnic press ignored the advertisement showed how little the Asian community valued their intervention.

The Guardian advertisement, entitled 'Statement from concerned individuals of Asian origin', was disappointing for several reasons. First, it was not clear why its signatories felt it necessary to respond to the Rushdie affair as Asians. The protest had been mounted by Muslims. Not all Muslims are Asian, nor all Asians Muslims. And therefore Asians qua Asians were irrelevant to the controversy. The advertisement invited the avoidable suspicion that the Asians were worried lest they should be tarred by the Muslim brush and wished to dissociate themselves from the protesting Muslims. The fact that nearly three-quarters of the signatories were non-Muslims, mainly from India, reinforced the suspicion. Second, the advertisement asserted the importance of the right to dissent, something no major Muslim leader had questioned. Their protest was not directed at Rushdie's right to criticize Islam, as was evident in the fact that none of the passages where he did so were included in the widely circulated list of offending passages; rather it was aimed at what the Muslims, rightly or wrongly, regarded as the 'obscene' and 'foul' language used in the discussion of Muhammad and his family and companions. Third, the signatories condemned the Bradford book-burning without inquiring what it meant to Muslims and whether it bore any resemblance to the Nazi burning of books. While the white intellectuals could be forgiven for exaggerating the nihilist intent behind it, one was entitled to expect a greater understanding from those familiar with the practices of the Indian subcontinent. Fourth, the signatories did not consider it fit to place the protest in a historical context, as Edward Said had done, nor to admit that the book might have been guilty of occasional lapses of taste. Had they done so and then gone on to urge Muslims not to push their protest too far in their own long-term interest, their appeal would have appeared less biased and would have carried more conviction. Finally, it was not clear what the advertisement was supposed to achieve. If it was meant to persuade the Muslim community to become more open-minded and accept the need for reform, then it or, preferably, a lengthy and carefully argued statement should have been placed in the ethnic press read by an overwhelming majority of them. Publishing it in *The Guardian* exposed them to the no doubt ill-founded criticism that they were not interested in arguing with their fellow nationals, but in signalling to the white establishment that they were not 'like the rest of them'. It is ironic that *The Satanic Verses*, which the advertisement defended, is at pains to argue that a racist society thrives on 'divide and rule', and perpetuates itself by co-opting the immigrant elite.

It is instances of this kind that have made the Asian community intensely suspicious of its intellectuals. When a colleague asked a group of educated and uneducated Muslims why they had not involved their intellectuals in the struggle, the reaction was immediate and fierce. A school teacher said:

> *Ye sub sale harami hai. Na kabhi hamare the, na honge.*
>
> [All these scoundrels are useless. They were never ours, never will be.]

Another, a graduate working in a textile mill, said:

> *Ye hain gore ke chumche, sahib. Struggle ki bat bahut karte hain, magar kab mar khaya, nokari gai, tankha kam hui inki? Ye apne ko bahut bade samazte hain, or hamse nafrat karte hain. Aisa lagta hai ki hamse ye sharminda hain.*
>
> [They are all stooges of the whites. They talk a lot about struggle, but when have they been beaten up, lost their jobs or suffered a reduction in their salary? They think highly of themselves and hate us. It seems they are even ashamed of us.]

Although the criticisms were highly exaggerated and bitter, the Asian intellectuals can only ignore them at their peril. They need to ponder over Gramsci's notion of organic intellectuals and Edward Said's point about the writer's responsibility to his community in an inhospitable environment.

VI

In the light of our discussion several important conclusions follow. First, throughout the various stages of the controversy, most of the national press made little attempt to articulate and explain to its readers the nature and grounds of Muslim complaints against *The Satanic Verses*. As happens so often in 'tribal' England, it instinctively ganged up against the Muslims, mocking, abusing, ridiculing, and morally bludgeoning them into silence. With several honourable exceptions, the racism of many a journalist was just below the surface. They attacked not just the protest, which they were entitled to do, but the entire Muslim community as barbarians unfit to be citizens of a civilized society. The widely used and never clearly defined term 'fundamentalism' became a popularly accepted disguise beneath which racism masqueraded itself. Catholic, Jewish, and Anglican fundamentalism were acceptable, but not Muslim. Every Muslim parent who disapproved of sexual permissiveness, mixed sports, or girls wearing shorts was dismissed as a fundamentalist. The term became a devious device for blackmailing Muslims into rejecting their values. Hardly any liberal realized that in countering Muslim 'fundamentalism' they were setting up a rival fundamentalism of their own and corrupting the great liberal tradition. Historically speaking, whenever liberalism has felt frightened and nervous, it has tended to become aggressive and intolerant. The Rushdie affair was no exception. It also showed how little the national press knew about the ethnic minorities and the kind of debate that had gone on for months in the ethnic press. It had very few ethnic minority journalists, and they either lacked contact with their communities or were too nervous to report accurately.

Hardly any journalist cared to point out that even the self-confident Christian in an allegedly secular society had taken quite a time coming to terms with films on Jesus. Until the 1960s a strict protocol governed his depiction and it was considered disrespectful to portray his face on the screen. *The Last Days of Pompeii* (1935), *Quo Vadis?* (1951), and *Ben-Hur* (1959) show him only from afar or feature only his hand or foot. In *King of Kings* (1961), Jeffrey Hunter, who played Jesus, had to remove all bodily hair because it detracted from his divinity! *The Last Temptation of Christ* (1988) was irreverent but not at all abusive or mocking. As the director Martin Scorsese himself said: 'I wanted to show a Christ you could agree with … a real earthy Jesus.' He went on, 'It was never my intention to … shake anyone's faith, but rather to ignite faith.' Yet his film provoked a public outcry unprecedented in the history of religious films. Militant Christians launched a media campaign condemning Universal Pictures, the film's distributor, and staged a mock flagellation of Christ in front of the home of Lee Wasserman, Chairman of the parent company of Universal. They so intimidated theatre owners that several movie chains refused to show the film, and unsuccessfully demanded its total destruction so that it could never again be shown to the public.

After initial resistance, Christians came to accept Jesus as a righteous rocker in *Jesus Christ Superstar* and as an innocent clown in *Godspell* (both were stage musicals in 1971, and filmed in 1973). But they took to the barricades when he was portrayed as a charlatan in *The Passover Plot* (1976). The film was picketed out of existence after lasting only a few weeks, and never heard of again. It would seem that the Muslims are only a few years behind Christians in these matters. Both need to develop a greater spirit of religious tolerance and scepticism. Neither is in a position to lecture the other.

Second, with isolated exceptions, Muslim spokesmen showed remarkable incapacity to state their case cogently and coherently. They did not, or would not, appreciate the force of the liberal case for free speech and the difficulties involved in deciding when and how to restrict it. They showed little understanding of British history and the British political system, and spoke and acted in a way that alienated most of their sympathizers and convinced very few. They drew untenable comparisons between *The Satanic Verses* and the Spycatcher trial,[6] and kept talking about apostasy as if a Muslim was never at liberty to give up his religion. Rather than dispute the charge of fundamentalism or define the term and analyse its various forms and levels, many accepted the dominant definition of it and turned it into a virtue. Some flamboyantly flaunted their fundamentalism and lectured 'decadent' Britain in the familiar, missionary tone of spiritual arrogance. The white converts to Islam, who were ideally placed to mediate between the two communities, tended to be particularly unctuous. It was appalling to see after the Ayatollah's intervention that no Muslim leader condemned the death threat or even realized how unacceptable and offensive it was to all those not blinded or rendered callous by religious dogmas.

[6] The 1987 autobiography of a former intelligence officer, which the British government made strenuous legal efforts to ban.

Third, the national press reflected, reinforced, and did little to bridge the racial divide in the country as a whole. Either the white writers discussed Muslim protests among themselves, thereby treating Muslims as passive objects and outsiders, or Muslim spokesmen were 'invited' to state 'their' case. Rarely did the two meet together to debate as fellow citizens the kind of Britain they wished to create and the terms of their membership of it. 'This is what we are. Live as we do or leave': this unspoken premise of the national debate hardly displays such values as moral equality, common citizenship, tolerance, diversity, pluralism, and dialogue, which British society rightly cherishes and without which it can never be stable and peaceful.

Fourth, most of the national press conceptualized the entire controversy in terms of the inviolability of free speech. This was a gross oversimplification. In Britain and elsewhere, free speech is rightly subject to several constraints. It is impermissible when it libels an individual, endangers national security, causes public disorder, and leads to incitement of racial hatred. The Muslims did not deny free speech; they only questioned the conventional criteria used to restrict it. Though they put their case badly, they had a case and threw up important issues of which we need to take note.

The concept of free speech is far more complex than is generally appreciated. Speech occurs in a variety of contexts, each unique and subject to its own distinct constraints. Communication within the privacy of a family or between friends represents one form of speech, and is generally the most free. That between doctors, priests, solicitors, or barristers, and their clients raises different issues and enjoys considerable legal protection. At a different level, parliamentary speeches are rightly regarded as privileged communication, enjoying protection denied to ordinary citizens. Scholarly, literary, and scientific speech is generally subject to professional self-discipline and enjoys a good deal of freedom. The press, which by its very nature is public, powerful, reaches out to millions, has no institutional check, and is capable of causing considerable damage to ordinary men and women, is rightly subject to greater constraints. In short, freedom of speech cannot be advocated and defended in abstract and noncontextual terms. It might be granted in some areas, but not in others, or granted to a much greater degree in one area than in another without incurring the charge of inconsistency. It is not indivisible and requires a more complex and differentiated justification than is offered so far.

While free speech is most desirable, it is not the only value. It therefore needs to be reconciled with such other values as avoidance of needless suffering, social harmony, protection of the weak, truthfulness in the public realm, and the self-respect and dignity of individuals and groups. Besides, such reconciliation needs to be achieved not in the abstract and once and for all, but in the context of the changing circumstances of the society in question. In a society with a history of constant inter-religious violence, free speech is rightly subject to greater constraints than in one free of it. Although the constraints are regrettable, they are necessary, and can only be gradually removed as the society in question becomes mature and harmonious. That was why the Indian government was right to ban *The Satanic Verses*, and Rushdie was wrong to lambast it. This also explains why Britain has a law banning discrimination on racial but not on religious and economic grounds, and why Northern Ireland bans discrimination on religious but not racial grounds. The Muslims were rightly asking whether the race relations legislation needed to be extended to cover religious groups as well, and whether it was right to privilege the Church of England under the blasphemy law.

Self-respect, dignity, and others' good opinion are rightly regarded as some of the highest moral values in every society, especially a liberal one. That is why libel is a punishable offence, and has in recent months attracted unduly heavy damages. An individual is not a free-floating atom but a member of a specific community, and his identity is at once both personal and social. His self-respect is therefore necessarily tied up with, and partly grounded in, the general respect for his group. A Jew, an Afro-Caribbean, and an Indian feel demeaned not only when they are personally attacked but also when their respective communities are described in crude and hurtful ways. To say that 'all Jews are mean, rapacious and selfish' is to implicate and demean every one of them. Or to say that 'all blacks are thick, stupid and sexy', or that 'all Indians are effeminate, devious and unreliable' is to degrade every black and every Indian. Such remarks amount to ethnic libel and can be no less hurtful than individual libel. A society in which such remarks are made publicly, with general approval and moral impunity, demeans those involved both in their own and others' eyes, and treats them less equally than the rest. A civilized society based on mutual respect and decency needs to find ways of discouraging such remarks.

How we do so is a matter of strategy. In some countries the concept of ethnic libel is incorporated in their legal systems. The government of New South Wales in Australia has recently passed a law declaring ethnic vilification an offence. Even our race relations legislation is informed by a diluted version of this. Even if we do not legislate against ethnic, racial, and other forms of group vilification, surely we need to find other ways of showing society's collective disapproval of it. The recent decision by newspaper editors to introduce self-discipline and provide institutional redress to those feeling hurt is an important step in the right direction.

A creative writer lives in a community of men and needs to reconcile his freedom to write as he pleases with the legitimate rights of others to their individual and collective self-respect. Think of a novelist writing about the tragic victims of Auschwitz. Suppose he mocks and ridicules them, trivializes their suffering, and presents them as a despicable lot thoroughly deserving of all the mindless brutality inflicted on them by their tormentors. He creates scenes of collective debauchery, wife-swapping, incest, and cannibalism, and presents Jewish women as betraying their husbands and offering themselves and their young children to the Nazi guards in return for a few more days of life. Not only the Jews but all decent men and women would feel deeply outraged by such a 'literary' work and rightly complain that it violates their deepest feelings, takes unacceptable liberties with Jewish collective memories, and insults the honour and integrity of the victims. Since the law is a blunt instrument, and since we are rightly uneasy about giving government the power to censor creative writing, we may not ask for such a work to be banned. But we would be right to express our sense of outrage against it and our disapproval of, and even contempt for, the author in the strongest possible terms. To dismiss such protests as ignorant or inherently illegitimate is hardly the way to build up a humane literary culture. Like the press, literature is a public institution and creative writers are public figures wielding considerable moral and political power, for the exercise of which they are accountable not just to each other but to the community at large. Creating a sensitive and compassionate community based on mutual respect and concern is a collective task, requiring the efforts of not just politicians but all men, including, and especially, creative writers. The point of the Auschwitz example is not that *The Satanic Verses* is even remotely like it, but rather that the question of the freedom of creative writing is not as unproblematic as liberals would have us believe. Despite all their murderous threats and strident and confused language, Muslim protests have sharply brought home to us that the individual is socially situated and defined, that respect for him involves respect for the collective memories and heritage in terms of which he defines his identity, and that no creative writer can lightly override the moral obligations that this entails. His freedom cannot include infantile iconoclasm and mindless mud-slinging.

VII

When we approach *The Satanic Verses* in this light, we begin to form a just estimate of both the propriety and dangers of Muslim protests. *The Satanic Verses* is a brilliant literary composition, exploring with great tenderness, sensitivity, and courage the immigrant experiences of migration and exile. The two controversial chapters are a daring and highly imaginative exploration of the process of creating a religion. There are, however, places where they are open to criticisms. First, some parts of the two chapters reflect bad taste and handle a great theme in rather crude, abusive, and offensive language. Second, they show bad literary judgement. Rushdie could have easily handled the theme in a manner that did not bear such a close historical resemblance to Islam. It is disingenuous to say that he did not mean Islam and yet use names and events that are all drawn from its history. The Muslim suspicion that he was being deliberately provocative is not easy to dispel. Third, Rushdie showed a remarkable lack of political judgement. He could not have been unaware of at least half a dozen riots in India caused by similar references to the life of Muhammad. It is therefore surprising that, rather than handle them more skilfully, he chose to become even more provocative than the works that had led to so much violence in India and Pakistan. At least when the protests began to mount, he should have become alert, taken the Muslim community into his confidence, and at least tried to mollify them by the kind of statement he later made in the aftermath of the fatwā.[7]

[7] Rahul Singh interviewed the author V. S. Naipaul soon after the fatwā (*The Sunday Observer*, Bombay, 26 February 1989). He asked him: 'Don't you think Khomeini's murder contract on him is too atrocious for words?',

Since the Muslims felt both hurt and provoked, they were right to protest vigorously. Although it was politically unwise, and an emotionally traumatic event for white society, their burning a copy of the book too was understandable in the context. They were also right to picket and peacefully pressure the publishers not to issue it in paperback. By these and other actions they successfully placed their grievances on the public agenda and raised several important issues. They were and are utterly wrong to threaten violence against Rushdie and his publishers. It is against the law which they are obliged as British citizens to obey. Besides, apostasy is neither a legal nor a religious category under British law, and cannot be a basis of public protest or threats. Although they are wrong to insist that the book be banned and withdrawn from circulation, their demand that it not be issued in paperback has a point. If sections of white society and the publishers sincerely believe that the book is at times guilty of bad taste and has deeply distressed Muslims, they should demonstrate their limited disapproval of it. Since they are rightly committed to the principle of

---

to which Naipaul strangely replied, 'It's an extreme form of literary criticism' (laughs). He went on, 'I don't know his books but I've been aware of his statements. I found them usually left-wing and trivial and antiquated.' It is difficult to see why literature and what he dismissively calls 'left-wing' cannot go together. Naipaul is convinced that Islamic fundamentalism is intellectually shallow and lacks self-confidence and vitality. He observes:

> That is why fundamentalism is so powerful in the world, because these countries are the countries which are technologically at a disadvantage. In the way the world is organised at the moment, they are hangers-on. You might almost say they are parasites on the activity of the rest of the world. It is a fragile faith but that doesn't mean one should ignore it. … When Darwin attacked religion, it actually led to a great enriching of English civilisation because it was a part of science and development and of intellectual growth. Apart from faith, such societies have art, philosophy, debate, culture in its highest forms. The culture that is possessed by the fundamentalist societies is a rather Old Testament kind of culture, where the culture is almost a total expression of the religious faith. Everything is the faith: the way you get up, the way you eat, the way you get married, the customs you follow right through your life. That is one kind of culture. All are expressions of your adherence to your religious faith. The other kind of culture is exercise of the individual mind, the exercise of choice. The places outside have no idea of this higher world.

free speech and cannot allow the book to be banned or withdrawn, the only course of action left open to them is to press against a paperback edition. This is not horse-trading, surrender to 'fundamentalism', or a messy compromise, but a matter of consistency and prudence; the former because it reconciles a vital principle with a limited and self-acknowledged disapproval of parts of the book; the latter because, if done publicly and honourably, it entails a reciprocal moral gesture on the part of the Muslim community and may offer a way out of a tragic situation.

The Muslims have made, and are making, the same mistake as the British press, that of concentrating on Rushdie rather than the issues raised by his book. If they are really serious about ensuring that creative writers should in future exercise a measure of self-discipline and avoid giving gratuitous offence to people's deeply held feelings and sacred heritage, they need the support of both the literary community and British society as a whole. And they will not get it until they openly and unequivocally dissociate themselves from the threat of violence, and abjure every intention of ever harming Rushdie. Free and safe Rushdie is more likely to promote their cause than one condemned to live in hiding. Despite occasional bad literary and political judgements in the book, he understands and cares and feels for them, and has a better record of fighting racism and articulating their deepest anxieties and aspirations than some of their upstart leaders.

4

Free Expression, Censorship, and Information Literacy on the Internet

Some Perspectives on Search Engines and Social Media, and Their Usage*

JOACHIM GRIESBAUM

Thanks to information technology, we live in a world where information is abundant. Many people steadily carry around small hand-sized devices that allow 24/7 access to electronic information resources and offer round-the-clock options to get or stay connected with so-called contacts. For some, this world seems like a utopia.

But is this information-abundant world really such an ideal place, or should we take a more sceptical view? Possibly. According to Williams

* This chapter discusses questions of control and freedom of internet services, with a focus on search engines and social media. In addition to political, economic, and technical aspects, user behaviour is also a subject of discussion.

(2017), the internet can be seen as a tool for the government rather than as a force for democracy, because it makes the establishment of comprehensive surveillance easier. Furthermore, the emergence of the internet economy is connected with the establishment of a small number of businesses that concentrate in themselves extraordinary economic power as well as civic influence (Moore 2016).

According to Silverman (2016), viral fake election news stories outperformed real news on Facebook during the final three months of the 2016 United States (US) presidential campaign. And reviewing the results of some experiments, Epstein and Robertson (2015) have argued the possibility of a search engine manipulation effect influencing elections. These examples provide a first insight into what can be assessed as civic influence on the most central and important internet services of today, even if such consequences were not necessarily intended by the service providers. At the same time, they point to the fact that our lives are increasingly influenced by algorithms. For instance, it is algorithms and not humans that determine search engine result pages, the content of the Facebook news feed, whether we qualify for a loan, where we get an education, and so on. As O'Neil (2017) argues in *Weapons of Math Destruction*, the mathematical models used in these algorithms are a kind of black box, opaque and incontestable. Although everyone is judged according to the same rules, the reality is that those algorithms reinforce discrimination.

Should we therefore take a sceptical view? Probably.

The above-mentioned aspects gain much of their significance because many users are simply overwhelmed by this information-abundant world. Users are often not capable of successfully wandering through the seas of sometimes incorrect, partly even misleading, information that is acquired so easily with search engines (Wineburg et al. 2016). Furthermore, partly de-humanized communication behaviour is not that uncommon. In fact, there is a significant amount of hate material available online (Hawdon, Oksanen, and Räsänen 2017).

In sum, we get a complex picture of our information-abundant world with certain distinctly dystopian implications. How does this relate to questions of free expression, censorship, and information literacy?

On the one hand, tendencies to establish surveillance indicate that there is a need to be aware of and to support a 'liberty perspective' to avoid and prevent rampant surveillance, to resist censorship, and to secure diversity of opinion.

On the other hand, it is obvious that a laissez-faire approach can also be linked to detrimental outcomes, as we observe (*a*) a power concentration on some key markets concerned with information access and social communication, (*b*) the establishment of a new kind of fake news media industry that successfully creates and spreads misinformation, and (*c*) the invisible influence of supposedly neutral algorithms that often skew our reality. Thus, there is a need for regulations that are able to secure free markets and ensure the transparency and accountability of the algorithms controlling our lives. Beyond that, on the level of the individual user, there is also a need to increase information literacy, to support humanistic communication behaviour and to sanction online hate speech (Jubany and Roiha 2016).

As we can see, there is probably not always a clear-cut choice between freedom, free expression, and regulation, including censorship, on the internet. One can argue that a certain amount of regulation is necessary to secure a pluralistic and valid information landscape. Furthermore, users need to be willing and able to discover the information that they need, and to initiate and maintain objective discourse and debate.

This text touches on these questions. First, the macro-perspective–oriented issues are summarized briefly: (*a*) open infrastructure, and state-imposed surveillance and censorship, (*b*) markets, (*c*) news media, and (*d*) algorithms. Following that, the micro-perspective of the individual users and their behaviour is outlined. With respect to that examples of dysfunctional or outright evil user behaviour patterns within these services are discussed. On this basis, some considerations with regard to the development of information literacy skills are provided. The essay concludes with the attempt to conflate both perspectives.

Of course, the reader should keep in mind that this text is not neutral, purely objective, or even free of values. The author is bound by his cultural (Western) and educational (scientific) background.

The Macro-oriented Perspective

Open Infrastructure and Censorship

The internet was built as a robust and universally applicable information and communication infrastructure, allowing users to easily access information linked throughout the globe (Leiner et al. 2009). Modern social media, for example, social online networks, allow the further lowering of communication costs and information provision. As 'everyone' can be a publisher, there is a tendency for everyone with an agenda to be one (Shirky 2008, 17).

A prominent example of this kind of information provision and distribution is *Wikipedia*, and the manifold social media artefacts and posts related to the Arab Spring (Wolfsfeld, Segev, and Sheafer 2013). Of course, this kind of information output is not always considered as valuable. There are many other cases in which governments aim to protect or shield their citizens from content that they see as bad.

One example would be when the Chinese government moved to 'forbid open discussion of the so-called "June 4th incident" (Tiananmen Square incident) in the country's media and on its internet' (Kaiman 2013). According to Zhong, Wang, and Huang (2017), the 'Great Fire Wall' in China even causes self-censorship. Furthermore, the news media report plans to increase web surveillance and censorship further, forcing a ban on unapproved virtual private networks (VPNs), to oblige users to use their real identities on online platforms; and even to introduce a 'social credit system' that analyses and estimates individual online behaviour, building up loyalty scores for everyone (Williams 2017). Thus, Chinese internet censorship practices are increasingly reinforced. As China's surveillance regulations are probably the most prominently discussed ones in Western societies, it is interesting to compare them with practices in Western countries.

In a recent move to combat hate speech and fake news, a new law to improve law enforcement in social networks (the 'Netzwerkdurchsetzungsgesetz') was passed in Germany that specifically targets social networks. The networks are obliged to remove 'obviously' illegal content quickly or risk fines as high as 50 million euros. The law was widely criticized as restricting free expression and leading to a privatization of censorship (Courtney 2017; Gierow 2017). Even the United Nations High Commissioner for Human Rights (its their website) expressed concerns.

Although, seen from a normative perspective, one can come to a very different estimation of the censorship practices in China and Germany; it is still possible to conclude that both countries enforce laws that aim to protect their citizens from information that the ruling regime regards as dangerous and/or that is seen as a danger to the political and societal community.

We may conclude that the internet as an open and democratic technical infrastructure (Berners-Lee 2010) is fundamentally still alive and permits 'any person [to] share information with anyone else, anywhere' (Berners-Lee 2010). This is even true for proprietary or 'walled garden' areas such as social networks. Nevertheless, it seems that political regimes are increasingly capable of surveillance and willing to control information flows. Therefore, one could argue that there is a tendency towards more state censorship and less free expression. A more difficult question is how to assess this trend.

Limited information access on search engines and social media is not always a great evil, for example, when it hinders communication between criminals, extremists, or terrorists. With regard to the exercise of this kind of information control, the 'truth' probably lies in the eye of the beholder. Instead of blithely characterizing internet censorship as clearly 'good' or obviously 'evil' one should aim at a more differentiated political assessment, which could, for example, depend on the type of political regime enforcing the regulation or on the type of information that is to be censored.

Information and Communication Markets

The competition in important internet markets, which has so far been widely free, has led to a situation in which a small number of enterprises have taken a dominant market position. This is true for internet search, an area that is dominated by Google, for social online networks, dominated by Facebook, and even for e-commerce, dominated by Amazon.

According to Haucap and Heimeshoff (2014), direct and indirect network effects, switching costs, reputation effects, and economies of scale are the determining forces of competition between platforms and online markets, and are often characterized by a situation in which one dominant player is followed by another. As switching costs can be assessed as fairly low, both Google's and Facebook's dominant market position does not necessarily need to be long-lasting. On the assumption that new innovators will steadily hassle the existing players, one might question the need for market regulations.

Nevertheless, one has to keep in mind that we are not talking merely about the consequence of the dominant role of Google and Facebook in their respective economic markets, but also about their influence in a wider sphere, meaning the web economy as a whole and the societal impact already hinted at.

Given that Google 'has become the de facto gatekeeper of information available on the internet' (Lee 2016, 15), one could argue that the information provided at the top of the Google result list is often not only the starting point of our universe of available and acknowledged information but also the end of it.

In both cases, it has to be said that these dominant platforms serve as a kind of media infrastructure that could be part of political regulation, as these companies have got 'the power, for example, to command public attention, the power to communicate news and information, or the power to give people a voice' (Moore 2016, 22).

But one also needs to consider their economic power and influence on neighbouring markets. If one takes into account the important role of Facebook and Google for the communication and information research needs of their users, then it is not that astounding that within a few years both enterprises achieved market leadership as publisher platforms for online advertising.

Google is suspected of misusing its market leader position in the web search area to promote its other commercial services, particularly its shopping search service, thus damaging competition in the field. After a year-long legal dispute, the European Commission found: 'Google has abused its market dominance as a search engine by giving an illegal advantage to another Google product, its comparison shopping service.' Google was penalized with an antitrust fine of 2.42 billion euros (European Commission 2017).

Thus in both cases, Facebook and Google, it seems reasonable to temper the free market spirit with restrictions and regulations which secure the markets in order for it to indeed remain free and diverse.

News Media

Recent years have seen a rise in the dissemination and discussion of so-called post-truth reports or messages in online news and social media (Speed and Mannion 2017).

According to Silverman (2016), such fake news acquires more interest and is shared more often than debunking articles or real news. The topic attracted special attention in the context of the 2016 US presidential election. Most false news stories shared strongly favoured one of the two candidates. Therefore, there is a discussion of the influence of fake news on the outcome of the election.

Allcott and Gentzkow (2017) trace the establishment of a fake news industry back to two main reasons. First, it is very easy to set up websites. Second, in addition to the possibility of pursuing a specific political agenda, there is the opportunity to employ fake news publishing as a business model and earn money by generating advertising-related income.

The prevalence of social media makes it easy to disseminate such news, as there is no *ex ante* validity assessment involved. As the authors point out, fake news 'may generate utility for some consumers, but it also imposes private and social costs by making it more difficult for consumers to infer the true state of the world' (2017, 212).

Apart from these theoretical implications, the question of the real impact of fake news is rather unclear. Reips and Matzat (2016) articulate a more sceptical view with regard to the real effects and influence of post-truth or post-factual messages, as they see no strong empirical evidence for a substantial impact on the election results. Nevertheless, the question of what to do about this situation still arises, and one can postulate that a libertarian stance that is tolerant of such fake news and fake news media will lead to the detrimental effects already mentioned.

One could argue for more control on presumably trustworthy media sites. This regulatory path, which is oriented towards the legal aspects of news publication, has already been referred to ('Netzwerkdurchsetzungsgesetz').

In addition, an economic route to limiting post-truth media also seems feasible. As explained, a part of the fake news media landscape tries to make a living from advertising-generated income. Thus, if the big advertising platforms would implement stricter access control on their publishing partners, a lot of fake news media would probably be drained. (We see a connection here with the dominant platforms mentioned earlier.)

Algorithms

As Monteith and Glenn (2016) write, decisions made by algorithms affect everyone. Extensive user surveillance on the web and the widespread usage of this data undermine the user's sovereignty on data disclosure, as tracking is hidden and private data partly revealed and/or correlated on the basis of information provided by third persons or parties. Monteith and Glenn argue that constant online tracking makes certain groups (here people with mental illnesses) especially vulnerable, as 'online self-disclosure and constant tracking blur traditional concepts of public versus private data, medical versus non-medical data, and human versus automated decision making'. Furthermore, they stress the lack of transparency and accountability of automated decision-making systems, and emphasize that used data may be inaccurate and that the algorithms may fail.

To go beyond the intuition of what is right or wrong with algorithms, Shneiderman (2016) proposes independent oversight systems (as exist, for example, in transportation) to continuously check the algorithm-based information systems. According to his argument, this would not only increase safety but would probably also lower costs and increase quality. Approaches such as the European Union's General Data Protection Regulation, which aims to restrict artificial decision-making ('on user-level predictors') and to establish a 'right to explanation', whereby a user can ask for an explanation of an algorithmic decision that was made about them, are important as a way to avoid or minimize discrimination and to enhance transparency (Goodman and Flaxman 2016).

Diakopoulos (2015) investigated a surge-pricing algorithm of Uber that was intended to motivate drivers to go online, thus increasing the supply of available transportation offers. Instead, his analysis concludes that the algorithm merely redistributed the drivers already on the road, thus failing to fulfil the original intention. He requests a standard for algorithmic decision-making that makes the following aspects transparent: (*a*) human involvement with regard to the stakeholders and their goals, (*b*) data included, (*c*) the algorithm itself, its features and variables, (*d*) the quality of the inferences made in the algorithm with regard of accuracy and error rates, and (*e*) the presence of the algorithm in the field—where and when the algorithm is actually employed (Diakopoulos 2016).

Once again, we see a strong need for regulations. The aim of such regulations at this point is connected less with restrictions on the actors within the state or economic sector, as was argued in the previous sections. The goal is to provide sufficient transparency in order to be able to establish basic systems of accountability and control.

Interim Conclusion

In the beginning of the present chapter, a spectrum was suggested for the range of possible approaches to mastering the challenges of our information-abundant internet world that positioned a libertarian perspective at one end and the need for regulations at the other.

The internet was (and still is) a unified infrastructure into which further technical inventions may be built. It is a technical sphere in which innovations may emerge and establish themselves as a mass or niche phenomenon or vanish again. It is a commercial space that fostered and fosters the development of new markets. It provides an ecosystem that has led to new forms of communication and knowledge generation. It establishes a world in which many decisions are made on the basis of automatic, algorithm-based systems. This progress is possible, was initiated, and is sustained because the internet was built with a libertarian perspective in mind. Nevertheless, as markets grow and mature, and as algorithms increasingly influence our lives, the need for stronger regulations clearly arises. Regulations may even be seen as necessary to uphold the 'free' character of the internet and even our lives.

This argument can also be applied to the topic of freedom of speech. Fake news and hate speech indicate a need for regulations, as unregulated 'free expression' could be the cause of disinformation. At the same time, suppressing the formation and dissemination of information is censorship. Hitherto, and especially in the internet, with its surveillance possibilities, there is very good reason to be alert when it comes to censorship, especially as there is a rising tendency towards more of it. This could easily lead to a situation in which the diversity of opinions is seriously limited and freedom of speech comes to an end. On the other hand, censorship is not necessarily bad if it helps minimize the advent of misanthropic communication and disinformation.

Of course, it is crucial *what* is defined as misanthropic and misleading and *who* is defining it. This is an interesting aspect. A Westerner would probably argue that it is important to be able to control the decision-making authority with a system based on separation of powers and the existence of a permanent opposition. Yet, even if the normative stance on this topic were clear (which is not the case), the views, the knowledge, the competence, and the actions of the individual users are also of the utmost importance, because, for example, disinformation only unfolds its detrimental power if it is perceived and handled as a kind of justified information.

The following section aims to gain further insights by focusing on user behaviour.

User Behaviour

Whereas the explanations in the previous section are primarily oriented to a macro-perspective on the internet, the emphasis in the following is on the micro-level, with a focus on the individual. This is the area that is under our own individual control. In the following discussions, the reader may therefore be tempted to compare the given explanations with his or her own behaviour.

This section is structured in three parts. First, important aspects and limitations of the information behaviour of (search engine) users are sketched. Following that, the communication patterns in social media referred to as 'hate speech' are discussed. Both these aspects reveal that the internet is not a place in which users dwell competently and comfortably. Instead, we often find dysfunctional or even outright inhumane behaviour. How can we address these problems?

The third part of this section is concerned with concepts that aim to improve information literacy on the part of the user.

Information Behaviour

There is a substantial amount of research covering the field of human information behaviour (Case and Given 2016). The academic discipline of information science is primarily concerned with the ways in which users research and apply information. Models of information behaviour usually encompass a (conscious) information need as a starting point to initiate (purposeful) information behaviour. The information behaviour is executed in an information (seeking) process which leads to a certain outcome. All information behaviour is context-specific and bound to manifold personal, task-related, situational, and (possibly) other factors. The information-seeking process is usually traversed in different, often iterative stages in which the need is stated and results are selected/gathered and analysed/evaluated until the need is satisfied or the searcher stops the information-seeking process (Case and Given 2016, 141–76).

Regarding the behaviour of web searchers, R.W. White (2016, 64–82) reports some central results of the research. In particular, he mentions behavioural biases, such as that people prefer top positions, since they trust the search engines to present the best results first (*position bias*). Searchers also prefer results that attract their attention by containing images or certain words (for example, 'official', 'free') or by means of formatting (for example, bold). They also favour certain resources (for example, *Wikipedia*).

A blog post on Moz.com includes statistical data on user interaction with search engines (Fishkin 2017). According to these, search sessions are rather short (with a mean duration of under one minute). The queries are also rather short, typically containing only three keywords. For each query, there is usually no more than one result selected. This broadly corresponds to the argument of Lewandowski (2008) that search engine users are easily satisfied. In other words, they often don't (think they need to) invest a noticeable effort in web search.

There are also cognitive biases. Although R.W. White (2016) states that cognitive biases are an under-researched field in information seeking, one may nevertheless assume that they are also present in web search as in many other aspects of human behaviour (Kahneman 2011). Knobloch-Westerwick, Johnson, and Westerwick (2015) investigated and confirmed the existence of *confirmation bias*, for example, the preference for information which supports one's own view, when selecting search results in the context of political information-seeking.

Wikipedia has a comprehensive list of cognitive biases (*Wikipedia* 2017), amongst them the *availability bias*, which is the tendency to overestimate the probability of the occurrence of events with greater presence in memory, and the *base rate neglect bias*, which is the tendency to ignore base rate information and focus on more specific, more unlikely information which is also listed. Both biases have already been covered as problems in web search. For example, White and Horvitz (2009) argue that availability bias and base rate neglect bias could lead to misjudgements during health-related web searches when search engines are used as a diagnostic tool.

It is therefore apparent that, with regard to information behaviour, users tend to minimize effort and are prone to errors due to biases in the perception and interpretation of results.

But the possible problems of web search go even further. The title of Carr's 2008 article in *The Atlantic*—'Is Google Making Us Stupid?'—illustrates this line of thought. As users get accustomed to effortless information access and they experience information overload, their informational habits and cognitive structures slowly adapt and are rebuilt.

A series of studies, as reported by Wineburg et al. (2016), indicate that the ability to estimate and evaluate information is poorly developed among young users.

For example, over 80 per cent of middle school pupils were not able to identify native advertising on a website as such.

In another test, where the task was to decide whether a photograph of what were assumed to be Fukushima flowers (showing 'nuclear birth defects') was evidence of the conditions near the Fukushima Daiichi Power Plant, nearly 40 per cent of 170 high school students were prepared to accept the photo at face value.

According to Metzger and Flanagin (2013), we can explain this kind of (at least sometimes dysfunctional) behaviour by considering that users try to limit their costs by minimizing effort and employing simple heuristics ('learning by doing') to evaluate the credibility of information. These heuristics are based on easy to grasp factors such as familiarity or popularity.

To sum up, at first sight internet search seems to be easy; in reality, it is not so simple. If we connect this realization with the establishment of a fake news industry and the spread of misinformation as argued in the second part of this chapter, then it is not difficult to see that there really can be cause for concern. Searchers do indeed seem to be vulnerable to misleading information.

Communication Patterns in Social Media—Hate Speech

While the detrimental effects of dysfunctional information behaviour can be assessed as self-damaging, hate speech can be described as a purposeful behaviour that tries to harm others. The Council of Europe refers to hate speech as 'covering all forms of expression which spread, incite, promote or justify racial hatred, xenophobia, anti-Semitism or other forms of hatred based on intolerance' (Council of Europe 1997).

The first question is whether hate speech is a significant problem at all. The answer is, it seems to be. According to a representative survey in Germany (Forsa Institute 2016), two-thirds of the respondents had already encountered hate speech. So at least in Germany it is a phenomenon that is known to most users.

If we ask who the victims of hate speech are, a statistical analysis by Mondal, Silva, and Benevenuto (2017) indicates that the great majority of hate speech falls into three categories: race (for example, against black people), behaviour (for example, targeting insecure people), and physical attributes (for example, referring to obese people). In another study, by Costello, Hawdon, and Ratliff (2017), in a sample of roughly 1,000 users from the United States of America (USA) aged 15–36, roughly 23 per cent declared themselves to have been the target of hateful or degrading material online at some point in their life. A survey-based regression analysis indicates that users of social online networks, people who discuss private matters online, and discussants who join in on online hate or confront users who publish hate posts, all have a higher probability of being a victim of online hate.

With regard to the perpetrators of online hate speech, Isasi and Juanatey (2016) emphasize that these can be divided into those with an extremist political profile and those with a personal agenda (haters and trolls).

Governmental measures to protect citizens from hate speech have already been mentioned earlier (in the section 'Open Infrastructure and Censorship'), and, as suggested, can be seen as a strong argument for regulation or censorship. Furthermore, as Jubany and Roiha (2016) propose, advertisers could and should boycott platforms that provide a publishing space for discrimination or even worse content, a kind of censorship by business that has already been mentioned (in the section 'News Media').

But that is only part of the story. The individual behaviour of the receivers and third parties, the so-called 'bystanders', is also important for minimizing the negative effects of hate speech. Quoting the *spiral of silence theory* (Noelle-Neumann 1974), Jubany and Roiha argue that if the virtual audience remains silent, hate speech becomes more normalized as people conclude that it represents a popular view or even the view of the majority. In addition, the results of Costello, Hawdon, and Ratliff (2017) imply that counter-speech could be detrimental to the users, as such behaviour increases the probability of their too becoming the victims of hate speech.

Some initiatives that aim to counteract online hate take an educational stance, providing users with background information to assess this phenomenon and to encourage and enable users to use counter-speech. For example, the BRICS project tries to foster 'media literacy and active involvement of web users and web content producers'. For that purpose, the project website (2015) provides information on the topic and concepts for workshops. Such initiatives show that there are ways to address the aforementioned dysfunctional patterns of information and communication behaviour other than through public regulation. The idea is to empower and motivate the user to behave in an information-literate or media-literate way. An information scientist would indeed describe this kind of competence as *information literacy*.

Information Literacy

Building up information literacy is the way to empower users with the ability to apply competent information behaviour patterns and to communicate online in a purposeful and humane manner. Information literacy includes both information-oriented and communication-oriented components.

The American Library Association (ALA), an authority in this field, provides a 'Framework for Information Literacy for Higher

Education' (ALA 2015). According to this, information literacy can be seen as meta-literacy that encompasses cognitive and ethical components with regard to information usage and online participation:

> Information literacy is the set of integrated abilities encompassing the reflective discovery of information, the understanding of how information is produced and valued, and the use of information in creating new knowledge and participating ethically in communities of learning.

The ALA defines six concepts that need to be addressed in order to be able to behave in an information-literate way. These concepts are as follows:

Authority Is Constructed and Contextual
Information Creation as a Process
Information Has Value
Research as Inquiry
Scholarship as Conversation
Searching as Strategic Exploration

Space doesn't permit detailed elaboration of these concepts, so suffice it to say that from them manifold specific capabilities and competencies can be derived, for example, that information literature users 'use research tools and indicators of authority to determine the credibility of sources, understanding the elements that might temper this credibility', that they 'recognise that a given scholarly work may not represent the only—or even the majority—perspective on the issue', or that they 'understand the responsibility that comes with entering the conversation through participatory channels'. We can therefore say that information literacy is a concept already developed and defined in an elaborate and specific way that takes into account the described aspects of information behaviour but also (at least partly) covers patterns of online communication.

In order to empower the user to behave in an information-literate manner, the ALA suggests an open-minded and collaborative approach in providing and implementing training opportunities. Ideally, these should not consist of one-time classes or learning activities, but be systematically integrated, as ongoing learning experiences, throughout a whole period of study, possibly also including community-based learning. A closer look at two online repositories (Association of College & Research Libraries [ACRL] n.d.; Primo 2017) that collect appropriate learning resources reveals that there is already a multitude of material available online that everyone can use, free of charge.

This brief look indicates that the provision of learning resources is probably not a big problem. The next question is how to systematically anchor information literacy–related learning into education, be that into higher education or otherwise. As the framework is focused on higher education, it may not be a perfect fit or applicable for all user groups (for example, children). Nevertheless, as it is oriented towards higher education it aims at a high standard that on principle would be desirable for 'everyone' and could serve as a baseline.

The ALA hints that the current approach is often 'via one-shot classes, especially in introductory level classes' (ALA 2015).

Nevertheless, even if the provision of learning opportunities were to be enhanced substantially in the near future, one question remains open. Would enhanced knowledge actually translate into more information-literate behaviour? The explanations by Metzger and Flanagin (2013), who state that users try to limit their costs by minimizing effort, seem to indicate otherwise. In addition, behaving in an information-literate way requires not only the necessary knowledge but also the motivation to apply it. For that, one has to be aware of one's own cognitive limitations and dysfunctional behaviour, as well as of those of others. This information needs to be included in information literacy training programmes.

Ultimately (and this is the main point here), information literacy depends on users' media discipline and openness. Discipline means the willingness to continue internet research beyond a few clicks and to be persistent in using information resources. Openness means being able to recognize different perspectives, to accept and even demand plurality, and to be able to consider information that does not correspond to your own view. Seen from this perspective, information literacy is as much an *attitude* as it is a *competence*. It could be worthwhile to emphasize this point in the ongoing discussion on information literacy.

It can probably be agreed that there is a comprehensive understanding of the necessary components that make up information literacy. In contrast to that, although there are many learning resources available, it is doubtful whether users receive sufficient training. And even when that is the case, the question arises of the transfer into real-life behaviour. At this point, it should become clear that information literacy is as much an attitude as a competence. Yet trying to expand information literacy, as sketched out by the ALA (2015), is undoubtedly the way to go.

But it is still a long way.

***

Conflating the main points made in this article will lead us back to the rather sceptical view put forward in the beginning of this chapter (and, if anything, understated). Users are indeed often out of their depth in this internet-based, information-abundant world. Extensive knowledge resources and multiple perspectives on many topics are widely free and available. At the same time, users are frequently in danger of acquiring (or maybe even aiming for) a distorted and very limited picture. They may not even be aware of this.

The obvious solution was mooted in the previous section. The idea of building up information literacy is nothing new, in fact it has been under discussion for some time now (ALA 1989). Nevertheless, as we increasingly rely on electronic information, it is now more important than ever. This is especially true with regard to current trends concerning questions of censorship, markets, media, and algorithms, as described earlier. Despite the ongoing debate on the dangers of censorship and surveillance, one can clearly argue the case for regulations. Regulations are vital, not to hinder free speech but to control developments and entities that have the potential to lead the internet away from its open infrastructure and freedom-oriented path, and in the direction of a more obscure and interest-driven appropriation by powerful organizations and mechanisms that may even come to undermine the foundations of democratic societies.

Interestingly, the idea of improving information literacy can be seen as a kind of empowerment through 'regulation', this time not on the macro- but on the micro-level. The framework of competencies and training offers ample opportunity to empower users, and should be expanded and enhanced. This approach is the best way to help users navigate and communicate in the information-abundant internet world in a self-determined manner. Information research and communication behaviour–related knowledge and awareness are prerequisites for the utopian internet world described at the beginning of the present chapter. So, at the risk of oversimplification, we can perhaps express the message of this essay in one sentence: In the present information-abundant world, we urgently need to regulate business, media technologies, and even our own behaviour if we are to secure freedom and freedom of expression.

5

My Internal Censor

JERRY PINTO

To begin with, I believe there is great value in learning. We learn to be human (or not). We learn to be kind (or not). We learn and we change. Our experiences shape us. Our friends shape us. Our decisions shape us. And who we are shapes the texts we create. This is as true of the literary writer as it is of the person who works in genre fiction.

How do we learn what we learn? There is positive and negative reinforcement, we know. We also know that we are all humans and do not work in these binaries. You might choose pain. You might choose risk. You might choose to walk away from rewards. The joy is not in the pain/pleasure, risk/reward binaries. The joy is in the choices and they are unlimited.

As creative people, we want our choices to be unlimited.

We want to be able to do as we please, only we know that we have never ever had that freedom. The freedom to be free would exist, we know, only in Utopia. Utopia is the good place and it is no place at all, in other words, the perfect place that does not exist. Why does it not exist? Because for my friend P, this would be a place where everyone would get to play cricket eight hours a day and get paid for it. Because for my friend Q, this would be a place where cricket would be banned. Because for my friend G, we would all walk around naked so that no one would ever be bothered again by the ghastly necessity of ironing a shirt. Because for my friend R … you get it.

But you could dream up a Utopia where we all get to do our thing, right?

My thing is to say what I think. I think you're a fool and I think you need to be told that.

Your thing is to live a life that is free of criticism. You do not think I have the right to judge who is a fool or not and even if I do, you cannot see why I cannot keep such an opinion to myself.

So here is my formulation: we have a society here and now. We can improve upon it or we can dream of Utopias. Or we can resist these foolish binaries. We can improve on our society by dreaming of Utopias too …

Wait.

This is not getting us anywhere.

Let me go back to the moment of creation.

Of course, every text—and I use this word as a synecdoche—has a starting point: a commission, an idea, the extension of an idea. In its first moments, the text is not dangerous as it does not exist except in dialogue with its creator. The creator wants it just so; the text resists. The creator shapes it, works it, reworks it, and all the time, the creator hopes that the audience isn't in the room.

It is.

It cannot be banished. Being aware of the audience is implicit almost in everything we do. Take two revolutionary phrases: *épater les bourgeois* (see Chapter 1, 'Drawing Lines') and 'make it new'.

The phrase *épater les bourgeois* imagines up:

- a bourgeoisie
- its characteristics and its sentiments, and
- what would then shock it.

The phrase 'make it new' brings into being an idea of what is old (and outworn) but surely not what is old (and classical). The phrase also assumes that this old and new would be something the audience would be aware of, or else who would be the judge of newness since no one invents the wheel without a touch of awe at the greatness and uniqueness of what has been invented?

I would go as far as to say that the audience is the co-creator of what I am doing. I am writing a piece for the newspapers. I would like to use the word 'zeugma'.[1] It is the exact word and I am happy that I know it, for our society puts a high premium on a good vocabulary. Not a very high premium but it is enough to make me happy. Now I write 'zeugma' and I rejoice in it. But only for a moment. Then I erase it because the unseen presence demands it be erased. This is not the audience, this is me, and my understanding of it, my understanding of its vocabulary, my understanding of how easy it is for the audience to turn away and consign the product of my thought to oblivion. I erase 'zeugma' because I think the audience may see this as me flashing my knowledge at them and because there are only so many words allowed in a newspaper article, I …

Excuses, excuses.

I am in charge and I remove 'zeugma' because I think it may cause an adverse reaction.

What if I leave in a word that causes an adverse reaction?

Is there any word that cannot, in the wrong circumstances, cause offence?

How am I supposed to walk this minefield?

***

The law is no help.

The law begins by inventing The Reasonable Man.[2] He is a useful legal fiction, this Reasonable Man, though he may have been updated to a Reasonable Person. The Reasonable Person has been around since 1837. The Reasonable Person reads the fine print on the contract. The Reasonable Person checks the weather forecast before setting out. The Reasonable Person would know that coffee is likely to be hot.

[1] The name for a figure of speech that is used especially in literary analysis; it takes its name from an ancient Greek word that means a 'yoking' or 'linking together'.

[2] In English legal tradition, he is known as 'the man on the Clapham omnibus'. Other legal systems use similar expressions.

The Reasonable Person knows that he should pay taxes on time … You get the idea.

The Reasonable Person therefore is a product of the world as it is known.

Now is art part of the Reasonable World? If art seeks to make new, what about it can be judged by the Reasonable Person who works from the past and its models?

If the Reasonable Person were to read the Marquis de Sade, what would she/he make of that corpus? Or if the Reasonable Person were to read Machiavelli's *The Prince*, with its injunction to the victorious princes to kill off all the heirs unto the last child of a defeated enemy so as to prevent a sentimental uprising led by that child when it is grown? What does the Reasonable Person make of Karl Marx if the Reasonable Person has been brought up in a capitalist society? What does the Reasonable Person make of T.S. Eliot if William Wordsworth is the model?

And if art takes no risks, is it art? There must have been thousands of sunflowers painted by hundreds of painters, flower painting being an avocation pursued by Jan Breughel the Elder and Hokkusai, and then along comes Van Gogh and had the last word on the subject but only because he risks it all by painting them dying. And when you think it is all over, Georgia O'Keefe reminds us that flowers are botanical genitals. That is how you move on, you move forward, you take risks. The risks are terrible, you can fail and never sell a painting (as Van Gogh did) or you may get stuck painting flowers and begin to hate them.

Here be dragons.

The point I am trying to make in my ham-handed way is that we need an Unreasonable Person. But as soon as I conjure her up, I kit her out to suit my particular needs of unreason. I need her to have a great sense of humour so she can see when I am laughing. And yet who among us has not known how painful it is to be laughed at? (This is why the comedian, the comic, the cartoonist are all universally hated by those in power and loved by those without it; though at the behest of those in power, those without can turn and rend the very things they love. Watch social media for examples.) Other artists and creators will have other needs and will construct her differently.

Thus the Unreasonable Person turns out to be as impoverished a fiction as the Reasonable Person is.

The world talks glibly about internal censorship and the external forces of censorship as if these exist in different compartments of a writer's mind. Actually, there's a near-constant interplay between the two. This is mediated by what we know and what we hope.

Each time any one of us pushes the envelope a little, it's a gamble.

Because no one wants to be silenced.

But if we don't gamble, we don't connect. The audience will eventually tire of the same routines, the same sounds, the same colours, the same shapes, and it will drift away.

This is how it is. We must. We have to. We shouldn't. 'Politic, cautious, meticulous'?[3] We try, we try.

And we will try to find our way through.

[3] This is how Prufrock describes himself in T.S. Eliot's poem *The Love Song of J. Alfred Prufrock*: he is not Prince Hamlet, but just 'an attendant lord' with a minor role to play.

6

Wittgenstein's Lion

Intercultural Communication and Foreign Language Competence

JÜRGEN BENEKE

> If a lion could talk, we wouldn't be able to understand it.
>
> —Ludwig Wittgenstein, *Philosophical Investigations* ([1953] 2009, 235e)

Even *within* cultures, people with different interests may clash, and try to impose their views on others (or find that others are trying to impose their own views on *them*). But whether it is about power, or politics, or greed, or religious world view, there will almost certainly be a massive component of misunderstanding, often in both directions. If such failure to understand each other is common *within* a culture, and difficult to resolve, how much more problematical and perplexing is it likely to be when people from *different* cultures interact?

Intercultural communication is the name of the discipline that has arisen to assume responsibility for the study and better organization of this interaction. Unfortunately, however, the term is now used in an increasingly inflationary manner, and often lazily invoked whenever foreign languages happen to come into play: thus, whoever communicates in a foreign language, or teaches it, whoever translates, or interprets, is necessarily, it would seem, involved in an 'intercultural' activity.

A close inspection of the relation between linguistic and cultural mediating activities suggests, however, that interpreters or language teachers are not automatically interculturally competent, and the average foreign language user even less so. Very often, when people communicate in a language that is not their mother tongue, they are unaware of the many pitfalls they either happily pass by or equally happily wade through. And, very often, people naïvely believe that they have understood each other.

Let us look at a number of the challenges that language and culture teaching has to master.

Challenge No. 1: The Inevitable Fuzziness of Signals

Two cases may illustrate this point. The first is an incident at a German railway station. The location is Hanover main station, during the international trade fair. The place is extremely crowded, it is almost impossible to move forward. A German visitor tries to explain the unpleasant situation to his—non-German—colleague. He says: 'It's the mess, you know.' The background to this relatively funny miscommunication is a well-known lexical 'false friend'—'*Messe*' in German means 'fair', and the word looks and sounds very similar to the English word 'mess'. Both parties believe they have understood each other, a clear case of pseudo-communication as a result of the fuzziness of the signals used.

Much less harmless is the following incident; it revolves around the concept of 'fair', a very English concept, as it turns out. Gerald Newman, a young American manager, has recently been transferred to Japan. He has been entrusted with the Japanese affiliate of his American 'mother' company. After a few days he organizes a meeting with all the employees in order to present them with his ideas on how to run the unit. On this occasion, he gives a speech, a typically American pep talk, which is intended to motivate his staff and make them share a common vision. He concludes his talk, which is met with friendly applause, with the words: 'I promise to be fair to every one of you.'

Everybody seems to be very pleased. After a few months, however, a general feeling of disappointment makes itself felt throughout the organization. Newman tries to get to the root of the problem, which, however, turns out to be very difficult. Nobody is prepared to discuss the issue openly; they even deny that a problem exists.

After some more weeks, a young Japanese member of Newman's staff, who had studied in the United States of America (USA), plucks up enough courage to talk to his boss. Newman finds it difficult to believe what his Japanese assistant tells him.

'Newman-san,' he says, 'you promised to be fair to us, but you have greatly disappointed us.'

Such a degree of directness, openly focusing on the problem and even suggesting who is responsible for the disappointment, would 'normally' be quite unusual in Japan—it is an extremely face-threatening act. But intercultural communication is not 'normal' communication. We find ourselves in a kind of no-man's-land, the 'realm of fuzzy signals'. In order to function smoothly in international settings, it is absolutely essential to identify and cope with the fuzziness of signals. 'Excellent' international communicators have trained themselves to feel at ease in the land of fuzzy signals.

'But how have I disappointed you?' Newman asks in deep bewilderment.

This incident, too, is a case of pseudo-communication, this time, however, with dramatic consequences, that is, the fundamental deterioration of the corporate climate.

What is the background? The American manager had implemented the typically American MBO ('management by objectives') system, together with a performance-related pay scheme. At every level, the respective manager has to negotiate and agree on measurable 'objectives', for example, sales figures per annum. At regular intervals, the employee's actual performance is then compared with the objectives agreed on. As a consequence, the pay every person receives is in direct proportion to their performance. Within the tradition of American business culture, this procedure is transparent and the epitome of 'fairness'—the better your performance, the more you get, and of course vice versa. The result is a considerable 'spread' of payment on each level. To rank every employee on a performance scale is seen as a typical responsibility of a manager. Consequently, the new American boss did not doubt for a second that he was entitled to evaluate his staff members' performance. He was convinced that this was exactly what he was paid for, and he was equally convinced that his behaviour was 'fair', because he based his decisions on measurable facts.

For the Japanese, on the other hand, 'fair' meant: Everybody on the same organizational level gets exactly the same pay. Differentiating on the basis of individual performance is considered to be the opposite of being fair. The Japanese 'collectivist' cultural tradition does not allow for differences at the same level. In actual fact, the Japanese employees used an *English word with a Japanese meaning*, a dramatic case of pseudo-communication.

Challenge No. 2: Closed Systems—the Hermetic Nature of Cultures

Cultures typically are more or less closed systems. When looking at them from the outside, the 'foreign' observer has an advantageous non-partisan position. But even so, it is difficult, if not impossible, to understand and to inventorize any culture exhaustively. We always have to reckon with the observer's bias, and many cultural features may escape even the professional eye. But even the members of a culture are very often unaware of the full range of values and beliefs that they subscribe to. As a rule, we only become aware of our values when they are challenged, when they jar with other people's values or even clash with them. According to psychologist Nancy Adler, 'culture is only a problem when it is a problem' (1997, 3). Her phrase is only seemingly a tautology. On the contrary, it very elegantly expresses the 'hermetic' character of cultures. As long as everything runs smoothly, like a well-oiled machine, we tend not to be aware of 'culture'—be it a foreign one or our own.

The intricate relationship between 'language' and 'national culture' has often been evoked since the age of Romanticism. Rarely, however, have we been shown indisputable facts to support this concept. In traditional language teaching in schools, it is usually taken for granted that the study of the works of the 'great' authors of any language community will automatically lead to deeper insights into the respective cultures. When it comes to so-called High Culture (literature, the arts, and so on), this assumption is justified to a certain degree. On the other hand, it is very often the 'best' national authors who transcend their cultural milieu and become part of the universal heritage of mankind, as world literature.

However, when it comes to using a foreign language for purposes such as working together in international settings, a familiarity with Goethe, Cervantes, Baudelaire, or Pushkin may occasionally be a door opener, but it will never be sufficient. What, then, is that particular area of competence that is necessary for working together successfully across national and linguistic borders? I suggest that it is the ability to cope with fuzzy signals in general (see earlier) *and* to recognize, understand, and deal with a broad variety of cultural and communicative styles. In a world where multicultural work groups have become the norm, not the exception, a competent response to the different cultural preferences that members of international groups may have is absolutely vital. And—equally important—every one of us will have to become aware of our own cultural concepts and preferences, bearing in mind, however, the caveat of Edward T. Hall: 'Culture hides more than it reveals, and, strangely enough, what it hides, it hides most effectively from its own participants' (1959, 29). The reason is that cultural concepts are taken for granted as the building blocks of our 'model of the world'.

For example, let us assume that a high-rise building has collapsed, killing several people. In the West, a committee would be installed in order to determine the cause and eventually to suggest measures to prevent a similar disaster in the future. Nobody would be content with anything less than a clear identification of reasons and responsibilities. The committee would look at a limited number of possible causes. The most likely candidates would be wrong statics, poor workmanship, a gas explosion, or something similar. The number of possible causes would be finite, and all of them based on the Western model of the world—based on scientific and engineering knowledge. The very moment that a member of the committee asked a question such as 'But what did the Ancestors/God/Allah want to tell us by this incident?' that person would have said goodbye to the Western model of the world.

But there are, of course, cultures where such questions are considered to be absolutely legitimate and 'normal'. It seems a deplorable fact that humans do not see 'brute facts', but rather only things they have learned to see. Consequently, we perceive any object or behaviour we encounter *in terms of our own culture*. The impact of this constraint is illustrated by the following case.

A group of French students of German visits a German university institute, where they are welcomed by the dean of the faculty. Before the encounter, the students were asked to keep a field diary and to pay particular attention to the non-verbal communication of the 'natives' (that is, the German faculty members). This is what they, therefore, note in their diary: 'As a greeting, all the professors banged their fists on their desks.' The students are certain that this is exactly what they saw. In actual fact, the German lecturers were using a ritual that is quite common in Germany, especially in an academic setting. As a form of greeting or applause, one raps one's knuckles on the surface of the desk or table. The student 'anthropologists' were indeed somewhat bewildered by this peculiar form of being greeted, which seemed extremely weird and conveyed aggressiveness rather than a friendly welcome. They had entered the realm of fuzzy signals, without, of course, being aware of it. Had they been trained in the art of coping with fuzzy signals, they might have discovered the discrepancy between friendly faces and a seemingly aggressive 'banging of fists'. As is so often the case, our students did not perceive the 'reality', but simply interpreted the signals *in terms of their own linguistic and cultural patterns*.

Anything that is not interpretable in terms of familiar patterns tends to be 'normalized' so as to be part of a well-known concept, which may, however, slightly deviate from the patterns we have grown up with. This tendency to normalize and to plane down smoothly what we perceive is characteristic of the hermetic character of cultures as 'things taken for granted'.

Challenge No. 3: The Meaning behind the Words

If we agree for the time being that intercultural competence is the most important learning goal both of language didactics and translation theory, we will have to ask ourselves whether this goal can really be seen as a by-product, as it were, of linguistic competence in the sense of mastering the grammatical rules and the standard meanings of the lexemes of the foreign language.

This assumption is evidently incorrect. The way we look at the world, our values, and our routine actions is the result of our socialization in a specific cultural environment. We learn 'the world' and how to operate in it to a large extent through our language, for example, in the form of 'scripts'.

In any culture, a fully socialized individual will, for example, have learned the 'correct' or 'usual' way to respond to the bereavement that a person close to them has suffered, including the 'appropriate' verbal and non-verbal responses. One such typical and routine response could be an embrace, accompanied by the words 'I don't know what to say'. By this choice, the speaker shows that he is trying to avoid the triteness of more conventional phrases such as 'my sincere condolences', but that he nevertheless honours the obligation to say something that is in harmony with how this particular culture looks at death and how to respond to it. The routine character of such phrases exempts the user from having to ponder every single time on the best choice.

Routine phrases thus help the user to cope with standard situations. But since they are so deeply 'soaked' in culture, there is the danger that they may not 'travel'. A non-native user of English, coming from a noticeably different type of culture, with a different attitude to death and propriety, may find a routine phrase that was coined for a British English setting totally inappropriate to express his or her attitude. The moment we use any language other than our own, we have to 'buy' a complete model of the world, including values and scripts.

For example, let us look at a medical practice in any Western country. A patient is told to get ready for an examination by the doctor. The doctor's assistant will typically expect the patient to take off any clothes that might obstruct the examination, which as a matter of course will involve physical contact, often across the gender barrier. Outside a medical surgery, it would be an outrageous imposition to ask a complete stranger, out of the blue, to 'undress, please'. This procedure tells us a lot about the way Western societies handle the concepts of 'nakedness' and 'shame', and a sentence like 'please undress to the belt' in an English or American setting is no great surprise. But what a shock this phrase might cause to an immigrant from—say—a Muslim culture. The extent to which the user of a foreign language is expected to subscribe to a complete model of the world leads us to the next challenge.

Challenge No. 4: The Lingua Franca Use of Language(s)

Surprisingly little attention has been devoted so far to the systematic study of the complexities and ambiguities inherent in using any language as a so-called lingua franca. The term denotes the use of a 'language of convenience', which is not the native language of any of the participants in a communicative exchange. The most widely used lingua franca today is, of course, English. Although we do not have reliable figures, a reasonable estimate is that between 70 and 80 per cent of all interactions worldwide, be it in the area of business, tourism, or politics, are carried out in English—and *with no native speaker of that language being involved.*

This has, of course, a tremendous impact on language use and behaviour. Take, for instance, the acceptable degree of directness in expressing disagreement in a business interaction. It tends to vary a great deal across cultures, ranging from a complete avoidance of any open expression of disagreement (which one might find most typically in Asian cultures) to a communicative style where the clear and outspoken expression of opinion is seen as a virtue. In such a culture, you say what you mean and mean what you say. Circumlocution and indirectness are seen as 'shifty' or 'treacherous'—'they say one thing and mean something totally different.' German users of English as a foreign language, for example, set great store on being 'frank' and take great care not to mince their words or 'beat about the bush', which very often provokes that loaded compliment by Americans: 'You are so refreshingly direct.' Although US–German interaction is not lingua franca use in the strict sense, the American attitude may serve as an illustration of how 'bluntness' is very often perceived. Bluntness in any culture bears the risk of coming across as a face-threatening act, and a good language trainer would warn his trainees of the American tendency to avoid it if at all possible. But what happens in a full lingua franca situation? It is not at all clear which degree of directness would be acceptable to a Russian or Spanish participant. What is certain, however, is that lingua franca settings per se are the territory of fuzzy signals, and its users very often despair at vagueness and ambiguity—'why do they not just say what they mean?'

There are no easy solutions. Every traveller who enters the land of fuzzy signals should always be aware that fuzziness is inevitable. A few suggestions might be helpful here. Don't be afraid to be redundant or repetitive (no matter what your teachers may have told you—it is a virtue, not a vice). Learn to paraphrase your message (if the first arrow has not hit the target, the next one may). Learn to give and call for constant feedback, a technique known as *active listening*. Learn to practise metacommunication, both linguistically and culturally, always bearing in mind, however, that these techniques may potentially be seen as face-threatening. Because who is normally so bold as to ask a high-ranking person for clarification or re-wording?

Challenge No. 5: The Intentional Fallacy—The Better Your Command of a Foreign Language, the More Dangerous It Becomes

As a foreign language user when you reach a high degree of competence in a language, especially in the areas of phonetics and intonation, you run the risk of being held responsible for anything you say—you will be taken at your word. But very often, foreign language users *don't* say what they mean, but use words or phrases that 'come to mind', just to overcome a possibly embarrassing pause. This widespread practice may lead to pseudo-communication (see earlier).

Still more dangerous, however, are mistakes on the level of acceptable forms of politeness. The following exchange between an English host (female) and a 15-year-old foreign exchange student may serve as an illustration. The two have just come home from shopping, carrying several bags in their arms. The host is trying to reach for something, which is difficult, with all the bags. The student says, 'Put it on the table.' In response, the English host yells at the girl: 'Who do you think you are, bossing me around like this?', grabs the telephone and complains to the exchange agency about the girl's 'rude' behaviour. The English host cancels the exchange, telling the bewildered girl to leave immediately.

The poor girl was unaware of the fact that a direct grammatical imperative is perceived by many British and also American speakers as an 'order' and is, as such, face-threatening and definitely out of place in the given situation. A more appropriate expression would have been: 'Why don't you put it on the table?' The avoidance of the imperative turns the phrase into a (helpful) suggestion. The girl was taken at her word, supposedly 'bossing' her host around. Had she shown clear signs of language deficits, the host might have put the 'rudeness' down to the girl's 'poor' command of English. In other words, when your linguistic output is faultless, a failure to adhere to conventions of politeness or other pragmatic rules is perceived as being intentional—he or she is *deliberately* insulting me!

Again, there is no simple remedy—it would certainly be somewhat ridiculous to recommend foreign language users to grade down their language competence. Principally, however, every foreign language-user should send 'handicap signals' at regular intervals during conversations, the message being that he or she is not a fully competent speaker, something such as: 'Please bear with me, I may occasionally sound harsh or I may have to ask you to repeat a sentence. You may put it down to my culture or my poor language skills.'

And again, since we are in the realm of fuzzy signals, it is by no means clear whether a violation of a native speaker politeness rule would be perceived as equally grievous by a lingua franca user.

Challenge No. 6: Mutually Negative Perceptions of the Other in Intercultural Interactions

The following two examples are taken from the sphere of non-verbal communication.

Example one: What constitutes a 'proper' handshake (if a handshake is at all seen as a 'proper' form of greeting in that particular culture!)? In every hand-shaking culture there are unconscious, but clear expectations as to the manner of 'doing the handshake'. There are, among others, the number of 'pumps', the intensity and nature of eye contact, smiling, and the degree of hand-pressure applied. This last should be neither 'too firm' nor 'too flabby'. Long-standing prejudices have developed around the quality of a handshake, for example in Franco-German (business) interactions.

To the German mind, the French handshake lacks the 'proper' degree of firmness. Germans often say that it 'feels like a dead fish'. The French, for their part, perceive the German handshake as 'bone-crushing'. Since the non-verbal element has a powerful influence on whether or not we feel attracted to a person, this whole area has a tremendous impact on the start-up phase of Franco-German business interactions (between male interactants). Frequently, mutually negative stereotypes come into play. Here are some French stereotypes: *This bone-crushing German is aggressive; he is trying to get the better of me. I have heard from others that all Germans are like that. It reminds me of the German tanks in the last war. I don't like this person.* German stereotypes run along these lines: *This Frenchman has an effeminate character; he is probably unreliable and shifty. I don't like this person.*

The tragedy here is that both sets of stereotypes are totally subconscious and mutually negative. And there is no likelihood that they will dissolve on their own with time. It needs someone to draw attention to the 'mechanism' of mutually negative stereotypes.

Example two is the well-known complaint about the 'grumpy' Germans and the 'silly' Americans. One of the first things that American visitors to Germany notice is that Germans don't exchange smiles whenever they meet someone, as would be the case in the USA. Instead, they keep a neutral face. This facial expression is usually interpreted by Americans as 'grumpy' or even 'hostile'. While Americans have been educated to smile at each contact (given that the other person is within one's perceptual space), even with complete strangers, Germans as a rule only smile when they know the person or have a particular reason for smiling. The American cultural routine is 'the contact smile', the German cultural pattern is: 'avoid intrusiveness'. On closer inspection, the German facial expression is neither 'hostile' nor 'grumpy', it is simply neutral. The American contact smile, on the other hand, is generally misinterpreted by Germans and others as 'silly' or even 'treacherous'—'they can't possibly be sincere in being so friendly towards someone they don't even know. It's only masquerading as friendliness, and goes to show how superficial Americans are.'

The only way to avoid falling into the trap of mutually negative perceptions is to learn to become a good observer ('What are the actual facts?'), and to avoid rushing to premature conclusions. A trained and careful observer, might, for instance, detect that the Germans' 'hostile' expressions are actually just 'neutral' faces, and the 'superficial' Americans are only trying to establish a positive atmosphere at the outset of an interaction, even at the price of glossing over hidden differences.

Challenge No. 7: Incompatible Discourse Rules

Discourse rules govern how face-to-face interactions are organized. Among these are rules for turn-taking and for interrupting, the acceptable degree of technicality, what level of volume is considered appropriate, and the extent to which face-threatening behaviour is tolerated.[1]

A look at turn-taking is most revealing here. Usually, people are not aware of their culture's hidden rules. An example of this is the rules governing turn-taking in non-moderated conversations, in spite of the enormous differences in how you 'get in a word edgeways' in different cultures. In Scandinavian countries, for example, children are educated not to interrupt the current speaker, but to wait for him or her to finish the sentence or phrase. Even short pauses between turns are common, before the next speaker begins.

However, in a foreign language interaction, a pause—be it ever so short—is often seen as embarrassing. The conclusion may be drawn that the speaker is looking for the right words, or it may simply be assumed that they don't have an answer ('Could he/she even be a bit *slow*?'). If the pause is felt to be 'too long', a well-meaning or impatient Central European speaker may be tempted to 'prompt' the Scandinavian, suggesting what he thinks he may be trying to say. In Central Europe, on the other hand, speakers will frequently interrupt the current speaker to indicate their wish to take over. The 'new' speaker speaks for about half a sentence while the current speaker has not yet finished, so that there is overlapping speech for a couple of seconds, until the first speaker 'hands over'. There are other cultures where the overlapping phase can be fairly long, leading to two or more speakers 'holding the floor' simultaneously. And yet people in such cultures don't 'lose the thread'. In Spain or Italy, for instance, people manage to take part in several conversations at the same time.

[1] For a more detailed discussion, see Schegloff and Sacks (1973); Sacks, Schegloff, and Jefferson (1974, 696–735).

Now take a multinational working group, moderated by a Finnish manager, where participants from 'overlapping speech cultures' tend to interrupt continuously or even speak simultaneously, and you can imagine the horror the manager will experience. The interrupting or prompting speaker will, of course, be perceived as 'aggressive'.

Still more bewildering in connection with interruptions is the completely different cultural meaning of interruptions. When a French speaker—and he still remains French even when he is speaking English—interrupts, this may mean that he is deeply involved and interested, even supportive, whereas a German speaker will tend to interpret an interruption as indicating disagreement or even as a display of hostility.

How to Find One's Way in the Land of Fuzzy Signals

As we have seen, Wittgenstein is right: the meaning of words or phrases is very often deeply ingrained in cultural deep structures. They are an invitation to negotiate their meaning in a given social context, bearing in mind that every user brings his or her personal and cultural biography to bear on the outcome.

The use of a lingua franca for international cooperation is like navigating uncharted territory. The many challenges discussed earlier call for the united efforts of both practitioners of and theorists on English as a lingua franca. There are no easy answers other than the development of awareness on every level through training and monitored experiences, and a readiness to learn how to cope with fuzziness in the use of linguistic and cultural tokens.

7

John Betjeman, the Subversive Conservative

JANE DRYHURST BECKERMAN

John Betjeman, born in 1906, died on 19 May 1984, aged 77. By the end of his life he had accomplished a great deal. He had campaigned successfully to conserve and retain many buildings of distinction that were threatened with destruction. His public life, most unusually for a poet, was connected with his passion for architectural conservation and he became a very well-known 'personality', appearing on radio and television and as an interviewee on many 'chat' shows. Not since Matthew Arnold, and Milton before him, had a poet led a crusading public life while continuing to regard himself primarily and seriously as a poet.

His image on TV was that of an 'old buffer' who liked churches, railways, and unfashionable seaside towns, and he talked about them slowly in rhythm or rhyme in his clear, uplifted voice as the camera panned over the English countryside, railways, and suburbs. These TV and radio programmes supported his active work in the Georgian and Victorian societies. As he enthused over churches, unfashionable buildings, and small towns, he wore a hat and an old raincoat and glasses, nicely complimenting the image of an elderly enthusiast who knew a lot and cared a lot, but who, despite the 'posh' accent, wasn't an academic, nor an intellectual. In his last televised interview in 1984, in a wheelchair, his knees covered with a plaid rug, that image was confirmed when he was asked what, if anything, he regretted in his life and he answered, 'I haven't had enough sex.'

He distanced himself from university academic life continually and carefully throughout his career. He taught for a term or two after leaving Oxford, without a degree, but ever afterwards worked for a living as a journalist, or a 'hack' as he called himself. Despite his lack of public involvement with politics, academics, or intellectuals, he was asked in 1960 to be a witness for the defence at the *Lady Chatterley's Lover* obscenity trial (see Chapter 1, 'Drawing Lines'), and enthusiastically agreed although he was not chosen to take the stand.[1]

He was made Poet Laureate in 1972 and called 'the People's Poet'; just as the life of Diana, Princess of Wales, 'the People's Princess', subverted the image of the British monarchy, Betjeman's poetry subverted literary and critical orthodoxies of the twentieth century. His poetry has received little critical attention, is not part of the university canon, and his perceived lack of 'seriousness' distanced him from the poetic mainstream of the mid-twentieth century. Today, Betjeman's lifelong concern for the preservation of an architectural heritage that he saw was under threat is widely understood and applauded, and by the end of his life he was one of the most popular poets of the century as well as a prescient conservationist. His was an indisputably dominating and influential presence.

He was certainly the best-selling poet of the twentieth century. Betjeman's *Collected Poems* were published in 1958 by John Murray, and Philip Larkin (1984) reported that sales reached 1,000 copies a week and shortly thereafter reached 100,000. Literary critics of the mid- to late twentieth century who had cut their critical teeth on Leavis, T.S. Eliot, Auden, Pound, and the early Modernists struggled mightily to come to terms with this degree of popularity,

[1] E.M. Forster, Aldous Huxley, Graham Greene, Iris Murdoch, Helen Gardner, and Bertrand Russell were also asked to testify. The two other poets asked were Stephen Spender and T.S. Eliot.

and mid-century critical writing about his work positions him firmly outside 'real' poetry.

Thus, 'the strength and appeal of what he writes lies apart from the discriminations that must be used when "real" poetry is in question' (Wain 1961). Or

> the man wasn't serious [...] all the creative effort of Eliot, Yeats, Auden, Richards, Empson, Leavis, has done no good at all [...] no one apart from mildly eccentric Oxford dons has ever taken [his poetry] seriously. He is a skilful, harmless, minor writer who writes about the delicious trials and tribulations of the upper middle class. (Alvarez 1959)

This point of view is underlined in an 'appreciation' by Kingsley Amis in *The Observer* of 20 May 1984, the year of Betjeman's death. '[Betjeman's] own work resists the application of critical tools [...] another defect from certain points of view [...] and the thought of a thesis on it is grotesque' (Amis 1984a). This comes at the end of a paragraph in which Betjeman is described as anti-academic; 'he stayed away from academic and literary circles', and indeed uncritical, responding to the work of poets he liked with commonplaces. 'Isn't that lovely?' or 'Frightfully good, old Newbolt, isn't he?' Here Amis percipiently represents Betjeman as living and working outside the literary life of his time. It is noteworthy that in Amis's opinion this disqualifies him from being taken 'seriously'. Betjeman was thought of as a poet who did not 'develop'; 'his style—as both man and poet—was consolidated early and expanded rather than developed' (Brown 1999, 3)

Geoffrey Grigson, born a year earlier than Betjeman, was another very influential critic and poet, who 'detested and still detests his verses, or most of them', and who recalled his reaction when Betjeman was appointed Poet Laureate in 1972. Perhaps Betjeman's appointment was a 'pointed joke' or a deliberate 'rebuff to modernism', or an effort to 'exalt' a politically neutral poet (Grigson 1984, 169).

Poetic 'nostalgia' was often attributed disparagingly to Betjeman. According to some obituary notices, he had a 'passionate nostalgia for the late-Victorian values of his childhood' (*Evening Standard* 1984), and struck 'familiar notes of celebration of a simpler style of life and worship' with a 'loathing of present tendencies' (Curtis 1984). Philip Larkin (1984) maintained that he was 'resolutely opposed to the spirit of his age', and that he developed an 'older tradition' of 'direct communication in unambiguous language'. His work, said Larkin, was a 'memorial of twentieth century English life'. Betjeman's so-called nostalgia was often correlated with a simplicity of style that begat ease of understanding. His poems were all apparently 'perfectly intelligible' (Ingrams 1984), written so that 'everyone could understand' (Amis 1984b). He was a 'living repudiation of the idea that poetry must be arcane or saturnine' (*The Times* 1984d), whose 'down to earth style kept him in the forefront of modern poetry for more than twenty years' (Bassett 1984).

Betjeman is portrayed as a picture-book Englishman, remembered for 'championing fast-fading values' and being 'a great British character who campaigned to preserve traditional institutions like music hall, village greens and Church bells' (Bassett 1984). He is described as 'a fervent Englishman [...] keeping alive [...] his country's heritage' (*The Times* 1984c). He was 'the most English of poets' (St John-Stevas 1984), whose 'poetry and campaigning zeal sprang from the same source [...] a passionate nostalgia for the late-Victorian values of his childhood' (*Evening Standard* 1984).

Betjeman's death was reported in Canadian, American, and European papers at some length but emphasis was placed on his work as a poet rather than as a pioneering conservationist, broadcaster, or architectural journalist. His literary awards were listed frequently and he was described as a 'refined, subtle writer' (*Toronto Globe and Mail* 1984), who 'ennobled the ordinary life of suburban England' (*The Washington Post* 1984), and 'relished using the English language' (*The Los Angeles Times* 1984).

British comment on Betjeman at the time of his death illustrated Philip Larkin's statement, in his Introduction to the Houghton Mifflin edition of the *Collected Poems*, that, 'the quickest way to start a punch-up between two British literary critics is to ask them what they think of the poems of Sir John Betjeman' (1971, 5). There was general agreement on his failure to write worthwhile verse as Laureate, on the importance of his work as an architectural conservationist, the depth of his interest in the Church of England, his success as a television 'personality', and the extraordinarily high sales of his poetry. Both his poetry and his personality occasioned conflicting opinions.

He was the 'eccentric but loveable Poet Laureate' who 'never quite grew up and never quite grew old' (*The Times* 1984a) and who 'like many an overgrown schoolboy loved railways [...] and was a familiar figure on TV usually pleading for the preservation of some monument or other' (*The Times* 1984c). He was described as having an 'impish personality' (*The Times* 1984c) and writing 'whimsical poetry' (Glancey 1984). The report of his memorial service, held on 29 June 1984, in Westminster Abbey, ended with a description of the congregation 'shuffling out to the good-natured melancholia of *Banana Blush*'. John Betjeman, we are assured, 'would have adored every archetypically English moment' (Hewson 1984). This characteriszation of Betjeman as childlike and unworldly is summarized in the unsigned obituary notice of *The Times* on 21 May (1984b):

> The amusedly self-deprecating view he took in public of his own literary work suggests a whimsical attitude towards himself that undoubtedly contributed to his public image, but it may well have limited his overall achievement.

The portrait of a poet and a man who is not to be taken seriously by virtue of his 'natural' lack of gravitas is accompanied by several accounts of Betjeman that suggest he was a willing participant in the creation of this image. 'He played the fool partly in self-defence' (Stamp 1984), and protected himself by hiding behind an 'act'. Hillier (1988) makes much of Betjeman's skill as an actor in the first volume of his biography.

Memories of him are contradictory. A lifelong friend and colleague, John Piper (1984), described Betjeman as 'a lover of the human spirit', and the *Daily Telegraph* leader column of 21 May 1984 wrote that Betjeman 'loved the human race'. Auberon Waugh (1984) said of Betjeman that 'of all the people I have ever known, I would say that he was the one who detested the human race most completely'.

Hugh Casson (1984) stated confidently that 'John Betjeman hated vulgarity (he couldn't see its vitality)', but Alan Ross (1984), writing about the commemorative Betjeman exhibition staged in the foyer of the National Theatre in October 1984, commented that the exhibition lacked 'something of the vulgarity and common touch that John Betjeman would have appreciated'. Gavin Stamp (1984) reported that Betjeman was irritated at being automatically identified with

Victorian architecture in the public mind when he knew 'what was good and fought for it'. Ivor Bulmer-Thomas thought that Betjeman 'looked at architecture like a poet, not a scholar', and that 'he lacked follow-through' (1985, 218–20). He is described as both 'whimsical and diffident' (Stamp 1984) and as possessing 'considerable resilience [...] toughness and pugnacity' (Larkin 1984).

The one aspect of his personality on which there is general agreement is 'a melancholy far more incisive than literary gloom' (*The Times* 1984d). Betjeman was 'the most guilt-ridden man I have ever met' (Hillier 1984), 'haunted by the prospect of death, guilt, insecurity and fear of punishment by God' (Lord 1984). His 'melancholy was striking' (Ingrams 1984) and 'he feared people' (M. Piper 1984).

A similar double vision operated in critical commentary on his work as a poet. Philip Larkin (1984) was almost the only writer among the admirers of Betjeman's work to confront his poor critical reputation after his death as a 'good writer of light verse with occasional deeper moments', a reputation which he suggested was not unconnected with the high sales of his poetry. Larkin praised the range and subtlety of Betjeman's poetry, the 'ease with which his poems range from comedy to pathos and ruthless honesty', his 'totally original vision of human topography' and his 'vigorous style' that had created a 'poetry of immediate response that [...] captured the reader even against his will'. Betjeman, wrote Larkin, had 'created [...] the taste with which he is relished'. Roy Fuller (1984) pointed out that, like Auden (and other 'modernists'), Betjeman liked to use traditional poetic forms but thought that no one subject was more 'poetic' than any other.

Betjeman himself is reported to have said that his poetry could be 'boiled down' to three themes, 'that you're all alone, that you fall in love, that you've got to die' (Lord 1984). The patronizing tone of many of Betjeman's obituary notices was commented on by Frank Delaney (1984), who suggested that it was Betjeman's very popularity as a poet and public figure that explained this.

Literary criticism of succeeding decades has overturned the orthodoxies of the mid-twentieth century and Betjeman's work has long outlasted that of many of his critics and contemporaries. Betjeman positioned himself from the very first as a poet who did not align himself with any contemporary poetic 'movement', a stance that could have been either foolhardy or, as will be shown, an extraordinarily brave and confident beginning.

Mount Zion, Betjeman's first volume of poetry, was published in November 1931 when he was 25. Its startling appearance and the range of poems within demonstrated his skill in manipulating traditional poetic form and his desire to experiment with themes and tone. Betjeman wrote poetry all his life, but to fully explore the development of his poetics is outside the confines of this essay. I propose here to discuss his first publication, *Mount Zion*, a tour de force of revolutionary poetics and a dazzling achievement.

The physical appearance of *Mount Zion*, often ignored, immediately signalled Betjeman's desire to claim his reader's full attention. *Mount Zion* was crammed with illustrations; some taken from Victorian illustrated poetry books, some drawn by contemporary artists. Ornamented initials decorated many poems that were bordered within art deco frames. The cover was bound in paper used for wrapping fireworks, obtained from Brocks, the firework manufacturers (Hillier 1988, 354).

Mount Zion was privately published by Edward James, a wealthy art collector, surrealist, eccentric, and friend of Betjeman's from Oxford. James and Betjeman were both anxious about the appearance of the book, and consulted one another on details of presentation and production. James wrote to Betjeman from New York that 'the type most suitable would be in awfully bad taste—possibly an abortive Gothic' (Betjeman 1994, 47).

Later, James decided that a single typeface alone could not reflect the full range of poems and that it might be varied from page to page. He continued: 'While the book may present an epitome of everything that is the worst taste in type and decoration [... we] must not allow the outside world one moment to doubt the deep intensity of our sophistication' (Betjeman 1994, 48).

Eventually, a single Victorian typeface was used and two different colours of paper, a pastel pink and cornflower blue. Bookshops may not choose to display a first slim volume from an unknown poet as a matter of course, but may be more easily persuaded when presented with such a glittering, eye-catching cover.

The subtitle of *Mount Zion*, 'In Touch with the Infinite', is a reference to *In Tune with the Infinite*, a popular self-help book by Ralph Waldo

Trine, published in New York in the late 1890s and re-printed in the UK soon afterwards.[2] On the front fly leaf, with the accompanying subtitle was a wasp-waisted female figure holding an old-fashioned telephone. This illustration, an engraved woodcut, was from *The Telephone, the Microphone and the Phonograph*, a French scientific treatise on the history and correct use of the telephone (Moncel 1882). By 1931, however, about 2 million people in Britain had telephones and the phones themselves were recognizably modern hand-held instruments that rested on a cradle from which one could dial (BT Archives). Betjeman and James had therefore chosen an illustration that would have been an archaic image in 1931.

The dedication page had a sepia photograph or engraving of Sezincote, a country house in Moreton-in-Marsh owned at that time by Colonel Arthur Dugdale and his wife, Ethel. Betjeman knew their son, John, at Oxford. The visual impression made on the reader before looking at the poems is considerable and ambivalent. A Brocks firework paper cover, promising sparkling, fizzing, and illuminating poetry is followed by a woman not of her time trying with an antiquated instrument to get 'in touch with the infinite'. The dedication page shows an exotic country house, home of the wealthy Dugdale family, where Betjeman acknowledged himself in his dedication to have been a grateful guest:

> Constantly under these minarets I have been raised from the deepest depression and spent the happiest days of my life, Mrs. Arthur Dugdale therefore, the hostess of Sezincote, I run the risk of alienating by dedicating to her this precious, hyper-sophisticated book.

The meanings of 'precious' are contradictory; one indicating value, the other signifying the essentially false. His description of *Mount Zion*

[2] The title was also used by E.M. Forster in a short story entitled 'The Purple Envelope', written at some time between 1903 and 1906. It appears last in a list of disappointing presents given to a young man on his 21st birthday by elderly, dull relations. The list of presents, symbolic of all that was least attractive to a young, physically active man who was hoping for a new rifle, are: 'Watt's *Hope*, Watt's *Love and Death*, Botticelli's *Madonna of the Magnificat*, a sovereign purse, a watch-chain, a tea-caddy, and *In Tune with the Infinite* by Mr. Trine' (Forster [1972] 1979, 65).

here as both 'precious' and 'hyper-sophisticated' creates an expectation of the effete, the epicene, and the camp—a nod to the last decades of the nineteenth century, and an almost deliberate thumbing of the nose at the prevailing, much more serious political and economic mores of the early 1930s. But the apologetic tone in his dedication may have also communicated Betjeman's anxiety on behalf of those readers whom he knew would not enjoy these qualities. This offer and withdrawal of a framework for reading the poems may be representative of Betjeman's inexperience or uncertainty as a public poet. It can also be read as part of Betjeman's desire to play a 'game'; to establish himself from the first as an ambitious, difficult, contemporary poet; arch, knowing, ironic, and at odds with other poets of his time. His project in *Mount Zion* is closely connected with what Lionel Trilling has called 'authenticity' and 'the doctrine of masks'. The opening pages of *Mount Zion* with their jumble of contradictory images and words do indeed

> [say] one thing when another is meant, not for the purpose of deceit and not wholly for the purpose of mockery (although this is usually implicit), but, rather, in order to establish a disconnection between the speaker and his interlocutor, or between the speaker and that which is being spoken about, or even between the speaker and himself. (Trilling 1972, 120)

In the next introductory page, entitled 'The Author' and framed, as are all the poems by a contemporary border, Betjeman positions himself defensively, grateful for the 'forbearance and understanding' of his printers and publisher and his 'good friends'. It prepares the reader for a crowded stage of contributors, muses, and distractions in the form of illustrations within the volume and can also be read as a cleverly ironic piece of self-promotion. However grateful he is for his 'good friends', we are informed that a fairly substantial list of magazines has already published his poems. Betjeman had begun to 'make it' in his own right. It is an effective piece of self-advertisement, an adroit, stylistic manoeuvre. It is also quite without precedent in the work of other poets of his time.

The title itself, *Mount Zion*, signals the ambitious nature of the project. It is 'one of the hills in Jerusalem, on which the city of David was built; [hence] house of God, the Christian Church, place of worship'

(*Oxford Dictionary of English Etymology* 1966, 1023). It is a symbol of home and of destiny for Christians and especially Jews. Psalm 137 recalls the Jews who were removed from their homeland and taken as hostages to Babylon: 'By the rivers of Babylon, there we sat down, yea we wept when we remembered Zion.'

The majesty of the title with its deep religious resonance, combined with a comic image of flawed communication (how is it possible to be in touch with the infinite?) and a welter of other pictorial images and stylistic effects, creates a field of clashing ideas and images, ambivalence, and deliberate confusion that is both exciting and daring. Betjeman undermined clarity in a way that has become progressively far more familiar as the twentieth century advanced. These images, grandiose, comic, and surreal, are a first indication of what Josipovici (1977) calls the two lessons of modernism: the lessons of *silence* and of *game*. Betjeman's interest in 'game', the creation of multivalent imagery in words and pictures which obscure easy identification and interpretation and undermine the reader's attempt to become involved in his project, is established here, at the beginning of his career.

There are 21 poems in *Mount Zion*, of which 12 appear in the *Collected Poems* of 1958, which ran to 10 editions in 2 years, and sold at least 100,000 copies. *Mount Zion* cast a very long shadow indeed, and the recurrence of these poems indicates an unusually strong and significant beginning for a young poet. And although the quality and quantity of illustrations that embroidered *Mount Zion* certainly contributed to a dazzling first impression, they have not created or ensured the longevity of Betjeman's popularity.

A surprising number of poems are concerned with religion—religious feeling, religious activity, and Nonconformity in particular. This was (and is) a daring choice for a young poet, and adds to the sense of confusion, strangeness, and ambiguity in *Mount Zion.* How is the reader to experience these poems with their clashing images and illustrations, conventional form, and startlingly unusual subject matter? I shall explore a number of poems from *Mount Zion*, including one or two that are relatively unknown, perhaps because they are the most 'experimental', the strangest in tone, subject, and form, and demonstrate just how 'far out' Betjeman, in 1931, was prepared to go.

'St. Aloysius Church, Oxford' (1931, 57) is an 'unknown'—the only poem in *Mount Zion* not to have been published before 1931, and not included in subsequent collections. It includes a peculiar feature in its second stanza: an asterisked note.

> Aloysius, rich and poor,
> Must enter by Thy grain'd oak door
> To realise with unreal eyes
> Reality* and paradise.
>
> *In its mystical sense.

This note on 'reality', in the context of the two similar words in the proceeding line, 'realise' and 'unreal', draws the reader back to the first stanza, with its lines describing the materiality, in contrast to the 'mystic reality', of the art in the church. The reader looks again at the 'paint', the 'glass', the 'plaster' that make up the 'many coloured master' of the 'sacred heart' and can now see a gaudy Christ figurine from a visitors' shop perhaps as well as a dignified Christ from one of the better-known Catholic churches in Oxford.

Betjeman's tone here is impossible to fathom. The excited, emphatic quality introduced by the use of exclamation marks in the first stanza is dislocated and undermined. Is this a side-swipe at Catholic 'bells and smells'? Are the 'paint', 'glass', and 'plaster' transformed spiritually by our 'art' of worship, or is the 'art' of the material Christ figure, ambivalent in the poem, the best we can do? The poem echoes William Blake's 'The Tyger' in its verse form and in the line 'what paint, what glass, what plaster'. The triple use of 'realise', 'unreal', and 'reality' in the last two lines leaves the reader with an uneasy final question: is 'paradise' 'reality', or is it 'unreal'?

The asterisked footnote creates even more ambiguity. Betjeman has chosen not to place the 'mystical sense' of 'reality' within the body of the poem, the main structure. It lies just outside, undermining the uplift of the final line. The reader may construe this as a religious commentary in its own right or it may be a deliberate lowering of the poetic temperature, a coming down to earth with the bathos of a footnote, a smattering of pedantry. It may be a device for distancing the poet from his subject, informing the reader that he is not entirely confident of his authority, or his commitment, to write on religious matters. This is a provocative poem, defying easy categorization and resisting interpretation; part of the excitement of *Mount Zion*.

In comparison, 'The Sandemanian Meeting-House in Highbury Quadrant' (1931, 32) has been reprinted many times. All the poems in *Mount Zion* share the same border but 'The Sandemanian Meeting-House' is richly ornamented, while 'St. Aloysius' is left unadorned. The effect of the ornamentation in the former poem is of a finely wrought container holding something precious enough to be cushioned and protected by these exquisite decorations. The poem, in harmony with this conceit, contrasts the secrecy and privacy of the small sect with the rush and bustle of London outside:

> Away from the barks and the shouts and the greetings,
> Psalm-singing over and love-lunch done,
> Listening to the Bible in their room for meetings,
> Old Sandemanians are hidden from the sun.

Sandemanians (or Glasites) believed that 'the use of political or secular weapons as a means of reformation, instead of the word and spirit of Christ, is wholly wrong' (Hastings 1913). Members washed one another's feet at the weekly 'love feast' and Sandemanians believed that the accumulation of wealth was unscriptural, that money was to be given away to churches or communities in need. There were at most a dozen Sandemanian chapels in Scotland and a few in England and the USA. Here once more is a visual essay, a snapshot, with no core of 'meaning', no agenda, no overt or covert message. There is the bustle and roar of London's streets, railways, and trams and amongst them, invisible, a tiny group of people who are 'hidden from the sun', left out of everyday life, unknown. Here is a snapshot, a moment in a busy city before the lens zooms in to the 'hidden world'. There is no personal tone here, no easily discernible opinion; perhaps a reminder that religious lives are always hidden but not less intensely felt.

An entirely different poem, 'Hymn' (1931, 17), expresses with considerable feeling Betjeman's anger at the way in which medieval churches have been 'restored', not only with no concern for the original integrity of the building but also to enrich local developers and improve the quality of the furniture in local homes. The poem, straightforward and deeply felt, is written to the rhythm of the hymn tune 'The Church's One Foundation'. It begins:

The Church's Restoration
In eighteen-eighty-three
Has left for contemplation
Not what there used to be.
How well the ancient woodwork
Looks round the Rect'ry hall,
Memorial of the good work
Of him who plann'd it all.

Three more poems concentrate on aspects of Nonconformity: 'An Eighteenth-Century Calvinistic Hymn', the aforementioned 'Sandemanian Meeting-House in Highbury Quadrant', and 'Competition'. Betjeman had originally decided to call this first volume of poems *Chapel and Spa* (Hillier 1988, 353), a less impressive title than the one he eventually chose, with fewer resonances, but one that reflects Betjeman's interest in Nonconformity and the buildings associated with it.

'An Eighteenth-Century Calvinistic Hymn' (1931, 23) is, in the style of 'Hymn', a comic satire on Nonconformist acceptance of suffering as its own reward, but written in the voice of a glad sufferer.

'Competition' (1931, 30) is another 'unknown'.

The independent Calvinistic *1810*
Methodist chapel is gone,
Dust in the galleries, dust on the stairs
There was no one to carry it on.
And a Norman New Jerusalem Church *1840*
Was raised on the sacred site
Where they praised the Lord and praised the Lord
By incandescent light.

The italicized dates on the right-hand side in each of the three stanzas probably refer to the opening dates of the four chapels described in the poem, and the competition in the title refers to their struggle for survival. The accompanying illustration shows an urban street with two chapel buildings along a road. One, the 'Norman New Jerusalem Church' (1840), originally the 'Independent Calvinistic Methodist Chapel' (1810), has a 'for sale' sign, and another is a 'pinnacled Wesley Memorial Church' (1860).

This is one of the many poems in *Mount Zion* that announce Betjeman's revolutionary agenda. No other poet of the twentieth century concerns him- or herself with the fortunes of a few Nonconformist chapels in an unidentified town, written as part history lesson, part celebration (the 'traceried windows [...] rock with song') and expressing concern over their future. This more serious note is undercut by the question mark after the final lines: 'What of Mount Carmel Baptists (Strict), [1875] / For they've central heating there?'—what indeed? The reader is left, as so often in this collection, juggling the various tones and effects Betjeman has so skilfully produced.

Is the poem mocking the conformity of the Nonconformists in their need for improved lighting and heating, or applauding the desire to attract and keep congregations in small chapels? Or is the poem a spoof history lesson, a stylistic joke on a subject that is utterly, eccentrically unfashionable, written for friends who would appreciate his humour? This is Betjeman as a subversive who refuses to provide his reader with a stable tone. Despite the thundering stresses of the rocking rhythm and rhyme, Betjeman avoids both clarity and certainty.

Two other extraordinary religious poems are 'Tunbridge Wells' and 'For Nineteenth-Century Burials'.

'Tunbridge Wells' (1931, 35) is empty of individuals, though the facing print foregrounds a young man. The people of the town are 'rung from rest' by 'the Gospel Bells', on a 'Lord's Day morning'; the town is revealed, as it

> Climbs to light through the mist adorning
> Towers and steeples of Tunbridge Wells.

The allusions here may be to the nature of enlightenment, and 'Lord's Day morning', Christmas Day. The reader then looks down at the illustration added underneath the poem, a line drawing of three bells, looped together with ribbon and entwined with holly. It could easily be a tracing from a cheap Christmas card.

The reader is finally thwarted. The poem with its illustrations has resisted any attempt to produce harmony or clarity. This is an example of Betjeman's early connection with what has become known as postmodernism: the capacity to destabilize text, to choose not to be taken 'seriously', and to create an effect that is neither contingent, nor deliberately provocative, nor pretentious, but indefinable within poetic discourse. Here is the source of Betjeman's reputation as a poet 'outside' poetry.

In contrast, 'For Nineteenth-Century Burials' (1931, 29) is one of the most affecting poems in the collection. It begins:

> This cold weather
> Carries so many old people away.
> Quavering voices and blankets and breath
> Go silent together.
> The gentle fingers are touching to pray
> Which crumple and straighten for Death.

In *Mount Zion* the poem is literally entwined with its illustration of a church surrounded by trees blown in a high wind. On the page, the words push against the illustration contained within the border, as the wind pushes against the chapel windows. The poem goes on to capture the atmosphere of a wintry country churchyard, cold and windy. The lines are broken up on the page to produce the visual effect of being crushed, blown to the very edges of the border. Each couplet reproduces the sensation of a different gust of wind, beginning with hard, active sounds and ending with a gentle fall. The visualization within the poem is of the wind as spirit, an active, almost human presence in the churchyard (a conceit found again in a later poem, 'The Heart of Thomas Hardy', 1937), 'old people' and 'bells' that are carried away on the air, the 'quavering voices' and 'stuttering tales of Gothic' that mingle together as they blow through the churchyard and against the windows of the chapel, creating a vision of humankind and nature blending at a graveside in the cold wind. The poem sets up contradictions with fingers that both 'crumple and straighten' and where the 'quavering voices' are also 'silent'. Betjeman creates a visualization of spiritual transformation as the dead are blown about by the wind and pressed up against the windows of the church, the home of their spirit.

Other poems in *Mount Zion* are written as dramatic or melodramatic narratives, stories strongly told of death, mysterious disappearance, and sex. 'The Outer Suburbs' (1931, 44), for example, is filled with light and shadow, illuminating an evening of suburban life. It is also a gothic portrait of suburban family life that includes a macabre and subversive sexuality, a powerful element in Betjeman's later poetry. The 'Jacobethan' bed, an ironic brand name mocking solid English oak and rollicking Shakespearean sensuality, looms over the events of the evening. Hubbie's 'gloom' after his 'weary walk' from the station is intensified by 'wifie', sitting knitting, like a spider spinning a web, 'hiding what should not be seen'. She is 'safe in the Drage-way living-room', all 'expectant for the bed' and seemingly impervious to hubbie's misery, which is possibly compounded at least in part by sexual reluctance. The suggestion that sex and domesticity are inimical is perhaps unsurprising in the young (Betjeman was in his early twenties when he wrote this), but despite a closing exclamation mark for comic emphasis this is a rather sordid and unsettling vignette, combining 'modern' life with a grisly view of marriage.

Betjeman wrote poetry that was 'modern' in quite a different way than his contemporaries. Here he uses brand names and the word 'suburbs'. 'Kitchenette' was a new word in the 1930s and stained glass a relatively new development in interior domestic design, part of the 'arts and crafts' movement. The idea that a bedroom, or a living room, could have a brand name and be mass-produced was relatively new. The poem uses the names of real places, and this linguistic modernity is combined with a cinematographic view of the 'weary walk from Oakleigh Park' to 'Rosslyn Avenue', described in terms of camera angles and light, reflecting another new cultural development: cinema.

The word 'Gothic' was used by Alan Pryce-Jones in his review of *Mount Zion* a month after it was published. The Gothic convention of mysterious horror contained within a building is here together with the suggestion of entrapment and cruelty, but the poem can more appropriately be read as 'mock' Gothic; a small flat instead of a castle, a nod to the Gothic convention of sexual exploitation but with no clear indication of who is oppressing whom. The poem refuses to be read 'straight', and Betjeman's poetics of theatricality and subtlety as well as his ambiguities of tone, a poetic strategy that marks him out immediately from other poets of his time, are established. His skilled use of the conventions of narrative and of mystery, a suggestion of wrongdoing, a story that does not have a happy ending, are demonstrated here as they are in 'Croydon', 'A Flight from Bootle', and 'Death in Leamington', though in these poems equally dramatic events are handled quite differently.

'Death in Leamington' (1931, 13), another narrative poem, is one of the most anthologized and best-known of Betjeman's poems. Here there are no secrets. An old woman has died in her bed in Leamington Spa. We know nothing about her. It may be assumed that she has been ill for a while, as the attending nurse has not even noticed the moment of her patient's passing, caught up as she is in the routine of bringing tea. We are present at the moment of the discovery of her death. Here there is no modernistic 'branding' and little theatricality; eight rhymed quatrains in ballad fashion describe an event that can be considered to be without intrinsic interest at all—a commonplace. But the reader is forcefully questioned in the sixth stanza, suddenly confronted with the reality of death. 'Do you know that the heart will stop?' The comparison between peeling stucco, falling plaster, and death is highly original, and a marker of Betjeman's enduring interest in buildings and in death. The plaster dropping from the 'yellow, Italianate arches', the suggested whispered sound of a flake hitting the ground is beautifully chimed with the gentle death of the anonymous old woman in Leamington.

The use of ballad form creates the narrative frame for this 'story'. There is no sense of haste. The reader knows nothing of the woman who has died nor the woman who has nursed her. Nothing 'happens', because the poem has captured a moment that can have no sequel. The only effect of this death is that the 'lonely crochet' will not be finished. The personification of the woman herself as a lonely, unfinished piece of wool or lace work, patient and 'unstirred', is a full and tender image.

The following image of death itself as 'the spoken word' packs a harder punch. The idea that the spoken word could be a dead thing is again unusual. Dead compared to the written word? Dead compared to the thought that engendered it? The emphasis is on the word 'dead' in the last line of the second stanza. Betjeman has chosen to leave out the word 'as' in front of 'dead', which would have leavened the impact. In the fifth stanza, the only spoken words are said by the nurse, in a 'tiny' voice, banalities uttered as she bustles around the room not noticing that the old woman has died. The reader is vividly aware of her bright insincerity, her 'chintzy, chintzy cheeriness' spoken to an unnoticed cadaver.

Death, the inevitable and inescapable, is at the heart of the poem. But as the falling of plaster does not threaten the house, so the death of a person does not threaten humanity. The nurse tiptoes 'gently' away, and the reader is left to reflect, as so often, on the *tone* of the poem. Betjeman is reporting an unremarkable event, the death of an anonymous old woman. After the climax of the sixth stanza, where the reader is so forcefully reminded that death is final, the poems ends with the gas lamps being turned off in the hall in the 'calm of a Leamington ev'ning'; a quiet, humbling image of death, of the light going out, as the nurse makes her way from the house.

Six other poems in *Mount Zion* can be described as secular meditations on human behaviour: 'The Varsity Students' Rag', 'The City', 'Camberley', 'Westgate-On-Sea', 'The Wykehamist', and 'The Garden City'. Each of these poems aims at a different target: 'hearty' students, businessmen, middle-class suburban seclusion, town planning, Wykehamists,[3] and the arts and crafts movement and its devotees. Vivid, waspish, comic, and enduringly popular, these poems provide startling contrast to 'Death in Leamington' and 'For Nineteenth-Century Burials', and with these poems in mind it is possible to consider Betjeman as a poet working within a definable genre, that of *vers de société*, 'light' verse.

In his introduction to an anthology, Kingsley Amis outlines the skills of the writers of light verse:

> Light verse makes more stringent demands on the writer's technique. A fault of scansion or rhyme, an awkwardness or obscurity that would damage the only immediate context of a piece of high verse endangers the whole structure of a light verse poem. The expectations of the audience are different in the two cases, corresponding to the difference in the kind of performance offered. A concert pianist is allowed a wrong note here and there. A Juggler is not allowed to drop a plate. (1978, xviii)

The light verse poems in *Mount Zion* certainly fulfil Amis's criteria, although where Betjeman defies easy categorization is in the fact that he deliberately does 'drop a plate', creating deliberate awkwardnesses here and there, and that his subject matter is so unusual.

The diverse and problematic poems and graphics in *Mount Zion* include serious and affecting reflections on death and religion but

[3] Former pupils of the elite British public school Winchester College.

exclude the personal and the more familiar subject matter of poetry. There is no love poetry, nothing remotely 'contemporary', nothing that could be described as 'nature' poetry, nothing that gives anything *away* about Betjeman himself. Many British poets of the early 1930s struck a more serious note, reflecting the economic, social, and political uncertainties of the time. The more experimental poets of the first decades of the twentieth century dispensed with traditional poetic form altogether, while Betjeman embraced both rhyme and rhythm.

In November 1931, the publication date for *Mount Zion*, Betjeman and James made good use of friendships made at Oxford when they sent it out for review. The 'old boy network' post-Oxbridge is well-chronicled, and Betjeman's career in the first years after leaving Oxford (without a degree) was typical (Cunningham 1988). The extent of his (and James's) contacts within the literary world is demonstrated by these reviews. For a poet's first volume to be reviewed in five leading London papers and magazines is impressive and three of the reviews were written by close friends at Oxford: Alan Pryce-Jones, Tom Driberg, and Randolph Churchill. But however close the friendships were—and Betjeman shared a house with Randolph Churchill and Edward James in London (Hillier 1988, 297), it is soon clear that the reviewers found it difficult to evaluate or categorize *Mount Zion*, expressing various degrees of contradictory bewilderment, and struggling to find a context for Betjeman's poetry and a language to describe it.

Tom Driberg's was the first review for the *Daily Express* of 12 November 1931. Driberg reports:

> [I have just received] an entertaining new book, a slim, precious and sophisticated volume of poems. It is printed on pale blue and pink paper and bound in the sort of paper that is used in the construction of fireworks. Mr. Betjeman has a curious complex about the monstrous architecture of the mid-Victorian temples of non-conformity (that strange mongrel Gothic), and about such kindred subjects as the arts and crafts garden cities and Camberley. He seems half fascinated, half repelled. I fancy it is a case of *odi et amo.*

Driberg does not change register or tone whether he is writing about Betjeman's poetry or cocktails, and a critical note is struck that recurred throughout Betjeman's career. Here for the first, but by no means the last, time we read that Betjeman's poetry is an eccentricity that precludes, perhaps even deliberately prevents, critical attention.

Randolph Churchill and Alan Pryce-Jones, in *The Architectural Review* and *The London Mercury* respectively, try harder to engage with *Mount Zion* and contemporary critical discourse. Churchill struggles gamely but unsuccessfully to characterize Betjeman's poetic project:

> If you like the genuine sublimation of the ridiculous you should read these poems. All the ugliness of the suburbs, all the vulgarity of human nature, are transmuted into golden beauty when touched upon by Mr. Betjeman's pen. This book contains some of the wittiest satires that have been produced for some time. The very beautifying of the grotesque in life and architecture with which these poems are principally concerned, brings a heightened sense of the ridiculous. (Churchill 1931)

Unlike Churchill, Alan Pryce-Jones (1931) was a professional writer and a regular reviewer on *The London Mercury*. He and Betjeman were, and remained, good friends and his review can legitimately be described as the first serious attempt to 'place' Betjeman as a contemporary poet. 'Mr. Betjeman has invented a completely new attitude of mind', he begins, 'and therefore he cannot hope to escape objections'. The 'new attitude of mind' is described by Pryce-Jones (1931) as

> a variation of what the late eighteenth century called 'horrour'. At the thought of Croydon, the Low Church, gas, an Irish peer in a bog, the Regent Palace, handicrafts; of any tortuous vulgarity, or obscure dignity, of lunacy in any form, of the colour mauve, of conifers, of drunk undergraduates, of Sandemanians, of stockbrockers, his sensibility becomes horrid, his indignation sometimes bristles as well, and simultaneously he is amused at the spectacle of himself in a rage. The sophistication of this is that the poems are deliberately not better. Whereas most poets, especially comic ones, polish their verses, Mr. Betjeman unpolishes his so as to make them scratch horribly on the reader. The ideal reader will be as tortured as the author and as abruptly amused. Mr. Betjeman is not wholly innocent of having read Osbert Sitwell, but otherwise his inspiration seems to have no parents at all. This book is worth buying because it could never happen again. Even Mr. Betjeman could not be so eccentric twice running.

Pryce-Jones recognized that Betjeman's 'completely new attitude of mind' involved not only the content of the poems but also their presentation, an opinion echoed by a later admirer, Philip Larkin. After Betjeman's death Larkin (1984) wrote, 'Truly he had created, as Wordsworth said all great and original writers must, the taste by which he was relished.' But in Pryce-Jones' final statement that 'even' Betjeman could not continue to produce such 'eccentric' poetry, it is possible to read a baffled dismissal, a suggestion that *Mount Zion* was a joke, an attention-seeking promotional stunt that would not, or could not, be repeated. In fact, from *Mount Zion* onwards Betjeman wrote and published poetry all his life. John Murray published *Continual Dew* in 1937, and Betjeman wrote to Edward James:

> Murrays [*sic*] are keen to publish the poems. I'm glad they're doing it because they will let me have some fun with the typography as you did. A further thing. Last week Auden wrote to me saying what a corking good 'comic' (I like that) poet I was. Eliot wanted to reprint *Mount Zion* for Fabers [*sic*]. But Murrays [*sic*] got in first. I am not sorry. It would not have been fun to come out uniform with Stephen Spender. (Betjeman 1994, 142)

Betjeman's '(I like that)', I think, denotes disappointment in Auden's judgement.

Pryce-Jones had defined Betjeman's new attitude of mind as a kind of horrour, and included in his list of horrour-inducing subjects several items that are not to be found in the iconography of *Mount Zion*. The Irish peer in a bog is taken from Betjeman's short story 'Lord Mount Prospect', published by *The London Mercury* in 1929 with the help of Pryce-Jones. The colour mauve, lunacy, obscure dignity, and tortuous vulgarity are also difficult to locate confidently in *Mount Zion*. Pryce-Jones does not attempt a definition of the word 'horrour', but Dr Johnson's *Dictionary of the English Language* (6th edition, 1785) provides four definitions derived from the work of various poets. 'Terror mixed with detestation' is to be found in Spenser, Davies, Milton, and Dryden, writes Johnson; 'dreadful thoughts' can be found in Shakespeare's *Macbeth*; 'Gloom, dreariness' is best illustrated by Pope; and the medical symptoms, described as 'shuddering or quivering as precedes an ague-fit', appear in Bacon's *Natural History*. These phrases have acquired a comic quality through time and overuse in popular literature. They can be described as mock- or pseudo-Gothic in the literature of the twentieth century.

Pryce-Jones highlighted another of Betjeman's poetics, writing that Betjeman 'unpolishes his [verses] so as to make them scratch more horribly on the reader', and described this as a 'sophistication'. This is the only comment on Betjeman's use of form in these first reviews, and again is a perceptive identification of one of Betjeman's more interesting and daring poetic strategies, commented on earlier.

Another noteworthy contemporary review of *Mount Zion* appeared in 'Brevities on Books' by an anonymous contributor to the *New Statesman and Nation* (1931):

> Mr. Betjeman is too good to be true. If Mrs. Ros had known what she was doing, or had Cornelius Whur tried to parody himself seriously—no even then *Mount Zion* could not have been produced.

Cornelius Whur and Amanda McKittrick Ros were minor Victorian writers who shared a propensity for overblown phraseology and exaggeration that resulted in comic bombast; all the more comic as they were wholly in earnest. The following is the 'Mr Collins' preface to Cornelius Whur's second book of verse, *Gratitude's Offering*, written in the style of Crabbe's *The Village*.

> The *title* which this volume bears, was adopted by the author in consequence of the unanticipated *patronage* he has received, and the success that attended his former work, 'Village Musings'—*three* large editions having been called for in a very short time. No one, he thinks, can have been treated more handsomely. To ladies and gentlemen who adorn the first circles he considers himself under special obligations. (Whur 1845, v–vi)

The dedication page to *Mount Zion* does bear comparison with this passage from Whur. There is the same obsequiousness and obvious desire to ingratiate, but Betjeman and the people he wanted most to impress were entirely and enjoyably aware of the comic effect he was producing.

Amanda McKittrick Ros was known as 'the World's Worst Novelist' as she continued to publish her own novels and poetry from the last years of the nineteenth century onward (Drabble and Stringer 1987,

876). Ros's lifelong themes of self-congratulation, fury at uncomprehending critics, and concern for social position are couched in comically absurd grandiosity. A typical example, 'An Epitaph', was published in 1933, and begins as follows:

What is my name pray—what to you
Standing there my slab to view?
If I surpassed my sex—what then?
By wielding as I did my pen.

The anonymous reviewer in the *New Stateman and Nation* (1931) presents *Mount Zion* as a highly successful joke on and in this tradition of overblown, pious, Victorian, sentimental ingenuousness. For this reviewer, Betjeman's work is a clever joke, a deliberate parody of the unfashionable writings of Victorian sentimentalists such as Whur and McKittrick Ros. It is, however, difficult to reconcile this reviewer's reading with poems such as 'Death in Leamington' and 'For Nineteenth-Century Burials' where the sparest detail and simplest language and form are able so movingly to illuminate death and change.

The visual presentation of *Mount Zion*, the ornamentation and Victorian engravings do (and did) create a 'Victorian' style. They were evidence that Betjeman and Edward James had indeed produced a 'hyper-sophisticated' and 'precious' work that had confused and disorientated its first reviewers, but the longevity of the popularity of these poems cannot be explained by their 'hyper-sophistication' nor by their 'preciousness'.

In *Mount Zion*, John Betjeman set out his stall as an adventurous, fearless, subversive, and revolutionary poet, who had no desire to be seen as a member of any contemporary poetic 'movement', and who led his readers on a tightrope over a waterfall of daringly experimental poetics. Changes in literary and art criticism of the last fifty years have made it much easier to find a vocabulary with which to approach Betjeman's work. Gone are the hierarchies of mid-twentieth-century literary criticism. Now readers can appreciate the excitement of confusion, and are able to enjoy what Betjeman may well have been the first twentieth-century poet to understand—that poetry is not simply about perfection of language or appropriateness of subject, or subtlety of tone. Betjeman created both 'For Nineteenth-Century Burials' *and* 'The 'Varsity Student's Rag' (1931, 19), which begins:

> I'm afraid the fellows in Putney rather wish they had
> The social ease and manners of a 'varsity undergrad,
> For tho' they're awf'lly decent and up to a lark as a rule
> You want to have the 'varsity touch after a public school.
> CHORUS:
> *We* had a rag at Monico's.[4] *We* had a rag at the Troc.,[5]
> And the one we had at the Berkeley[6] gave the customers quite a shock.
> *Then* we went to the Popular, and after that—oh my!
> I *wish* you'd seen the rag we had in the Grill room at the Cri.[7]

There are fun and games with a lorry in Trafalgar Square, and the students nearly get arrested by a policeman.

> But that's nothing to the rag we had at the college the other night;
> We'd gallons and gallons of cider—and I got frightfully tight,
> And then we smash'd up everything, and what was the funniest part
> We smashed some rotten old pictures which were priceless works of art.
> CHORUS: We, etc.

Oh dear! But you can tell the 'varsity man' by his blazer and tie, and 'you know that he's always ready and up to a bit of a lark'.

Street rap, Oxford-style, of the 1920s! And John Betjeman's work continued to light up the twentieth century.

[4] Café Monico (a restaurant).
[5] The Trocadero Restaurant.
[6] The Berkeley Hotel restaurant.
[7] The Criterion Restaurant.

PART TWO

8

A Failed Dream*

SANJUKTA DASGUPTA

(With sincere apologies to Rabindranath Tagore)

Where the mind is full of fear and the head hangs down
Where knowledge is controlled
Where the world is broken into tiny cruel fragments
By narrow domestic walls
Where words spill out from the dark depths of untruth
Where tireless endeavours strive towards diabolic oppression
Where the clear stream of reason is clogged with glutinous effluents
The dreary wasteland of dead habit is all around
Where the mind is trapped in serpentine gyres of malice
Hatching more and more Satanic thought and action
Into that Hell of horror, O unfortunate citizens, let not my country dive!

2 July 2017

* Sanjukta Dasgupta's poem *A Failed Dream* refers to a poem in Bengali by Tagore (*Gitanjali 35*), which begins (in Tagore's own translation into English), 'Where the mind is without fear and the head is held high ...'. See also Chapter 23, 'Where Is the Mind without Fear?' by Sashi Kumar, included in this book.

9

Four Poems*

PEER KHAN

Khajuraho

The coupling figures bend, and thrust, and merge
In lust or ecstasy. I can't see how
Not to respect that passion's lasting surge
Down all the centuries from then to now.
A million tourist cameras click their fill
Of pictures frozen by the figures' grace
In (kindly) for a moment holding still,
Before resuming their debauched embrace.
Why should this worry *them*? What do *they* care?
Their temple is in India, but *they*
Are *not*. They want no part of that despair
—From joyless prudishness they step away.
For why should this be *our* concern, they sneer:
This 'caste'? This 'honour'? Dowry? Duty? Fear?

* The poems included here comment on how the relaxed sensuality of the earlier Indian tradition has given way to prudery and repression ('Khajuraho'); on the 'saffron terror' of recent years ('Saffron'); on the intolerance of caste ('Outcaste'); and on the rise of thuggish vigilante terrorism by Hindu extremists ('From Ape to Ape').

Saffron

Saffron's a friendly name for Sixties girls,
Who broke your heart (but pulled you into bed),
Who rolled their joints and tossed their hippie curls,
As Peace and Love were screwing with your head.
Saffron's a treasure, and this god-like spice
In any kitchen wouldn't go amiss.
Risotto, biriyani, any rice:
A pinch of saffron wakes it like a kiss.
Saffron's a symbol, too, though much abused
By godly men (or those who claim to be)
Who lead whole armies of the mad, confused,
And vicious, all of them too blind to see
That, as they throw their victims to the flames,
God watches, unimpressed—and marks their names.

Outcaste

'The people of your race are dark as sin,
Your sinfulness is filthy like your breath.
Your breath is black and rotten like your skin.
The people of your skin are twinned with death.
You have no right to share our dal or bread;
You have no right to water from our well;
No right to shelter, comfort, or a bed;
Your only right is to a place in hell.
You screw my light-skinned woman with your eyes
And throw your shadow on my bowl of rice.
For this, your sluttish whore, before she dies,
Spreadeagled on her back will pay the price.'
—This land is sick: a cancer in its gut.
The time has come: the cancer must be cut.

From Ape to Ape

(For M.M. Kalburgi)

Thoughts are what make us, and our thoughts are free.
Thoughts become words, and since our age began
(When nervous apes descended from a tree)
Those words have shaped the history of Man.
A gathering on a hillside in the sun:
Here words were said and shared, and in the raw
Exchange of needs and interests, one by one
Ideas were born: 'the people', 'freedom', 'law'.
There came a time to write them in a book,
For everyone to read, debate and learn.
If you seek knowledge, this is where to look;
If you seek wisdom, this is where you turn.
Now apes on motorbikes their will impose,
And bullets bring our story to a close.

10

The Censor's Tail

MANJULA PADMANABHAN

A censor's life is filled with **WOE**
Every day, I go to work feeling **ill**.
MI OF CEN
I arrive feeling **ill**
I settle down to work feeling **ill**
And I will leave work feeling **ill**
BLASPHEMOUS
ANTI-NATIONAL
OBSCENE
PERVERTED
All writers are **SICK**. Utterly and wholly **SICK. SICK. SICK.**
MY NEW NOVEL IS ABOUT...
BLAH BLAH BLA BLAH
STAMP PAD
They write non-stop filth and rubbish ...
BUT IT WILL CORRUPT THE YOUTH!!
I HAVE NO CHOICE!
ON

... then they cry when their books are banned! Fools.
Film-makers are just the same.
NO CHOICE!
TOTAL BAN!
Artists. Poets. Playwrights. All the SAME.
They all want our APPROVAL...
... and all they produce is SHIT
MMPHH!! EEEARGHHH! YECHHH!! ISH!!
I don't flinch. I don't complain. I just do my duty.
And go home.

On the surface, people look so ordinary and normal. But that's just the surface. Underneath, they look ... different.
DELUX TOWER
LERN 2 TIPE
TOLET
JUICI
GENERAL STORE
AIR-CONDITIONED
ELECTRO
ISD
S.T.D.

VERY different. Filthy. Twisted. Monsters. All of them. And I'm the only one who can see them for what they really are.
DELUX TOWER
LERN2TIPE
TO LET
JUICI
GENERAL STORE
AIR-CONDITIONED
ELECTRO
ISD
S.T.D.

So I do my best not to think about them.
I watch TV. I wait for dinner.
I eat dinner early. My servant makes whatever he likes. I don't interfere.
I wait restlessly for the day to end.
Finally, I am alone. Alone with my tail.
My own sweet tail. So perfect and so pure.

Everyone has a hidden tail.
Like every nation has its secret agenda. Things that must remain HIDDEN.
All tails are SECRET. And SACRED.
That's what makes my job so important. I save the nation's TAILS.
I keep them tucked safely. Out of sight.
Only TRUE PATRIOTS can enjoy them. And sleep soundly. At night.
The End

11

Two Poems

ARUNI KASHYAP

At Age Eleven, My Friend Tells Me Not to Wear Polyester Shirts

I really don't know why you still share
your lunchbox with him because he belongs to the other tribe
and he hates us now; but until yesterday he used
to love us quite a bit because he had come
to my birthday party with a pencil box; though
my aunt had sniffed saying that a pencil box
didn't cost too much, I had liked it so much,
had sat down together beside my sister's harmonium,
drawn Mickey mice on plain sheets and Ma had
said cheerfully when she found us with those pictures asking everyone

to come see come see

but I was so embarrassed because
his Mickey was better than mine, with the ears done very
sharply, my Minnie was too bad; instead of looking like Minnie,

she had looked like Mickey, like a Mickey who is sad just like
the way my mother sits sad these days after a hand came flying
on the roof of our grandma's village because the tribals like
him have started hating us; when his mother met my mother
at the market place, she wore a *dokhona*,[1] spoke to my mother in Hindi
when my mother asked her questions in Assamese. I have watched
many Hindi movies you know, *Mainey Pyar Kiya* and all, so I wanted
to correct her Hindi, tell her that she wasn't making sense but I didn't say
anything because our driver had told me that they would throw bombs
on our roofs; I couldn't risk that. You shouldn't talk to him because
he hates you, talks to you only in English, that strange Hindi,

haven't you heard
about the busses that were up in flames in Rangia last month?
The car bomb that went off at the market place in Kokrajhar last week?
I have seen the photos when Ma fed me cucumber salad:
burnt flesh turns red
when your face comes near fire, clothes stick to you. You
should never wear polyester.

My Aunt Talks about Being Raped by Soldiers

My husband
...
had never put it in my mouth before
because
...
I had never imagined it could be even put
in such places. At sixteen when I eloped,
clutching the collected coins that I wrapped in a hanky after breaking
my earthen piggy-bank shaped like an elephant, I carried nothing
but the cotton clothes I had on,
the notebook where I used to note down
teasing-songs so that we could sing those in weddings
to irritate grooms who came from faraway villages
on carts drawn by tall hornless bulls.

[1] Traditional women's dress of the Bodos, an ethnic and linguistic group in Assam, West Bengal, and Nepal.

My man was gentle to me.
On our wedding night, he took time to slide himself into me,
asked me again and again if I was ok; stopped whenever
something oozed out of my mouth: a sound, a muffled yes or no,
a long breath. Unlike the other women of our riverine village—
women with whom I sat popping in chopped olives
dressed in rock salt under the sun
during breezy late fall months—I never had tales
of strange positions; so I had fainted
I had
fainted

fainted; when they
took his body away for cremation,
I had pulled at the fully bloomed red rose plant
in front of our courtyard,
uprooted it in one go
until my palm and the roses were of the same colour,
until the women had screamed that I had gone mad,
that I would faint,
that my blood-pressure would reach my head and
no cold water on the scalp,
no coconut-oil on the hair,
on the forehead,
would bring me back to life

but

it was only just that moment
when I had lost control.

I wanted to live
for the smile of my two-year-old son,
for the four-year-old daughter
for the thirteen-year-old son who had just started
to be a little distant from me,
who had just started to have broader shoulders
than he used to have two years ago;
there was time still left for his shoulders to broaden up slowly
like an inflated balloon; like the moon that moves
from the sickle-moon night to the full-moon night
in fifteen days; there was still time

for his voice to wear a new skin
like snakes changing the upper layer of their body after
a certain age to gain new skin. I knew, I would have to live for them,
without the gentle touch of the man I loved
who asked me if it hurt
caressed my hairy groin with his rough farmer hands
before slipping into me
who never asked me to put it into his mouth
who left me alone during those months when
I told my children that I was
hiding a pumpkin under my sari.

But this man in green clothes
who had come with a gun
had asked me to do things to himself
I had never done to my husband
if I did, he would leave
my ten-year-old daughter.

I am so thankful my son wasn't around
who was sent away to his uncle's house
ever since his father's death for a better life and education.
I am so thankful the officer didn't kill me unlike
the other women in the village who were left to die by
other soldiers and officers. He was a high-ranking officer
with soldiers around him who waited outside
when he came every alternate day after dinner

until it had become my habit to wait for him,
until it had become my habit to put the children away to sleep
after cooking early on the hearth and wait for him so that
I could go to sleep after the regular ordeal,
until it had become my habit to stop resisting,

I always burnt the notes
he slipped between my breasts before dressing,
before walking away. I don't know if you have seen
burning bills, but it looks good when notes
burn in green flames, and please note this down too
that he paid me though I didn't ask, write about this also in your
report

so that everyone knows; I can't believe
I have to narrate such things to an unknown man

but please do write everything
on your paper's front page
along with my picture.

12

Five Poems

R. RAJ RAO

Swastika

(for Sachin Labade)

Commuters stripped me on a Berlin train.
I was wearing a white Fab India sweat shirt
with a swastika engraved on it in orange.
You can't walk our streets
with that satanic symbol on your clothes, they said.
It means you celebrate the elimination of homosexuals and Jews
in the gas chambers of Auschwitz and Dachau.
I'm homosexual myself, I told them, and also a Jew.
But it didn't wash.
To save my sweat shirt from being ripped to shreds
(a present from my mother)
I tried saying that the swastika was a sacred symbol in India.
It represented the elephant god Ganesh.
Ganesh will take care of you in a strange land, my mother had said.
But words failed me.

I was tongue-tied
like a man with speech impairment.
When I found my voice
I told the mob that the Nazis were in India too.
They were known by strange three-letter acronyms: BSS. RJP.[1]
The mob lit a fire.
I saw my sweat shirt slowly turn to ash
but I had no regrets.
The German cold made me shiver.

Bed and Breakfast

Checking into a Bed & Breakfast,
we collected our keys and went to our room
with a view of the sea.
Though it was a double room the beds were disjoined.
We marched back to the lobby
to ask for a room with conjoined beds.
Those are given to couples, the manager said.
We *are* a couple, we protested.
The manager thrust a dictionary into our hands
that defined a couple as a man and a woman.
I'm a woman, my friend said.
He had shoulder-length hair and a girlie walk
and wore earrings.
He even offered to undress.
But the manager was a walnut.
All hotels being full,
we went back to our room with the disjoined beds.
In the verandah, a sparrow had given birth to chirpy chicks.
Ships waited to berth.
We showered, ordered fried fish and wine.
As evening came we joined our beds,
getting rid of the wooden side-table placed between them.
We smoked a joint, then cuddled up and switched off the lights.
A midnight knock.
We opened the door.

[1] No existing organizations with these initials are being referred to here, but if the reader plays with the letters it will become clear which Indian organizations are meant.

It was the manager asking us to leave.
What is our crime, we asked.
But he pushed us out the front door,
flinging our backpacks behind us.
Faggots, he spat
and violently slammed the door.

Man Friday

Robinson Crusoe
had a Man Friday.

I too have a Man Friday,
but also
a Man Monday
Man Tuesday
Man Wednesday
Man Thursday
Man Saturday
and Man Sunday.

A man for every day of the week
to make my bed creak.

Outlaw

Since you won't marry
you cannot be stooge son-in-law.

You are not a woman
so you cannot be docile daughter-in-law.

As you don't have siblings or wife
you cannot be buddy brother-in-law.

You are not a woman
so you cannot be servile sister-in-law.

Since you do not have offspring
you cannot be phallocentric father-in-law.

You are not a woman
So you cannot be matriarchal mother-in-law.

What are you then?
You are an ostracized outlaw.

KU Lecture, 3 June 2015.

The Department of English, Kashmir University
cordially invites you to lecture
on the Poetry of Agha Shahid Ali,
their email said.
I gracefully accepted.
I was holidaying in Srinagar with a friend
and had just returned from frost-ridden Gulmarg
where gondolas took us to the clouds.
The invitation came with a brief:
I was not to refer to Ali's homosexuality.
I could only speak of him
as a poet of Azad Kashmir.
The brief came from the Begum,
the formidable head of the English department.
But so many of Ali's poems express his longing
for male companionship, I protested.
While acknowledging his desire for Kashmir's independence,
aren't you suppressing his other desire for a male lover?
The Begum was aghast.
She meant business.
I began my lecture with a bout of coughing.
Bottled water was quickly brought, lest I choked to death.
Drinking the water,
I was emboldened to blurt out that Ali was gay.
The Begum was shocked.
This was insubordination at its worst.
Unable to look me in the eye,
she fixed her gaze on the tiled floor.
I went on to state
I had once created a menu in my fiction
where the chef's special
was a dish called Chicken Agha Shahid Ali.[2]
After all, Ali loved his *roganjosh*.[3]

[2] In gay slang, a 'chicken' is a very young gay man.

[3] *Roganjosh* is an aromatic Kashmiri meat dish containing tender pieces of lamb.

The audience, made up of teachers and students, laughed.
The Begum wasn't amused.
She was unable to take her eyes off the floor,
so embarrassed was she.
Something got into me.
I let out a secret:
When Ali visited my university for a seminar
some twenty years ago,
I caught him cruising in the gents' washroom.
A militant student rose.
'Sir, you are saying dirty things about our national poet,'
he yelled.
The audience agreed.
The Begum felt vindicated.
The student whipped out a gun.
When he put his finger on the trigger,
I ducked.
Armed guards whisked away the student.
I let myself go.
Ali hated the ghetto, I said.
He was as American as he was Kashmiri.
That's why he lived and died in America.
Besides, he could be a homo in America,
but not in Kashmir.
The Begum signalled to her faculty to end the blasphemy.
My coughing fit returned.
This time they didn't offer me water.
The tea arranged in the Begum's cabin remained undrunk.
I was hastily ushered out of the classroom,
bundled into a waiting Uber cab
and driven to my hotel on the Dal Lake.
My honorarium for the lecture was withdrawn.
Rain replaced a day of sunshine.

13

Much Ado about a Bridge*

M. MOHANKUMAR

This river was a blessing to us; but it cut us off
from the mainland and, during the rainy season,
was furious, and hazardous to cross. Our demand
for a bridge fell, for long, on stone-deaf ears.
We launched an agitation, led by a freedom-fighter,
holder of the *tamrapatra*,[1] who undertook a fast
unto death. Then they put it in the 'works budget'.[2]

And there it remained, buried deep amongst
a thousand other works, waiting for 'better times'.

* Nowhere is the gap between words and actions greater than in government bureaucracy (and this not only in India).

[1] *Tamrapatra*: a copper plate engraving; a decoration awarded by the Government of India to freedom fighters in recognition of their role in the Indian Independence struggle.

[2] A budget document carrying the names of numerous works demanded by the public but having little chance of getting executed for want of funds.

We picketed the Collector's[3] office and courted
arrest. We met the Minister, man of the masses,
who sounded sympathetic, read through our
petition, and wrote on it: 'Immediate action'.

Nothing happened; nothing but ravages, year
after year, the rains lashing, the river flooding.
We took our protest to the state capital, staged
demonstrations in front of the State Secretariat.
Blind eyes. Deaf ears. Our panchayat[4] president
undertook a fast. A young man threatened to set
himself ablaze. Then the Minister held a meeting.
Pressed, the officers gave it in writing that they
would take up the work on a 'priority basis'.

Heavy rains again. The river broke the banks
More than once. A boat capsized and we lost
five of our school-going children. We planned
to *gherao*[5] the officers. There was a snag, they said;
they needed a bit of land for the approach road—
on the other side—but the owner had gone to court
and obtained a stay order.

Then, over the years, what we feared happened:
the river started drying up. Not an act of God
but man's handiwork. Now it remains a trickle.

Now we cross it on foot, negotiating our way
through the wild thickets and the brambles.
And they say that what we need is not a bridge
but a motorable road—across the river-bed.

[3] The Collector is an IAS Officer who is Chief Administrator, Revenue Collector, and local Magistrate of a district in India.

[4] Local council.

[5] 'Encirclement': a tactic by which protesters in India surround someone and refuse to release him until their demands are met.

PART THREE

14

Here Is a Country ...

NAYANTARA SAHGAL

In 1986 my novel *Rich Like Us* received the Sahitya Akademi Award. The Akademis were set up as autonomous institutions during the 1950s, as guardians of the creative imagination and promoters of its finest products in literature, music, art, and theatre. But the Sahitya Akademi, India's National Academy of Letters, remained silent when a distinguished Kannada scholar, M.M. Kalburgi, himself an Award winner, was murdered by gun-toting vigilantes on 30 August 2015 (Sahgal 2015). The killers had come on a motorcycle, rung his bell, shot him dead when he opened the door, and sped on their way. This was a repeat performance of the earlier murders of two distinguished Maharashtrian writers, Narendra Dhabolkar on 20 August 2013 and Govind Pansare on 20 February 2015. Both men were rationalists, well-known for their anti-superstition activism. Dissenters among intellectuals and artists were thereby warned that they would meet the same fate. But it soon became clear that the war on dissent—through threat, persecution, or murder—went beyond writers and artists. It now covers every area of life and lifestyle in the name and under the protective umbrella of the ruling ideology known as Hindutva.

Hindutva is the rejection of India's pluralism, with its multi-religious, multi-cultural heritage. Hindutva regards India as a Hindu country and has partitioned us into Hindus and Others, although its intolerance and militancy are no part of Hinduism but a perversion of it for political purposes. The majority of Hindus, apart from other Indians, do not accept it, as the general election of 2014 showed. Only 32 per cent of voters voted for the present Bharatiya Janata Party (BJP) government, but in our first-past-the-post electoral system its victory has enabled Hindutva to flex its muscles and to target Muslims with a particular vengeance. Not long after Kalburgi's murder, a village blacksmith, Mohammed Akhlaq, was dragged out of his home in Dadri, outside Delhi, and lynched to death by a mob on the suspicion that beef was cooked in his home. As the Indian Constitution guarantees every Indian the freedom to live, think, speak, worship, and eat as he/she chooses, Akhlaq had every right to eat beef. The fact was that no beef was found in his house. A false rumour was circulated and an excuse invented to kill a defenceless Muslim.

I returned my Sahitya Akademi Award in October 2015. In a letter to the Akademi which I titled 'The Unmaking of India', I ended with the words: 'In memory of the Indians who have been murdered, in support of all Indians who uphold the right to dissent, and of all dissenters who now live in fear and uncertainty, I am returning my Sahitya Akademi Award.'

Vigilante lawlessness has continued and multiplied. Truck drivers transporting their cattle have been halted by persons of no authority, accused of illegally transporting cows, and killed. This has been the work of self-styled '*gau rakshaks*', or cow protectors, who would have us believe that the lives of cows are holier than those of humans. In effect it is one more way of targeting Muslims. Most recently, a dairy farmer called Pehlu Khan, who was returning to his farm with milch cows he had just purchased, was stopped on a public highway, within sight of passers-by and the police, and lynched to death by a mob. His cows were then taken possession of by one of the mob. In another incident that made national news, men armed with knives entered a train and stabbed to death a fifteen-year-old Muslim boy who was returning home to his village after his Eid shopping in Delhi (Bhardwaj 2017).

A deeply disturbing aspect of these murders is that, to date, it is mostly minor participants (if any) who have been convicted, despite abundant evidence, and in a bizzare reversal of justice, the families of Akhlaq and Pehlu Khan have been targeted (for other offences) as the guilty parties (Baruah and Angad 2018; Mukherjee 2019). We can only assume that the evil-doers have the protection of the law. The ultimate horror of this ongoing situation is that it is being allowed to happen in a democracy, under a ruling dispensation that wishes to be known as democratic.

The latest in this grotesque series of murders is that of Gauri Lankesh, a high-profile, outspoken, highly respected journalist known for her political activism and her opposition to the prevailing Hindutva ideology. Gauri, too, was shot dead outside her own front door by vigilantes who did the job and sped on (*Wikipedia*: 'Gauri Lankesh'). So the crushing of dissent in today's India is not confined to censoring or banning unwelcome 'texts', films, TV programmes, and the like.

I called my letter to the Sahitya Akademi 'The Unmaking of India' because what is happening goes against all that India has stood for and striven for since Independence. I am a writer of fiction, and each of my novels has drawn on that political material and has reflected the political atmosphere and aspirations of its time. Politics is my natural material because I grew up during the non-violent fight for freedom under the leadership of Mahatma Gandhi, to which my parents had committed their lives. My father, in fact, died in the course of his fourth imprisonment under British rule. My childhood was steeped in the sights and sounds of the fight for freedom, and imbued with an Indian identity that cut across caste and class, region and religion, and my novels have turned out to be about the making of modern India.

Here was a deeply religious country of many religions and cultures that rejected a religious identity and chose at Independence to become a secular republic under an agnostic Prime Minister; a country whose civilization has an ancient tradition of discussion, disagreement, and debate, even within its Hindu scriptures. It is that secular democratic ideal that Indians from all walks of life and different political parties are now defending in their refusal to be party to its undoing under Hindutva. Historians are protesting against the substitution of myths for history. Scientists are protesting against the destruction of the scientific temper and the spirit of enquiry without which no nation can call itself modern. Students and professors have rebelled against the assault on freedom of thought and expression. Dalits have risen up against the outcaste status assigned to them and have refused to do the job of scavenging and disposing of cow carcasses. What we are seeing is a fight for reason against unreason, a demand that the doors to knowledge and creativity be kept open, and that the fresh air of different ideas, diverse viewpoints, and different ways of life and thought should continue to invigorate and enrich India as it has done for centuries past.

15

The Spark in Their Words

The Texts Lived by Basava and Kalburgi

GITHA HARIHARAN

If the reformer and poet Basava were alive today, we would call him an activist or even a radical. Back in the twelfth century, when he spearheaded a movement in Karnataka, this is how he described the plethora of demanding gods who keep common people in their thrall:

> Certain gods
> always stand watch
> at the doors of people.
> Some will not go if you ask them to go.
> Worse than dogs, some others.
> What can they give,
> these gods,
> who live off the charity of people
>
> O lord of the meeting rivers?
>
> (*Speaking of Siva* 1973, 83)

It was not just the gods who 'lived off the charity of people' or were, sometimes, 'worse than dogs'. There were also the places where these gods lived—the temples—and more important, the men who ruled this temple culture, fattening themselves in the name of religion. The rich temples that allowed priests to be powerful doorkeepers of orthodoxy kept people in their miserable places. Basava's ideas and words criticized both temple and priest, the entire conservative and exploitative system, as 'static'. And he insisted that there was a 'dynamic' alternative:

> The rich
> will make temples for Siva.
> What shall I,
> a poor man,
> do?
>
> My legs are pillars,
> the body the shrine,
> the head a cupola
> of gold.
>
> Listen, O lord of the meeting rivers,
> things standing shall fall,
> but the moving ever shall stay.
>
> (*Speaking of Siva* 1973, 19)

Basava went further than a just path to spiritual salvation. Why, he asked, can't reason and spirit co-exist? Why should spiritual experience be devoid of reason? Basava scorned the irrational ritual:

> They plunge
> wherever they see water.
>
> They circumambulate
> every tree they see.
>
> How can they know you
> O Lord
> who adore
> waters that run dry
> trees that wither?
>
> (*Speaking of Siva* 1973, 85)

Basava took his critique of the establishment to its logical end. Building on reason, on the dynamic, on the opposition to man-made ritual, priesthood, temples, and their gods, Basava issued the most powerful challenge: all men are equal, regardless of caste; and all women are equal to men. When King Bijjala questioned him about the radical inter-caste marriage planned by Basava's colleagues in the movement, he asked the king, 'Are we not all born of the same source, a woman's womb? No man ever came out of his mother's ears.'

Basava did not merely mouth platitudes against caste oppression. Just as he ate with the lower castes and welcomed them into his movement, he insinuated himself into the lineage of those considered inferior by the orthodox. Basava may have been born a Brahmin; but he shed the sacred thread, the *agrahara*[1] culture of the Brahmins, the priests, and temple culture. He became a child of butchers, water-carriers, fodder-gatherers. He became a child of the lower castes, of the lowest 'untouchables'. This is how he made himself human.

> Nimbavve's my mother: she lives
> By fetching water,
> Cennayya is my father:
> He fetches fodder for the royal stable …
>
> (Basava, *Basava Vachanajali*, 352)

Or:

> The son of the slave in Untouchable Channayya's house,
> The daughter of the maid in Butcher Kakkayya's house.
> Those two went to the fields to gather dung
> and fell in love.
> I'm the son born of these two;
> the lord of the meeting rivers is my witness.
>
> (Basava 1984)

Was Channayya's son superior to Kakkayya's daughter? They are equal in our movement, said Basava. When his men had trouble learning to live this equality, Basava used words and images to remind

[1] *Agrahara* is the Brahmin quarter of a town or village, land often given to Brahmins free or at low cost.

them of the rational basis of equality. He sang words, for instance, by the weaver poet, Devara Dasimayya:

Suppose you cut a tall bamboo
in two;
make the bottom piece a woman,
the headpiece a man;
rub them together
till they kindle:
tell me now,
the fire that's born,
is it male or female,
O Ramanatha?

(*Speaking of Siva* 1973, 110)

Basava's own poem about men and women used a bisexual image to say that gender equality is only natural:

Look here, dear fellow:
I wear these men's clothes
only for you.

Sometimes I am man,
sometimes I am woman.

(*Speaking of Siva* 1973, 87)

So Basava's text, in its search for a meaningful life, whether of the individual or the community, foregrounded equality and reason:

How can I feel right
about a god who eats up lacquer and melts,
who wilts when he sees fire?

How can I feel right
about gods you sell in your need,
and gods you bury for fear of thieves?

(*Speaking of Siva* 1973, 84)

Equality and reason, but also confluence. The dynamic, the ever moving, instead of the static and stagnant. It has to be emphasized that even the spiritual in Basava's philosophy included the social, political, and economic aspects of the community. Unlike other Bhakti or devotional movements, which put individual salvation first, Basava's *sharana*[2] movement, and the Lingayatism he founded, advocated a more egalitarian Bhakti—eschewing traditional temple worship, idol worship, meaningless rituals, and even renunciation. The spiritual was firmly located in people's lives in the real world of society. Anyone, regardless of caste, gender, or community could become a *sharana*. The movement gave the common people of the Kalyana kingdom a sense of their human value, while moving them from the periphery toward the mainstream. The weapon of the movement was a body of literature: poems called *vachanas*—'what is said'—in language that connected to the common people.

It didn't last, of course. The crisis point for the movement came when the *sharanas* organized an inter-caste marriage. The fathers of the bride and groom were executed, dragged by an elephant. The king of Kalyana was killed; anarchy followed. Basava was forced to leave the city, and his end is shrouded in mystery.

Over the years, the movement which had equality at its heart became another caste. Today, the Lingayats form a considerable number in Karnataka. They are somewhere in the middle of the caste hierarchy, but wield economic and political power. And, in a sad irony, Basava's legacy has been appropriated by conservative elements supportive of the new right wing in India.

For someone who is inspired by Basava's text today—his words, his ideas, and his life—what is the way forward? How do you combat the distortion of Basava's ideas and words, the casteism born out of an anti-caste movement? How do you keep his challenges alive today, and challenge both old and new temples, priests, and gods? How do you challenge the old inequalities that persist, and the new inequalities that create deeper division?

Malleshappa Madivallapa Kalburgi, known as M.M. Kalburgi, was that rare scholar who had multiple personas. There was the folklorist, the teacher, the researcher, the vice-chancellor of a university, the

[2] A *sharana* is a seeker or follower who has 'surrendered' his ego and taken refuge in Siva.

public figure. There was the poet, the playwright, the translator. His research interests ranged from ancient to medieval literature, from grammar to poetics, from inscriptions to cultural studies. There was the prolific scholar; but there was also the outspoken critic of contemporary religious, cultural, and political practice. He used his scholarly research and speculation to intervene boldly in matters of contemporary cultural politics, including the distortion of history to gain or maintain political dominance. Vikram Visaji, writing on 'the tireless scholar and fearless critic', quotes Kalburgi:

> Of late artificial changes are being introduced instead of genuine ones in society thanks to religious and political leaders. The researcher needs to unravel actual history in order to stop the exploitation caused by such false history. Research is not a purely historical exploration but a struggle with those who invoke false history to profit from the present. (Visaji 2016, 74)

What guided Kalburgi in this struggle he speaks of?

Kalburgi knew intimately, through years of work, the extraordinary flowering of people's literature during a movement against orthodoxy in twelfth-century Karnataka, and the man who led this movement, Basava. Kalburgi's research and writing were inspired by Basava's idea of equality, his insistence on putting an end to caste and gender discrimination, and upholding the dignity of labour. Kalburgi was also a leading authority on the *vachanas*.

Kalburgi was a Lingayat too. But his interpretation of this literature and current Lingayatism, as well as his application of Basava's ideas to the social and political scenario today, angered the community's establishment. The struggle of the researcher that Kalburgi spoke of was the need to resist 'those who invoke false history to profit from the present'. For Kalburgi, these peddlers of false history included the growing new right wing in India; but first and foremost, the Lingayat establishment that had lost Basava's radicalism—the essence of the movement he spearheaded.

It was 8:40 in the morning on Sunday, 30 August 2015, in Dharwad, a place rich in cultural tradition, from literature to music. Seventy-seven-year-old Kalburgi was at home in Kalyan Nagar—an apposite address for a man who read and wrote so much about Basava's

Kalyana. Kalburgi was talking on his cell phone. There was a knock at the door. Kalburgi opened the door; two men shot him at close range; the bullet pierced his head. The men apparently sped away on a motorcycle; there were no eyewitnesses. When the family rushed to the verandah, Kalburgi lay dead on the ground.

There was widespread outrage over the assassination, and citizens from writers to scientists protested the fatal censorship of a scholar and writer. Kalburgi's murder was an addition to a list: the murder of anti-superstition and anti-caste activist Narendra Dabholkar in Pune, and that of anti-caste and anti–false-history activist Govind Pansare. This linked list—which has grown with the murder of journalist Gauri Lankesh in Bengalaru—is important to those who seek to challenge the offensive against freedom of expression and dissent.

In the case of Kalburgi, there is a clear textual link between his scholarly dissent and his murder. There are specific texts which the conservatives in the Lingayat community objected to. His collection, *Marga 1*, had two articles perceived as 'derogatory' of Basava, his wife, and sister. On the basis of several *vachanas*, Kalburgi had concluded in the first article that Basava's relationship with his second wife Neelambike was platonic. In the second article, he argued that the *veerashaiva* poet and leader Channabasava could have been the son of Nagalambike, Basava's sister, and a cobbler poet, Dohara Kakkaya. Such a birth, the product of an inter-caste marriage, said Kalburgi, had been obfuscated by false history.

The Lingayat temple chiefs brought immense pressure to bear on Kalburgi to recant—very much like their counterparts did with Basava centuries back. Kalburgi did recant, saying later: 'I did it to save the lives of my family. But I also committed intellectual suicide on that day' (interview for *India Today*, quoted in Narayan 2015). It was not just these and similar 'controversial' incidents that earned Kalburgi the enmity of the current Lingayat orthodoxy—it was his holding the religious and politically powerful in the community up to the radical standards of Basava's ideas, and finding them, and their reinvented Basava in contemporary cultural politics, miserably wanting.

In a tribute to Kalburgi, Shivanand Kanavi wrote in *Outlook* magazine:

> In today's India very few would of course stand Basavanna's test. This led Prof. Kalburgi to not only take on casteist and conservative forces in general but also some powerful conservatives among Lingayats. [...]
>
> For example, a remark he had made about superstitions in a public meeting in Bengaluru which had been organised to discuss the draft Anti-superstition bill prepared by Karnataka Government led to screaming headlines in one of the newspapers leading to death threats and cowardly acts of vandalism at his residence last year.
>
> But he carried on and when I asked him once about such threats he quoted me a *vachana* by Basavanna himself:
>
> Let what could happen tomorrow come to us today,
> Let what could happen today come to us here and now,
> Who is afraid of this?
> A person born will also die
> Neither Hari nor Brahma can override what my Koodala Sangama
> Deva has written.
> (Kanavi 2015)

The 'contested text' today is the body of Basava's ideas, his demands for political, economic, and social change combined with the interpretation of Kalburgi and his historical findings based on scholarship. Basava's movement, and Kalburgi's internalization of the ideas and words behind this movement: together they present a challenge to the powers that be, whether the powerful religious institution of the *mathas*[3] or their friends, or their preferred political ally, the new right wing exemplified by the Vishwa Hindu Parishad, the Bajrang Dal, and the Sri Ram Sene groups. The link between Basava and Kalburgi was apparent to many.

> The overarching concern expressed at the Town Hall in Bengaluru was that a culture of lethal violence might overwhelm the hallowed culture of discussion and questioning in Lingayat society. Indeed, one of the first victims of the temptation to violence was Basava himself—martyred at the end of the celebrated period of social reform, when he was thought to have gone too far by marrying a Brahmin girl to a Dalit boy. One protestor on the Town Hall steps had evidently thought of this: 'Yesterday Basavanna,' his sign read, 'Today Kalburgi'. (Karnad 2015)

[3] *Matha* (mutt) is a Sanskrit word referring to a cloister, monastery, institute, or college.

Perhaps the text that brings all these strands together is a play by Kalburgi called *Kettithu Kalyana*, translated into English as 'The Fall of Kalyana'. The play is about the struggle led by Basava for caste and class equality. But it also reflects the loss of the gains made by this struggle, centuries later in our times, through 'false history'.

The play begins with a powerful scene in the Brahmin *agrahara* of Bagewadi where Basava lived with his parents. It was full moon, and time for Brahmins to change their sacred thread. Fifteen-year-old Basava refused a new thread; in fact, he was about to tear off his old one. Two priests held on to his hand, telling him that being Brahmin meant access to 'the prestige of being called gods on earth' (Kalburgi 2003, 2). Basava resisted. His thread snapped, hung loose. 'I don't want this sacred thread which makes me a Brahmin instead of a human being,' he said.

> A man becomes a Brahmin as soon as he wears the sacred thread. From that day, he starts classifying society into Brahmin, Kshatriya, Vaisya and Sudra ... the sacred thread divides society ... (Kalburgi 2003, 21)

Basava dashed to the ground the text which exemplifies the traditional practice of division, the *Manusmriti*. Basava and his family were excommunicated.

(Kalburgi too was threatened, and with more than excommunication. The conservatives among the Lingayats took offense when he suggested that Basava's nephew, the *sharana* Channabasava, was a leather tanner. Kalburgi was threatened with death; he was summoned to a Lingayat *matha* in Dharwad and forced to recant [Narayan 2015].)

From the first setting of Kalburgi's play—the powerful Brahmin village culture—Basava moved to the second stage of his life, his exploration of temple culture. Basava went to Kudala Sangama, the centre of monasteries and temples, hoping to learn from the 'literature of ideas and freedom of expression'. But here too he found the same authoritarian, close-minded priestly culture, empty ritual, the mechanical reading of texts and reciting of mantras. The Shaivas' intelligence was also tarnished, he found, like the Brahmins, 'by the smoke of the sacrificial fire' (Kalburgi 2003, 12). Superstition was pervasive, resulting in irrational, often cruel practices: 'barking like dogs after worshipping God Mailara, walking about naked after worshipping God Bhairava, walking on cinders, torturing the body, sacrificing women …' (2003, 26). In addition to the wasteful practices of libation, palanquin processions, and religious rituals such as grand *pujas,* the poor ended up borrowing from the rich to offer their devotion to deities, and 'pots and bowls, roadside stones and trees enjoy the status of gods' (2003, 25).

(Kalburgi too was critical of the Brahmin-like practices followed by a section of the present-day Lingayat community, who pay lip service to Basava as a saint, but turn his ideas on casteless equality upside down. Kalburgi also supported writer U.R. Ananthamurthy's ridiculing of idol worship. And Kalburgi criticized the Lingayats' celebration of festivals such as Ganesh Chathurthi [Nayak 2015].)

Basava moved on from Kudala Sangama. In Kalyana, his father-in-law introduced him to King Bijjala and Basava was given a job in the royal treasury. His honesty was so exemplary that he was soon made finance minister. This was when Basava's idea of equality led to practical action. He cut grants to temples and Brahmins, redirecting resources to the poor and marginalized to whom, he announced, the treasury really belonged.

> These days, the kings have been exploiting the subjects; the priests have been exploiting the devotees and the men have been exploiting the women … society has been divided into two streams, the exploiters and the exploited. (Kalburgi 2003, 33)

Basava took cognizance of both divisions of class and caste:

> The caste difference between the privileged and the underprivileged is born out of 'religion' whereas the difference between the poor and the rich is born out of labour. (Kalburgi 2003, 40)

(Basava in Kalburgi's words: Basava's ideas and his times meet Kalburgi's reading and times seamlessly.)

The movement grew; there were followers from all castes, potters, weavers, boatmen, and both men and women. Many *sharanas* other than Basava became leaders in different ways. All of them had to face, of course, stiff opposition from priests, Brahmins, the rich, and finally the king himself. The crisis came when an inter-caste marriage took place, between the daughter of a Brahmin and the son of a cobbler. Then king, city, Basava, the movement—all collapsed into anarchy. The king was assassinated; Basava driven out of the city. Many *sharanas* were slaughtered. *Vachana* manuscripts were seized and burnt.

The status quo crept back over time. The Lingayats became a caste. Basava became a saint, rather than the bearer of a more just world. Many of his 'descendants' lost all connection with his legacy. But there were, there are, others who search for it, find it in text, word, idea, and action. They bring Basava back to our times, times which see both old and new manifestations of caste, community, gender, ritual, superstition, hypocrisy, and unreason. And the same big gap between the powerful and the powerless.

Kalburgi was one such man. He saw the gaps and the hypocrisy, the betrayal of Basava's rational, egalitarian, and rational approach to both social life and the life of the spirit. Kalburgi saw all this. And he was not just a scholar mining old words; he wrote, he spoke, he challenged. He was a practitioner of Basava's thought. His claim that the Lingayats are not Hindus angered the powerful Lingayats. In addition, his exploration of the positive aspects of Muslim rule in Karnataka, as well as Persian and Urdu texts, antagonized the Hindutva groups in India today.

Basava, Kalburgi. Neither was an atheist, but both believed in, and practised, a radical form of religion. Their words—indeed their lives—were texts that challenged the powerful status quo. Basava's end in exile is shrouded in mystery. Kalburgi's murder remains an ongoing 'case'.

But Basava's words remain:

> Earth is one and the same
> For pariah street
> And Shiva temple;
> Water is one and the same
> For washing shit and ritual cleaning;
> All castes are one
> For a man with self-knowledge …
>
> (*I Keep Vigil of Rudra* 2010, 59)

And Kalburgi's words too, the ones he put into the mouth of an old 'untouchable':

> You fear words. Men who fear words exult in human blood. You can silence me, but you cannot silence truth. Truth and fire are ever inextinguishable. They will always keep burning somewhere. One spark is enough to create a conflagration. (Quoted in Satchidanandan 2015)

Basava and Kalburgi. Their words are sparks that will not die.

16

Freedom of Expression and Values*

PERUMAL MURUGAN

This chapter attempts to discuss the relationship between values and freedom of expression in caste-ridden Tamilian society and, in a broader vision, in Indian society as a whole, on the basis of my experience.

I had never-ending questions on the subject of values even as a youth. I did not know what exactly 'values' were at that time. Even now I do not claim to possess any great knowledge of the principles of values, the ongoing research into them, or the ways of interpreting them. I am able to feel what a 'value' is, but incapable of explaining it. If you consider the well-established definitions, the meaning of a 'value' is that it is a characteristic of humankind supposedly intended to develop the lifestyle of the individual within society and make it more meaningful.

* This text was written in Tamil. A first translation into English was made by Sankara Narayanan.

If you ask what all these values are, you might come up with a list of qualities such as the following: kindness, courage, *satya*,[1] patience, peace, wisdom, happiness, non-cruelty, ability, learning through listening, self-learning, remembrance, non-violence, discipline, equality, kind words, friendliness, and fairness.

Both the definition and the list of qualities raise a number of questions. How can we find out *which* qualities make human life more meaningful? How do we define the qualities? If kindness is a value, are there not very many interpretations of that? There are contrasting views on kindness. Which one of them should be accepted as a value? Can we say that the views on the quality of kindness should be treated as the value? Yes: only the views constructed about the qualities can be treated as the 'value' and not the quality itself.

It is very difficult to explain whether beliefs, proverbs, rituals, and so on are in themselves values. Beliefs and proverbs are only opinions. Rituals are the actualization of views. Though it is hard to describe them all as values, I can certainly say that the quality of a value exists in each of them. If one is asked to follow in the footsteps of the ancestors without any criticism or questioning, then that takes on the quality of a value.

It is difficult to define what a 'value' is. A notable Tamil dictionary, (*Kriyavin Tarkalat Tamil Akarati* 1992) defines it as the right one or as per norms (regular), or the wrong one, and it is also described as a belief constructed by society and individuals (1992, 1071). It is a belief. A few say that only those things considered as good by society are its values. In keeping with the dictionary, rights and wrongs are also considered as values.

What is transmitted through parents and ancestors to the next generation is also considered as a value. This only describes how the value is guarded and is not a definition of the value. It can be said that, though I am unable to define it, I understood the meaning of the value according to my convenience. My simple understanding is that those things which cannot be questioned are values. Opinions constructed on how to conduct one's life (not necessarily righteously) are rigidly believed in by mankind, though it is a different matter whether people actually follow them fully in their lives. Believing firmly in those

[1] *Satya* is truthfulness—going in the direction of 'authenticity'.

opinions, insisting on them, imposing them on others, and insulting those who are unable to practise them are regular occurrences. Opinions on which such dictates are based can also be considered as values.

Belief in God is only a value. Different views on God prevail. One view says that God created all things. But this opinion must not be subjected to questioning. History tells us what happened to those who subjected this opinion to questioning. They were subjected to a great deal of misery! Even today people face huge risks if they question belief in God. Society does not accept those who challenge such values.

Opinion makers divide values into two kinds, namely individual-based and culture-based values. I can't completely agree with this view. The individual is a part of society. How can the individual be separated from society? Society creates the individual-based values, and when they are applicable to every individual in it, how can you separate them from society? But we have to categorize values in some way. For me, a division into natural and non-natural values appears more appropriate. It fits in with my aim too.

Nature-based values describe the relationship between human life and the ways of nature. There is a widespread belief that you should not insult time. Time here means the Sun. The Sun is the basis of all life. My grandmother began her daily chores in the morning only after offering a *namaskar*[2] to the Sun. It was not necessary for her to go to the temple to worship. In all parts of the world, worshipping the Sun as a God is or has been a traditional value. People touch their cheeks to worship God when the light is switched on in the night. This is an after-effect of traditional Sun worship. Living beings can function only when the Sun rises and gives light. Throughout the course of time, this value has remained.

In a poem from Sangam Tamil literature, *Kurunthokai*-157 (*Online Tamil Poetry* 2018), the heroine and her lover are having a good time in the night. She does not want the night to end. She calls the dawn Sun a sword that separates her from her man. She insults the Sun, and the value.

The sparrow comes and builds its nest in the roofing of our houses. House owners happily welcome it. They don't chase it away. It brings

[2] A greeting.

in and throws sticks and so on and leaves behind garbage. People clean up after it happily. It lays eggs there. Young sparrows are hatched. Till the sparrow family leaves on its own, they are allowed to live there safely. How and why? There is a belief that if the sparrow comes and makes its nest, the family will get a child too. It is also believed that if the sparrow's nest is disturbed the family will also disintegrate.

There is a belief that if a crow makes noise near a house, guests may arrive there. So a wife separated from her husband will request the crow to come and make noise near her home, expecting the crow's cry to bring her husband back. The crow is a better companion to humans than any other bird. Not a day passes without you noticing a crow. We can't sleep if we do not hear the crows. The food we offer to the crows is considered food to be eaten by our ancestors.

Such values provide protection to the sparrow and establish a relationship with the crow. In some places, trees are worshipped as God. Not even a small branch of the tree will be cut. If a big tree falls, people congregate and cry as if someone from their family had died. The deaths of cattle are also mourned and relatives come to express their condolences. These values relating to the sparrow, the crow, trees, cattle, and so on have established a bond between mankind and nature.

Some values are based on the five elements, namely, earth, water, air, fire, and sky. There are many changes, destruction, new creations, and so on that are inherent in such values. They don't cause much disturbance in human relationships. They are by and large accepted as being part of the changes that take place over time. But the values created for humans to live by in society are entirely different. Even a small violation creates great tension or disturbance among the stakeholders. Questions regarding values are fiercely detested. Values are treated as being more important than human beings. There is no tolerance of any questioning of values. And when there is no space for questioning, there is little space for freedom of expression.

There are many values based on the mother. There are hundreds of films that centre on her. They all treat the mother as a goddess. A mother's word is the Almighty's word. The *Aathichoodi*[3] is a collection

[3] A collection of one-line precepts, the work of a female Tamil poet of ancient times known as Avvaiyar ('the respectable woman').

of social values (*Wikipedia*: 'Aathichoodi'). The first value listed in that booklet is 'Mother and father are your first Gods.' Values such as 'Don't disobey mother's words' and 'There is no better mantra than father's instructions' derive from the concept of divine status for parents. A proverb in Tamil says, 'You may insult your mother; but not the water.' Even though this stresses the importance of water, the superiority of the mother's dictates nevertheless prevails. The order of priority in respect is defined in another verse: Mother, Father, Guru, and then God.

The mother being a goddess is euologized as the symbol of love and sacrifice. She acquires this divine status because she has dedicated her thoughts, deeds, and life wholly to her children, paying little attention to her own feelings. I doubt whether the other regions in India have such an image of the mother in their films as Tamil Nadu does. Why should the mother be a goddess? Why can't she just be a woman, fulfilling her own wishes, feelings, likes, and dislikes? Aren't women being forced to be like that? Those who raise such questions are treated as lowlifes who do not know how to respect the mother. My students in their poems attach as much importance to the exalted image of the mother as to love affairs. This exalted image of the mother is deliberately constructed in order to make her a domestic servant in actual life. But this bitter truth is unwelcome to many.

We should never disobey our parents. They are our creators. Therefore they have every right to guide us and dictate to us. We cannot argue with them. Mother and father are our first gods.

The hero of a particular film is a ruffian. He gets angry over even quite trivial matters and beats other people up. His distraught mother extracts a promise from him that he won't do this anymore. At a critical juncture, he is being beaten unfairly by others. But he won't retaliate because he is keeping his promise to his mother. His mother sees what is happening and tells her son to fight back. Only then does the hero strike back and thrash his tormenters. This stupid and boring scene is a familiar one in all our films. But people by and large get emotional over such ludicrous scenes because the status of the mother as a Goddess has been so deeply ingrained in them. In many of the films, the mother will be a widow. If the father is there in the movie, he too will be a paragon of self-sacrifice. Thus the value that tells us that mother and father are the first Gods is reaffirmed.

I have a very simple question regarding this value. The whole world of my grandparents was contained within ten miles. My aunt was married and sent to live at her husband's place five miles away. My grandmother used to make big plans to go there. Except for our village, the only place known to her was where my aunt was. Going to the nearest town for the market or festivals was a big journey for her. Everything was restricted to a maximum radius of ten miles.

My parents' world was a little bigger than that: about twenty to thirty miles, though only my father travelled that far for his business. It was too much for my mother. Occasionally, she visited the nearest town, fifteen miles away, but only because she was compelled to stay with my father when he was admitted to a hospital in that place for treatment.

Since I was of the first generation to get an education, I had to travel three or even four hundred miles.

My mother created very many obstacles for me to travel to such places. She was ignorant and afraid of the outer world. If her son travelled to far-off places, some untoward thing might happen to him; he might not return; he might, without asking her permission, fall in love with and marry an outsider. Such were her fears. (And, as she had feared, I did indeed marry an 'outsider'.) She expected her son to cultivate the family's small piece of land and live there, where she could see him. She was afraid of anything new that might destroy their lives. One should be content to keep on walking on the familiar path.

In my time, plenty of schools have been created to impart education to the oppressed. A new generation from races that were excluded from education for centuries was given the opportunity to learn to read and write. But their parents were not interested in education for their children. They had their doubts: 'What is the use of education for the toilers and tillers? Are they going to work as Collectors[4] after they have been educated?' Their superstition led them to believe that jobs such as the Collectorship were unfit for their children. They had a firm belief in manual labour, not in education.

Above all, there was a lurking fear that their educated offspring might not listen to their words. Several Tamil films produced in the 1950s and 1960s reinforced that fear. In one particular box-office

[4] Local administrators.

hit, the educated children were portrayed as arrogant, without love and affection, self-centred, lacking in respect towards their parents, and absolutely disobedient. The domestic servant in their household was uneducated. But he loved his master and his master's wife. He respected their words and was very obedient. And he was shown as the only male in the family who tried to save the elderly couple. The title of the film was *Uneducated Expert*. Foreign-educated young people were portrayed mainly as villains. Educated women were also portrayed badly in many Tamil novels and films. All this created a negative impression of educated young people.

If 'values' require me to obey the words of a mother who knows nothing about the outside world, who does not know the importance of education, and who is afraid of anything new to her, it is only natural for me to question those values. And I did raise questions. I asked tough questions. My mother merely complained that I was raising those points because I had received a little bit of education without bothering about the logic and fairness of my questions. There are still plenty of parents who think that educated children will ask unnecessary questions. Many of the villagers egged my mother on. 'Children will no longer be ours after they have been educated' was a well-entrenched view in their minds. This naturally led to a number of disputes between my mother and myself. She tried to keep me under her thumb by persistent abuse and intermittent tears. The plight of my mother at that time was really pitiable. My own plight, in having to face my mother and win her over, was equally sad.

I used to save my pocket money, wages that I had earned through petty jobs, and gifts in the form of cash given to me by relatives during festivals. I started purchasing books by mail order using this money. My mother opposed this vehemently. Relatives and fellow villagers gave multiple warnings to my mother: 'If he reads too much, the boy will be spoiled. And he may even go mad.' To bring me around to her wishes, she used to warn me that she would burn all my books.

Another complaint was: 'He just wants to avoid farm work. He's looking for an escape route through books.' I was struggling a lot to purchase books clandestinely. To keep them away from my mother's eyes was an equally daunting task. I could not find a safe place for my books in my home. I had a lurking fear that at any time they might be thrown out or sold to a waste-paper merchant or burnt. My first task after returning from college was always to check whether my books were safe. Under these circumstances, when people advised me not to disobey my mother's dictates, what should I have done? After several fights and tearful scenes, she gave in and allowed me to follow my chosen path, though very reluctantly and with a heavy heart.

She knows nothing about my education, my college, or the town where I stayed in order to study. So if she wants to know she has to listen to what I tell her about them. Only a person who knows a thing can explain it to another person who does not. This is a universally applicable rule. But our value-merchants insist that mother and father are the primary gods and that we have to obey whatever they say blindly. How is that possible? After the demise of my father, there was a big tussle between my mother and me. She was of the opinion that I was wasting money on books and study. If I had told her about the grades I had achieved, or the prizes I had earned for my poems, in public speaking contests, or essay competitions, it would have meant nothing to her. Books used to be given as prizes at that time. But there were no hands to receive the books in my home. My younger days were spent like this, with no one with whom I could share what I was doing. It was a really frustrating and disappointing time. Had I listened to my mother's words, I would have remained uneducated and led a life not to my liking. The blunt questions posed to my mother only made me want to press on.

Nowadays private schools and colleges in Tamil Nadu glorify our parents as gods. In the name of honouring their parents, children are encouraged to wash their feet. This is conducted as a festival: Pada Puja is its name. In some castes, washing the feet of your parents is a ritual during weddings. This ritual has now been converted into a major value and brought into the educational institutions. What age are we living in? Is washing the feet of your parents the truest way to show them your respect?

There are many benefits here for the educational institutions. The most important thing is the good impression created among parents about the school. Society apparently believes that washing their feet is the best way to show respect to your parents. So when the school makes the children do this, the parents are confident that this school will take their children in the right direction. A majority of the parents believe that those children who blindly obey parental wishes are the best.

On 19 March 2018, a Tamil newspaper described the Pada Puja programme conducted in a women's college in this way:

> The students were advised that the world is within our parents. Mother should be worshipped as a Goddess. There is no better temple than one's mother. No mantra is better than the words of the father.
>
> After that the students conducted Pada Puja. They washed their parents' feet with milk, curd, turmeric and water. Then they applied sandalwood paste and kumkum.[5] Flowers were placed, followed by archana[6] and aarti.[7] 700 students at a time performed the puja. Later they prostrated themselves at the feet of their parents to get their blessings.

Another Tamil daily (on 27 February 2018) published a report on Pada Puja conducted by boys and girls in a school. A popular Tamil speaker was the special guest at the function. He advised the children that whatever big success was achieved by them it would be owed to their parents.

The Pada Puja programme is thus a business development scheme by the school management using an age-old value. The customer-parents are immensely pleased that this school will guide their wards properly. The children will obey their parents, respect them, marry the boy or girl selected by them, take care of them when they get older, and so on: these are the impressions created among the parents by this feet-washing festival.

The children are unable to talk to their parents freely and frankly. Is there some way for them to express *their* wishes? Many students are compelled to join courses in higher education as dictated by their parents, though their personal preferences would have been different. Parents do not allow their children freedom of expression. If some opinion is expressed, it is simply treated as a sign of disrespect for the parents.

[5] Kumkum is a bright-red powder made from turmeric or saffron. It is used in various rituals, and symbolizes the fiery and creative power of the Goddess.

[6] Archana ('honouring, praising') is a part of the puja in which the name of the devotee is recited or the deity's name is chanted.

[7] Aarti is the ritual offering of light, also part of the puja.

Similarly, there is a value: 'The words of the elders are like *amrut*.'[8] So the youngsters have to accept the words of the elders—whatever these might be. The elderly have had plenty of experience in life. Their advice can only help!

There are different kinds of people. Only a few reflect on their experiences properly and learn from them. Many people are incapable of learning much, even if they live for a hundred years! Elderly people generally feel proud of their younger days. They tend to feel contempt, irritation, or even hatred for young people. They do not recognize the changing times. What can young people learn from such people? But our society insists that we listen to the elderly and follow their advice.

These values lend authority to the elders. An authority to impose their views on youngsters. The way this is done is regressive and contemptuous. Elders consider that they have a singular right to address young people. They think that the youngsters know nothing. And so they subject them to long lectures. We routinely see young people desperately trying to escape from such ordeals. How many elders have the patience to listen even for a few minutes to what youngsters think about an issue? The youngsters are expected to bend down before the elders to receive their sermons. How many of them have the freedom to express their own opinion without hesitation? All that 'freedom of expression' means for them is standing before the elders with knees bent, hands folded, and mouth shut.

Apart from parents and elders, we have attached a similar value to the teacher, the guru. Many from the lower castes are illiterates, so the teacher who imparts education is held to be at par with God. Our educational system also informs us that whatever you are told by the teacher is Veda.[9] Even if the teacher gives you false information, you have to accept it. You can't point out the mistakes. If you do that, you are branded as an outcaste and an undisciplined person. Ours, perhaps, is the only educational system in the world which thrives on *non*-questioning.

I have written a few articles pinpointing the unprincipled conduct prevailing among teachers. But the reactions to these articles were not

[8] *Amrut* (*amrit*) in Indian mythology was the nectar of the gods, an elixir of life.

[9] Here 'Veda' stands for 'knowledge', with the association of 'holy teaching'.

over the conduct of the teachers. Instead, many people asked, 'How can you write such bad things about teachers?' (Since we can write critically about every other section of society, why should teachers be exempted?) Others questioned, 'You are a teacher, so how can you write such damaging things about them?' Well, I could write such bad things about teachers precisely because I was a teacher myself and had been able to observe them closely. But neither the teaching fraternity nor the general public has shown any appreciation of my comments because our value system has elevated the teacher to the status of a demigod. A guru teaches. So he is an authority. No one has the right to question an authority. And this authority also enjoys a divine status. Once you raise an authority to divine status, you cannot question it. Authority prevails wherever you have to go to gain knowledge. And authority has never been on the side of freedom of expression.

We have no freedom of expression in our dealings with parents, elders, and teachers, and this is true in many other fields. A dominant, higher-caste person might be a complete idiot, but you are still obliged to listen to his words. With the master–slave relationship prevailing in the caste system, where is the scope for freedom of expression? If you are a resourceful person, your words should carry weight. But the words of the downtrodden don't reach the right places. This extends to those holding power in the government. So our value system is full of rigidity, on upper and lower levels, right through.

The values pertaining to gender relationships also go against freedom of expression. 'The husband is a god'; 'He is her virtue'; 'Even if he is made of stone or grass, he is her husband'—these are all popular proverbs. There is no salvation for a woman excepting her husband. He is the person who gives her life. He must be worshipped as a god. A woman touching the feet of her husband in the early morning before starting her daily routines was once a common scene in all Tamil movies, though not today. Yet there are still many ingenious ways to continuously assert the exalted status of the husband. She must put up with him despite all the cruelty inflicted by him. She must obey his words. She should not object to his dictates. If a wife expresses her opinion while a family issue is being debated within the family, her husband will yell at her that she does not know anything and order her to go inside the house. This *is* a common scene in many Tamil films.

'Never listen to a woman's words' is another rigid value. A woman has freedom of expression neither within her house nor outside it. Even if she says something, it should not be considered or followed. This is the status of women in gender relationships. If you search for a place where a woman can express her opinion freely in our society, you will find none. She may be described as a 'better half'. But our prevalent values show very clearly that she has no opportunity to express her views.

Our values do not allow a person to communicate normally/naturally with another person. Expression is a one-way traffic. You can't reject parental advice. You have to listen to the elders. What a teacher says is Veda. A woman can never talk. You have to be a yes-man in the presence of your boss. Only the officer's words will carry weight in a *sabha*.[10]

It is immaterial whether the opinion expressed is right or wrong. Who is giving it is what matters. But we can't express our views about an issue. We have scarcely any opportunity to express contrarian views. Even if you disagree with someone's opinion, you can't say it. You have to keep it to yourself. If you dare to express a differing view, you are disrespecting the strong and mighty. In the guise of ensuring respect and regard for our fellow beings, our value system prevents even a normal exchange of views between people. Only the free exchange of views can bring out different opinions, and differing opinions are the mark of a healthy debate.

As far as our society is concerned, there is no equality in expressing one's views. Dialogue between fellow human beings is not possible. There is no issue-based debate. Logical debates exist only in books; they are completely absent from everyday life. Wherever the question of freedom of expression is raised, our value system brings in words like 'prestige', 'honour', and 'respect' to suffocate freedom of expression. All men are equal is the basic philosophy of democracy. But this philosophy is new to us. For generations, we have treated people unequally. And we have manufactured corresponding values to sanction this inequality. Our talk about democracy is only in theory, on paper. What we practise is the opposite of democracy.

[10] Meeting, gathering.

If we are to discuss freedom of expression, we must first deal with the existing inequalities in everyday life and those social values which sanctify such grinding and glaring inequalities. We should re-examine and re-investigate them. We should interrogate them. Natural debate must take front-stage. The antiquated and outmoded should be challenged and rejected, and we should be prepared to abandon sick and moth-eaten values. Only then will we create a minimally acceptable platform for freedom of expression on the basis of equality.

17

Caste on the Plate

DIPTI NAGPAUL-D'SOUZA

In 2009, students and teachers of the Women's Studies course at the Krantijyoti Savitribai Phule Women's Studies Centre (University of Pune) undertook a project. As part of the 'gender studies' module, they studied Dalit food practices and documented culinary memories and recipes of the community. The project was researched by 22 students, guided by professors Deepa Tak, Sangeeta Thosar, Tina Aranha, and course coordinator (the late) Sharmila Rege. The team eventually published their work as a book—*Isn't This Plate Indian? Dalit Histories and Memories of Food*—in 2010.

The book triggered a debate in academia as well as in mainstream media on how food practices are used as a means of exclusion and oppression in the Indian caste system. There have been academic papers and also news features on the subject.

It is, however, important to note that in a culture where food plays a crucial role and recipe compilations are published by the dozen every year, *Isn't This Plate Indian?* is the first book to study Dalit food practices. Are Dalit food practices not worthy of study? Are they not considered knowledge that should be documented? The publication of this book raised these questions.

According to Arjun Appadurai, the documentation of culinary practices in India is a postcolonial process because 'cooking in India is deeply embedded in moral and medical beliefs and prescriptions' (1988, 5). The trend of cookbooks in India, thus, is not more than 50 years old and the audience—as well as authors—have largely been urban middle-class women. Appadurai further points out that leftover food in Hindu belief is equated with contamination, degeneration, and loss of status. While he emphasizes class as the dominant factor in deciding the nature of Indian cookbooks, he does not mention the role of caste.

In terms of cookbooks and the lack of any Dalit narratives in that space, the two points made by Appadurai are connected. A majority of the urban middle and upper-middle classes is also upper-caste. Therefore, their tastes and 'moral' preferences are reflected in the cookbooks available in the market. An example is the common perception across the world that Tamilians are vegetarians, whereas, in fact, only Tamil Brahmins are vegetarians. However, because Tamil Brahmins were more affluent and among the first to migrate, their cuisine travelled with them.

Various Dalit narratives and autobiographies lay emphasis on the importance of food in practising caste discrimination. Dalit feminist Urmila Pawar, for instance, recounts in *Weave of Life* (2003) that she would be excluded from the invitations to eat at the houses of her upper-caste classmates. In *Baluta* (1978), Daya Pawar recounts how the marginalized Dalits, expected to dispose of the dead cattle of their village, ate the flesh of the dead animals, as it was a rich source of protein and they could not afford nutritious food. The very title of Omprakash Valmiki's *Jhoothan* (1997)—'leftovers'—points at the deprivation and discrimination through food practices that the Dalit-Bahujan community has had to suffer. Valmiki recounts how, at weddings, the leftovers after the *baratis*[1] had left were relished by the *chuhras* (slang used by upper castes for Dalit-Bahujans).

Food has always been central to the practice of untouchability, as the authors of *Isn't This Plate Indian?* point out: it was first 'because who could eat what was regulated by the brahmanical order of the

[1] The wedding party.

society and then this itself became a marker of pure and impure status'. The book also cites several examples where Dalit women recount not disclosing their food preferences (especially for meat) to upper-caste classmates or colleagues so as not to be ridiculed for the food they eat. This, when their diet was barely a matter of choice but for generations depended on what the upper castes decided they should eat.

The recipes in the book also reiterate this. Ramwati Kudiya of the Valmiki caste recounts how the dried, leftover *pooris*, given to them by the upper castes, would be soaked in water to make a gruel, which was eaten with much delight at her home (2010, 78). Ashabai Kharat, a neo-Buddhist, speaks about *rakti*, a dish made using goat's blood (2010, 83). While in certain parts of the world, this would be considered a delicacy, in India it is difficult to imagine upper-caste members of society consuming *rakti*. The list goes on and on.

The upper-caste morality, which lays focus on words such as 'purity' and 'hygiene', also uses these terms as a means of exclusion and censorship. Meat, which comes from a dead animal, is considered impure.

This is reinforced through the term 'non-vegetarian', the usage of which is limited to the Indian subcontinent. By coining a special term for 'what is not vegetarian', meat has been 'otherized' or made to seem different from normal. In other parts of the world, where eating meat is not taboo, food that is 'non-meat' is pointedly labelled as 'vegetarian'. However, the stress on politicizing meat has evidently increased in the last 100-odd years because the Hindi term for 'non-vegetarians' is *maasahari* (literally, 'meat-eaters') and vegetarians are called *shakhahari* ('those who eat what comes from plants'). The Sanskrit word for meat, on the other hand, is *amish*, while vegetarian food, ironically, translates to *niramish* ('what is not meat').

This plays out well beyond cookbooks on store shelves; food continues to be used as a means of censorship as well as 'otherization'. In the last three-and-a-half years, since the Bharatiya Janata Party (BJP) came to power, it has emerged as one of the key factors defining national politics.

Dhoklas[2] are replacing *samosas* in Central Government canteens, Madhya Pradesh started to leave eggs out of poor tribal children's

[2] *Dhoklas* (originally from Gujarat) are made from chickpea and rice flour; *samosas*, on the other hand, baked or deep-fried pastries with a savoury filling, often contain meat.

midday meals, beef and other meats have begun to vanish from restaurant menus, and the debate over the politics of food is set to intensify.

In 1955, under Congress rule, India banned 'cow slaughter' (the cow is considered a sacred animal among Hindus). After Narendra Modi took over as the country's Prime Minister (PM) the ban was intensified in 2015 to include bulls and buffaloes (except water buffalo). In the time since, there have been several episodes where people, mostly Muslims, have been lynched on suspicion that they were in possession of beef or were trading a cow for slaughter. Teams of *gau rakshaks* ('protectors of the cow') are near-legitimized as the government has not taken action against the perpetrators of crime in the aforementioned cases.

There is even a weekly newspaper under the title *Gau Bharat Bharti* that is dedicated to the 'welfare of cows'. Published in Mumbai, it is distributed across Maharashtra, Delhi, and Gujarat. The editor, not surprisingly, is a member of the Hindutva group Rashtriya Swayamsevak Sangh (RSS) and heads the *gau rakshak* teams of northwest Mumbai. A large part of the newspaper content spews hate for 'beef lovers', urges people to opt for vegetarianism as a way of life, and praises the work of the ruling party, the BJP.

However, *Gau Bharat Bharti* is a very small part of the deliberate attempt to encourage the perception that India is a vegetarian country. It spills over into popular culture in many ways. *MasterChef India*, the local spinoff of the highly acclaimed cookery show *MasterChef* (originating in the UK and redeveloped in Australia), has had vegetarian seasons. In the telecast of the international editions of cookery shows, the word 'beef' is systematically muted.

The government's success in this sphere is largely because the public space and popular culture have—for a long time—been dominated by Brahmins, a chiefly vegetarian community among the Hindu majority. As a result, there has also been a rise in the number of vegetarian-only restaurants, and eateries offering meat options have also increased the number of vegetarian dishes on their menus.

This has made meat, primarily beef, the centre of communal and caste politics. The culinary practices of the weaker communities, such as Dalits and Muslims, are used as a means of demonizing them.

In fact, new research by US-based anthropologist Balmurli Natrajan and India-based economist Suraj Jacob indicates that the numbers projected for vegetarianism in India are likely to be inflated estimations. 'So people under-report eating meat—particularly beef—and over-report eating vegetarian food,' claims a BBC report by Soutik Biswas (2018) on the research. He adds that only about 20 per cent of Indians are actually vegetarian—much lower than common claims and stereotypes suggest—and that Hindus, who make up 80 per cent of the Indian population, are predominantly meat eaters. He further claims that 'at least closer to 15% of Indians—or about 180 million people—eat beef. That's a whopping 96% more than the official estimates'.

A careful look at India's vibrant culinary practices supports these claims, especially the fact that those practising vegetarianism are a minority. The way we eat is mostly dictated by geographical and climactic circumstances. Thus, seafood forms a large part of the diet of those who live along India's very extensive coastline, including Konkani Brahmins, who view fish as 'vegetable from the sea'.

In fact, a number of academic papers and pieces of research written over the last two centuries—some by celebrated Indian scholars—show that meat, especially beef, has been commonly consumed by people of all castes since Vedic times.

In his book, *The Myth of the Holy Cow*, first published in 2001, historian D.N. Jha (formerly Professor of History at the University of Delhi) maps the changing narrative on the cow and its sacredness over time. Citing the Vedic texts and epic mythologies, including the *Rigveda*, Mahabharata, and Ramayana, he talks about how the cow, among other animals, was used for sacrifice as well as for its meat. The meat of the cow was consumed not only by the gods but also by Brahmins. Jha supports his arguments by citing works by such Indian scholars as P.V. Kane, a conservative Brahmin and Bharat Ratna[3] recipient; and archaeologist and Sanskrit scholar H.D. Sankalia, among several others.

The practices around meat and beef consumption, Jha points out, began to change only after the idea of *ahimsa* (non-violence) was floated in the *Upanishads* (post Vedic texts written between 800–500 BC) and started to gain ground. The sacred status of the cow—and the practice of vegetarianism—has been on a slow rise since.

[3] The highest civilian honour awarded by the Republic of India.

> Needless to say, then, that the image of the cow projected by Indian textual traditions, especially the Brahmanical-Dharmasastric works, over the centuries is polymorphic. Its story through the millennia is full of inconsistencies and has not always been in conformity with dietary practices current in society. (Jha 2009, 136)

Jha adds that it became a tool of mass politicization much later, and its roots can be traced back to contemporary history. In 1882, Dayanand Sarasvati made the cow 'a symbol of the unity of a wide ranging people, challenged the Muslim practice of its slaughter and provoked a series of serious communal riots in the 1880s and 1890s' (2009, 19).

Not surprising, then, that Jha's book became a subject of censorship, first at the hands of its original publishing house, which backed off until Matrix Books stepped in. The printed copies of the 2001 edition, however, could not be distributed in India: religious fanatics called it blasphemous and got an order from the court restraining its circulation. Jha also became a target of threats and abuse.

In his book, while mapping the change in dietary practices pertaining to meat over the millennia, Jha has also quoted from the infamous *Manusmriti* (a Hindu social and religious text that lays out laws on diet and social conduct and which hardened the pyramidal caste system),which considers eating the flesh of the cow a 'minor sin'. Yet he does not touch upon the connection between the consumption of beef and the practice of untouchability. He admits this in the 2009 Navayana edition of his book, and attempts to make up for it by publishing excerpts from Dr B.R. Ambedkar's 1948 work *The Untouchables: Who Were They and Why They Became Untouchables*. Taken from Chapters 10 to 14, the excerpts appear in Jha's book as an appendix under the title 'Untouchability, the Dead Cow and the Brahmin'. This essay fills in the blanks, explaining how the Brahmins adopted vegetarianism and how the consumption of beef came to be associated with untouchability.

There is a legend in West Bengal, a state whose people famously love their fish and meat. In 1757, following the victory of the British in the Battle of Plassey, the Debs of Kolkata's Shovabazar, then a powerful clan of moneylending princes, invited Robert Clive for a grand Durga Puja (a festival in honour of the Indian goddess Durga). A *pandal*[4] was set up and beef and alcohol, among other 'blasphemous' items, were served even as the Brahmins conducting the puja rebelled. Although the Deb family, which continues to reside in Shovabazar, denies this, it is widely believed that the event set the precedent for Durga Puja *pandals*, where meat consumption is an integral part of the festival. Therefore, Brahmins across Bengal as well as Assam do not shy away from meat.

More importantly, it is said, the incident helped Nabakrishna Deb earn the title of 'Maharaja Bahadur', which forms an interesting albeit ironical parallel with what happened in 2016.

In an attempt to please the powerful Jain minority, the government imposed a ban on meat slaughter during the period of Paryushan (a Jain festival) across five Indian states—Chhattisgarh, Maharashtra, Rajasthan, Haryana, and Gujarat. Maharashtra was later excluded from the list after the Bombay High Court put a stay on the ban. In fact, the ban evoked massive protests by the Shiv Sena, which had supported the beef ban a few months earlier. However, the right-wing party could not have afforded to upset its Maharashtrian supporters, most of whom are meat eaters. However, the BJP would not be the first rulers to appease the Jain minority by banning meat slaughter during Paryushan. It is said that the Mughal rulers Babur, Akbar, Jahangir, and Aurangzeb also used the strategy and gained favour by the move (Jha 2009, 18).

In India, however, the ones who suffer most due to such bans are the minorities. A large number of the butchers are Muslims and beef forms a crucial part of Dalit and Adivasi (tribal) diet, a major source of protein for the community, many of whom are unable to afford pulses or milk products.

Similarly, central India is home to a number of royal cuisines, which feature game meat extensively. Deer, rabbit, peacock, ox, and other 'exotic' meats once found a place of pride on the dining table. This was until the culture of vegetarianism gained popularity, and forced these meats into obscurity.

But the matter of 'purity' is not linked to meat alone. Nor should it be believed that Hindus and Jains alone use this as a way of executing censorship through food. Take for instance Jains, who consider all root

[4] A temporary stage with a shrine open to people.

vegetables dirty and hence unfit for consumption. Similarly, certain Hindus avoid onion and garlic because these two items, high in anti-oxidants, are considered aphrodisiacs and hence propellants of 'impure' thoughts. It is hygiene that makes pork *haram* ('forbidden') for Muslims. Jews have their own dietary laws, imposed as part of their religion.

In a country where food has been used as a means of discrimination, it has also emerged as a form of protest. In Maharashtra, during the 1970s, when Dalit literature was a burgeoning movement, festivals would be organized where beef was served as snacks. It was a way of protesting against the *savarna* (upper-caste) literary festivals, dominated by Brahmins, which did not acknowledge or allow space to Dalit writers and poets.

In the current political climate, serving beef has re-emerged as a mark of protest. A beef festival was organized by students in Tamil Nadu. While Tamil Nadu is chiefly perceived as a vegetarian state, in truth, this dietary preference is limited to the Brahmin population of the state. The state is home to the famous Chettinad preparations of chicken, mutton, and beef. In addition, beef is consumed as a stir-fry with desiccated coconut (among Hindus), as tikka and kebabs (Muslims), and as a red chilli roast (Christians).

The state, where popular culture has been dominated by the upper-caste Iyers and Iyengars, has also been home to the Dravidian movement, led by Periyar, who famously used 'non-vegetarian' food as a primary argument against the Brahmin discourse of 'purity'. But despite the anti-caste Dravidian movement, segregation on the basis of food continues.

In 2015, at one of the country's premier educational institutions, Indian Institute of Technology (IIT) Madras, the Ambedkar Periyar Study Circle (APSC), an independent student body, was briefly derecognized by the Dean following complaints regarding their 'political activities'. Among other things, this included circulars by the APSC, which has a number of Dalit members, opposing the shutting down of the non-vegetarian mess at IIT Madras. IIT Madras originally served only vegetarian food at its main mess, but this rule was changed in 2013, only to be reinstated in 2015. The institute is home to students from all parts of India and many consume non-vegetarian food, but it has also had a long tradition of Brahmin teachers, a fact that once again connects caste with privileges.

In another incident, a documentary short by students of Tata Institute of Social Sciences, Mumbai, titled *Caste on the Menu Card*, was denied permission to screen at a film festival in 2015. The 21-minute film, which highlights issues similar to the ones faced by students in IIT, was to screen at the 12th Jeevika Asia Livelihood Documentary Festival, 2015, in Delhi until the Ministry of Information and Broadcasting denied it the requisite permissions to screen.

Each of these incidents highlights the debate on the politics of food, which *Isn't This Plate Indian?* addresses. While the debate on the subject continues to rage on, the publishing of the book was unable to alter what goes into the cookbooks that are published in India. Although many cookbooks now showcase the cuisines of minority communities such as Muslims, most steer clear of beef or pork. As a result, recipe books even today not only continue to chronicle upper-caste culinary practices, but also glorify caste in the process.

Take, for instance, food writer Anoothi Vishal's 2016 book, *Mrs. L.C.'s Table*, in which she writes about Kayasth food practices. This shows that there is an acute awareness of caste and therefore also a deliberate oversight of Dalit food. The failing is not on the part of the book itself but because of the rigidity of the caste system that makes Dalit food unmentionable.

There has been only one exception: Shahu Patole's 2015 book *Anna He Apoornabrahma* ('Food Is an Incomplete Creation'). A former journalist and an officer in the Ministry of Information and Broadcasting, he documents the food history of two Dalit communities from the Marathwada region: the Mahars and the Mangs. In his book, Patole examines Dalit food practices through the prism of religious texts and explains why he does not believe meat is impure (*tamsik*) while vegetarian food is pure (*sattvik*):

> I also looked at Hindu mythological texts where the four varnas have been mentioned along with what each should eat. We come under tamasic, perhaps even below that. A common proverb in our religious texts is that you become what you eat. But most people do not have a choice in what they eat and yet certain qualities are associated with each food group. I have tried to bring together all these different ideas in my book. (Quoted in Tarkare 2016)

However, it would be unfair to place the sole burden of documenting Dalit food practices on members of the community. Their dietary 'preferences' are surrounded by taboos and many have adopted upper-caste diets in order to avoid segregation. Openly speaking about their culture and traditions can place the individual under the scrutiny of upper-caste members of the society he or she is engaging with, leading to further discrimination.

18

A Petition to the Minister*

Shri M. Venkaiah Naidu
Minister for Information and Broadcasting
Shastri Bhavan
New Delhi-110001

Dear Sir

We, the undersigned, are deeply disturbed at the news of three films being denied screening at the 10th edition of the International Documentary and Short Film Festival of Kerala (IDSFFK) 2017.

We want to question the basis for denying screening permission to these films. A brief perusal of the themes of the films denied screening—the suicide of research scholar Rohit Vemula,[1] on artists in

* This petition, sent to the Minister for Information and Broadcasting in June 2017, was signed by 160 Indian filmmakers, actors, sound recordists, authors, journalists, curators, academics, and others actively involved in the Indian film industry.

[1] *The Unbearable Being of Lightness*, directed by P.N. Ramachandra.

Kashmir,[2] and on the student protests at JNU[3]—indicates that each one of these films is dealing with prominent political issues that have led to much discussion within the country. It is also clear that the government of the day is resorting to draconian action to stifle all such political debate and indeed Article 19 of our constitution, which guarantees the right to freedom of expression to every citizen of this country.

We also note that the Ministry of Information and Broadcasting has not given any reason for its withholding of screening permission.

We are part of a community of filmmakers and artists who are deeply disturbed by these attempts to restrict artistic voices. We cannot support actions that deprive audiences of meaningful cinema and endanger the democratic values of our country.

We unequivocally condemn this action by the Ministry of Information and Broadcasting and lend our unqualified support to IDSFFK and the filmmakers who are being prevented from screening their films.

We urge the Ministry of Information and Broadcasting to immediately issue an exemption letter to the three films and ensure that films at festivals do not face arbitrary censorship in future.

With Regards

(Signatures)

[2] *In the Shade of Fallen Chinar*, directed by N.C. Fazil and Shawn Sebastian.

[3] JNU stands for Jawaharlal Nehru University in New Delhi; the film is *March March March*, directed by Kathu Lukose.

19

If There Isn't a Free Press Don't Blame Modi

KINGSHUK NAG

Viewers were askance when they watched India's Finance Minister Arun Jaitley fumbling while delivering his annual budget speech in the Parliament on 1 February 2018. Speaking partly in English and at times in Hindi, Jaitley stumbled as he switched from one language to the other.

Four years earlier, unveiling the first budget of the Narendra Modi government, Arun Jaitley did something that had never happened before. He asked the Speaker of the Lok Sabha[1] for a time-out in the midst of the budget speech. After he renewed delivering his speech, Jaitley, in another first, read out the text *sitting*.

All this has not dented Jaitley's image, and in informed circles in New Delhi he is referred to as COB. That's the short form of Chief of Bureau and this is a reference to the control he reputedly has over the media in India's capital. Maybe this is an exaggeration but many

[1] The Lok Sabha (literally, the 'House of the People') is the Lower House of the Indian Parliament.

believe that the media eats out of the hands of Jaitley and plays up stories that he wants to highlight. Since becoming Prime Minister, Narendra Modi has not held a press conference,[2] and the only time he has met a group of senior journalists was at the residence of Jaitley. The finance minister had invited some senior media men for dinner and Modi made an appearance halfway through as if he had dropped in 'casually'.

Though with general elections slated in mid-2019 the Indian media has become slightly critical of the Modi government, for the better part of its tenure, with a few exceptions, the press have been demure. They have been like the proverbial three monkeys of Mahatma Gandhi: they see no wrong, speak no wrong, and hear nothing wrong ('wrong', here, refers to the lapses of the government). This is something strange, because the Indian media in the past was seen as robust, critical of actions of the government, and defenders of the rights of the poor and underprivileged. So what happened that the media took the oath of silence as soon as Modi became the Prime Minister?

Strangely, sections of New Delhi's media were quite enthusiastic about the prospect of Narendra Modi becoming Prime Minister. Modi had been a resident of Delhi a decade and a half ago as secretary of the Bharatiya Janata Party (BJP). Accessible always to the media, Modi was friends with many journalists and Delhi's journalists had made their assessment on this fact. But what they forgot was that in the meanwhile a lot of water had passed through the river Yamuna that flows past Delhi.

As soon as Modi became Prime Minister, media persons swarmed in huge numbers seeking to meet him. But to their dismay even Jaitley could not help. What was worse, dispensing with the past practice, Modi appointed no high-profile media advisor. In the past, all Prime Ministers have had media advisors who acted as the bridge between the top representative of the government and the fourth estate, and helped to disseminate the viewpoint of the government. Modi, however, appointed a low-profile Public Relations Officer (PRO) whom he brought along with him from Gujarat, the state where he was Chief Minister for thirteen years before he became Prime Minister.

[2] True at the time of writing of this article (April 2018).

The PRO, Jagdish Thakkar, had been a mere dispenser of press releases in Gujarat, and not a spokesman articulating the government point of view to the press. Past the retirement age of sixty, Thakkar was extremely media-shy. Finding no access to Modi directly, the press in New Delhi (most of whom had no inkling of his role in Gujarat) sought to contact Thakkar. But even the cell phone number of Thakkar was not available!

Prime Ministers in India traditionally have a large entourage of media persons accompanying them on their trips abroad, and all of them are accommodated on the plane carrying the chief executive of the country. But Modi, who as Prime Minister has displayed a penchant for going abroad at the drop of a hat, abandoned this practice from his first trip. This set the media aback because such trips allowed them proximity to the Prime Minister and an occasion to interact with him informally.

Soon it became clear to the media that Modi was not interested in meeting representatives of the press and opening up to their queries. What he was interested in was a one-way communication that allowed for no dialogue. He began addressing the nation on his *Mann Ki Baat* (literal translation: What's On My Mind) programme aired on the government-run All India Radio (AIR) in which Modi spoke on a variety of subjects. If sources are to be believed informal instructions were issued to ministers and the officials of the government to be less open to the press.

Panic gripped Delhi's press, which was used to being pampered. Many ran to Jaitley, a Delhi boy who had been on good terms with large sections of the press for decades. Though Jaitley continued to feed the press with news, he was not as forthcoming as before. Under normal circumstances, the press would have been expected to be critical of a government that slams the door in their faces. But quite the reverse happened. The fourth estate, as if rendered inert by an injection of anesthetics administered by Modi, soon began mouthing the government line on all subjects. All this happened even though the Modi government did nothing to bring in censorship rules or gag the press. What then silenced the Indian media? Though there is a complex set of reasons, the following example is illustrative of what happened.

A few years ago, one of India's largest media groups, which is obsessed about how much profit it can make, decided to set up a university in one of India's largest states. The group, which publishes many dailies, averred that newspapers were a sunset industry and that education (what with the recent privatization of university education) was an evergreen sector in a country where the population was steadily growing. The managers of the group were able to convince the Chief Minister of the state to part with approximately 70 acres of land at dirt cheap rates for setting up the university.

If at all there was a quid pro quo, then it was unwritten and on an 'understood' basis. The Chief Minister, however, assumed that he would get favourable coverage in the group's newspapers in future in return for the favours done. But the journalists of the group were innocent about the land deal and soon the Chief Minister—unhappy about what he perceived as unfair coverage—was all fire and brimstone. This was especially because elections to the state legislature were close at hand. Top managers of the media group swung into action and soon the newspapers of the group were singing paeans in praise of the Chief Minister.

Elections involve competition, so when you praise the Chief Minister and his party and portray them in a favourable light, this means that the competitor is necessarily shown in a relatively poor light. In this case, the competitor was none other than the ruling BJP and it was now their turn to get miffed. Ministers and other important dignitaries of the party conveyed, in their own way, to the journalists of the group, that the coverage of the elections was 'not realistic'. But all that fell on deaf ears. And, in any case, the BJP swept the polls, as the Chief Minister and his party were routed.

The profit-conscious media group in a bid to boost its bottom line has recently entered into a new business: that of conferencing. Scheduled a few days after the poll results was a mega investment conference where participation came at 1,700 USD per delegate. That was a small price to pay, considering that the media group had used its influence to convince Prime Minister Modi to attend, along with his top ministers and officials. But in the event neither Modi nor his mandarins turned up. Word was out that the Prime Minister was mightily upset at the 'unfair coverage' in the recently concluded elections, and that he was showing his annoyance by boycotting the conference.

The promoters of the media group were alarmed. Now they hastened to the Prime Minister to sue for peace. But the Prime Minister's

Office spurned them and asked them instead to call on BJP President Amit Shah, who is well known as Modi's 'go to man'. Shah was ready: the moment the promoters called on him, he fished out a 60-page report detailing the 'unfair' coverage of the elections in the group's papers. The promoters were speechless and chastened too.

Back in their office the promoters must surely have issued orders to the journalists. Not long after, the news coverage became extremely favourable to Modi and the BJP, so much so that many journalists have become wary of owning up to their stories. Modi must have been satiated, because when in the following year (2018) the group held the same conference the Prime Minister, along with many ministers, attended.

Another reason for newspapers to keep on the right side of the Modi government is the pernicious practice of 'paid news' that is growing by leaps and bounds. Newspaper barons justify this patently amoral practice by playing the same old record:

> We are a sunset industry, the newspaper that is sold at Rs 3 to consumers costs Rs 25 to produce. We need to diversify our sources of income and even advertising is difficult to come by. (And so on and so forth.)

Some even argue that 'paid news' does not cover all news coverage but is restricted to coverage of events such as fashion shows, parties, book and product launches, and the like. A chief executive of a newspaper group (who does not want to be named) told this author, in what sounds like a rather crude utterance:

> The holders of the events are willing to pay for the coverage. Sometimes the correspondents themselves make money by giving coverage to the events. We have institutionalized the practice by ourselves taking the money and boosting our revenue and at the same time plugging the scope for corruption amongst journalists.

Although the Modi government has done nothing to hit out at the practice, many media groups apprehend that sooner or later they could come under the scanner. Hence it is better to be good boys. At least one big newspaper carries an inconspicuous announcement in small font in its supplement that carries 'paid news'. It reads that some part of the news carried could be paid for.

In recent months, 'fake news' has become a concern. Although India is a multicultural democracy, and members of different religions and cultures have lived here together for centuries; online media is now somehow managing to bring out the worst in some people. Rumour-mongering and the purveying of fake news have become a common practice, leading even to riots, violence, and the resultant destruction of life and property.

To curb fake news, in April 2018, Modi's brash Minister of Information and Broadcasting Smriti Irani (a former television star) suddenly came out with a series of guidelines. With this, 'accredited journalists' both in the print media and in television stood to lose their accreditation if found guilty of purveying fake news. What is worse, the accreditation would be suspended even before an inquiry to establish the truth of the accusations was completed. Realizing that the move had the potential to damage the image of the government, Modi's office moved fast and rescinded the move within hours. But hackles had been raised. Accreditation is a kind of licensing mechanism by which journalists who are accredited get access to government offices and certain other privileges. In the good old days, this also included government houses for a few! Only a small proportion of journalists are 'accredited'. Almost all of them are in the capital, New Delhi (state governments have their own system of accreditation, but Smriti Irani's move was directed only at correspondents accredited to the central government). As journalists were up in arms, the Editors' Guild issued an uncharacteristically strong statement. A laid-back organization, known for doing nothing of consequence, the Editors' Guild declared that

> fake news is something that cannot be left to governments to initiate action [on] when, on many occasions, the government and parties in power—both at the Centre and in states—are charged with propagating fake news themselves. (*NDTV* 2018)

The statement added that

> news organisations are not the only source of generation of fake news with the country awash with digital platforms of all hues and opinions that operate without constraints and have the potential to cause far more damage.

The only other time that journalists had strongly reacted was when the Ministry of Information and Broadcasting had ordered Hindi TV channel *NDTV India* to suspend transmission for one day (9 November 2016). This was the penalty for revealing 'strategically sensitive information' in the coverage of the attack by terrorists on an air force base in Pathankot that is located on the Indo-Pakistan border. The ban order had been rescinded after the protests. But the promoters of the NDTV group—which was the first private TV channel in the 1990s—got on the wrong side of law with allegations that they had violated tax and foreign exchange laws and were subject to investigations. This again drew howls of protests from sections of the press.

The day after the government ordered, and rescinded, the fake news order it was the lead story on page 1 of most national newspapers. The reasons are not too difficult to figure out: the move hit out at the privileged journalists of the National Capital and they felt threatened. Hundreds of other (non-accredited) journalists who work in Delhi and other parts of the country could not have bothered less. It was also a lesson for Modi: if you treated the top news organizations and journalists indifferently they were ready to fall at your feet. But if you pushed them too hard, they would react!

Even as the Editors' Guild reacted strongly to the fake news order of the government, they strangely remained silent on an exposé on fake news by investigative portal *Cobra Post* in a sting operation in March 2018. Code named Operation 136 (because India ranked 136 in the Reporters Without Borders World Press Index, 2017), the sting showed that representatives of seventeen media outlets were willing to carry community-polarizing news before the national elections slated for 2019. The media outlets included newspapers, both English- and Hindi-language, and television channels (in Hindi, India's national language). They were also ready to carry 'negative news' on many top opposition leaders and some from the ruling party. All this would be for payment of cash, for which no receipts would be given, as per the revelations of the sting operation.

Though the results were publicized at a press conference in New Delhi's Press Club, the newspapers and television channels that were *not* part of the sting were strangely silent and, barring a few exceptions, did not report them.

In a way, as far as the media in India are concerned, history is repeating itself. In the Nehru years, from 1947 to 1964, when India's first Prime Minister Jawaharlal Nehru occupied the Prime Ministerial office, the press was strangely docile. These were the first years after India became Independent after 200 years of colonial rule and there were all round hopes that the country would build its own destiny. Both the people and the press reposed great faith in the government and whatever it was doing. As a result, newspapers covered what the government told them and what ministers said at press conferences. The reporter's job was like that of a stenographer! Taking down what ministers and high officials said and reproducing it in the newspaper (there was no television then). Since stenographers are good at taking dictation, what with their knowledge of short hand, many stenographers actually became reporters in newspapers and in due course of time some of them also graduated to the position of Editors! It was only after Mrs Indira Gandhi as Prime Minister declared an Emergency (that curbed civil rights and brought in news censorship) that there was a lot of resentment. When, nineteen months later, the Emergency was lifted in March 1977, genuine investigative journalism began to flourish in India. The curbs had impelled the press to rise and do their duty without fear or favour.

The period from 1977 to 2005 was the golden age of Indian journalism. There was nothing specific that happened in 2005 to end this golden period. It was just that the results of the process of liberalization that freed India from the clutches of 'Control Raj'[3] began to show. Control Raj had kept India's economy back and kept private entrepreneurship on a leash. This was because the commanding heights of India's economy were controlled by the largely inefficient and low-productivity public sector. On the positive side, India's growth rate, stuck at an average of 3 per cent per annum (called the Hindu Rate of Growth) in the control era, began to accelerate, creating more income and leading to better standards of living. But on the flip side, with no proper corporate governance norms in place a lot of unscrupulous entrepreneurs began to accumulate wealth.

[3] A suffocating system of central economic planning, also known as the License or Permit Raj, with controls and regulations imposed on different forms of economic activity, which was dismantled after 1991.

Much of this wealth went into the real estate sector and many of the entrepreneurs started entering politics. Some of them set up media channels to ensure that they got good press or at least to prevent negative reports about them. With more money being poured into the media sector, competition intensified and old media outlets began to feel the heat. Investments had to be made to ward off competition and this meant that there were pressures on profit margins. More advertisements had to be sought and, with this increased pressure, the advertisers began to flex their muscles. They wanted their pound of flesh: no negative reporting and no exposés, they stipulated. The advertisers were not merely large corporates, but also governments of various states and the central government itself.

By the time that Modi became Prime Minister in 2014 the media had been virtually compromised. Not that Modi is a great champion of press freedom, but if there isn't a free press in India you can't blame it on him.

20

Five Plays and This City*

RAMU RAMANATHAN

Thank you for letting me deliver the 20th Gulestan and Rustom Billimoria Endowment Lecture.

Today is 22 December 2017.

On 22 December 1989: it was the day Samuel Beckett died. Of course we didn't know it that time. We had a show of *Krapp's Last Tape* on the terrace with a garden. At Sakina Mansion in Colaba. Fittingly, there was no one in the audience. Just Meher Pestonjee and one fern plant.

The house belonged to her. It was our theatre *adda*.[1] You asked her, you wanted to perform a piece, she said yes. There was no fuss about applying for dates or faxing the proposal. We organized the *beedies* and booze and breads. Meher invited her artist friends and comrades and bohemians, some of whom were high and mighty folks. Not that we knew. Not that we cared.

Beckett matters. He always does. Simply because good taste is important.

* A talk given at the Asiatic Society in Mumbai on 22 December 2017.

[1] Meeting place.

After works by William Shakespeare, Bertolt Brecht, Henrik Ibsen, Anton Chekhov, *Waiting for Godot* is perhaps among the ten most performed plays in this city. It has been played on the stage, a ship, in pubs and discos, and classrooms and *bastis*,[2] at the IIT campus, in a children's park, and one of my favourite shows was at the Bowen Methodist Church in Colaba. Naseeruddin Shah and Benjamin Gilani blended their Laurel and Hardy antics with ecclesiastical theology.

Samuel Beckett would have loved it. The man who was born in Dublin and is buried in Paris.

Whenever I travel to Paris, I visit his grave at the Montparnasse cemetery. There are other graves around. Sartre, Duras, Ionesco, Proudhon.

I am an atheist. So I don't pray. I have a simple ritual. I recite *Krapp's Last Tape* in front of the Master.

Today, I am tempted to do the same. But I won't.

Instead let me share a few lines from *Krapp's Last Tape*.

'Perhaps my best years are gone. When there was a chance of happiness. But I wouldn't want them back. Not with the fire in me now. No, I wouldn't want them back' ([1986] 2006, 223).

This brings me to the beginning.

But to begin at the beginning is predictable. Every two-paise writer has been doing it. From Gurudev Bhasa to Gurdev Borges.

So, let me start at the ending.

Since I am a playwright, let me share a bit from an unpublished and unperformed play called *Sky View—Plot Number Two*.

Sky View—Plot Number Two

First the context: 'Sky View—Plot Number Two' is a typical Mumbai apartment block which is located in Vakola. The building is dilapidated and beyond repair. Like most apartment blocks in Mumbai.

It is privy to the lives of its occupants and three centuries of Mumbai's history.

In all this a man and a woman try to fall in love.

Unknown to everyone, the Arabian Sea has been creeping into the city.

[2] *Basti* is a poor housing area, shanty-town.

I read from the last four scenes in the play.
Cut to Scene 9.

SCENE 9.
THE LAST OF THE SCENES.

Me: It is December 25th.
As the year has passed by I see the Pumpkinification of Sky View—Plot Number Two.
The only certainty is the sky.
The sky is my Santa Claus who makes me smile, always.
Merry X'Mas.

END OF SCENE 9.

SCENE 10.
ALSO, THE LAST OF THE SCENES.

Me: December 29th.
The birthday of my favourite-most Rajesh Khanna.
Also the happywalla birthday of the Unknown Office Bearer.
It's a day of nothingness at Sky View—Plot Number Two.
She rings the doorbell.
He opens the door.
She stands on her toes. Even though she is not short.
She says, I have seen Lauren Bacall do it to Humphrey Bogart.
She: I have seen it in the movies. Bacall and Bogie.
He: Ha. I am your Bogey-Man.
Me: She kisses him on his lip. It is the gentlest peck he has ever received.
He: That's gentle. Tastes really nice. Like kaddi patta.[3]
She: Happy birthday, my love.
He: What about him … er your husband?
She: Fuck him.
He: Oh. Okay.
She: Kiss me.
He: Here? Mishra may be watching through the key hole?
She: Fuck Mishra.
He: Why would you want to do that with Mishra?

[3] Curry leaves (seasoning).

Me: The two of them laugh. There is laughter. For 2.5 seconds.
Me: Then the two of them search for his medicines.
Me: He hobbles around the house with a mean swagger, saying, I'm Digambar Samiar.
He: Watch me. I'm Digambar Samiar da.
Me: And she says, I am Digambar Samiar's sidekick.
She: I am your sidekick, da.
Me: Together they find his missing pills. The ones he pops for his depression.
Thus begins the case of Digambar Samiar—the detective with a law degree and Brahmin prejudices.
They draw the curtains. The lights are switched off. She says, I have three hours, till my husband returns. Yes, till my husband returns.

END OF SCENE 10.

SCENE 11.
ALSO, THE LAST OF THE SCENES.

Me: December 31st.
Last day of the year.
In the basti I hear a bhajan[4] programme.
The songs are recycled and remixed and regurgitated. That's what the organizer, who believes in Swami Satyanarayan,[5] demands.
It is almost midnight.
Dark-darkish sky.
No 10 o'clock ban tonight.
The bhajani packs his paya peti.[6] He is very drunk. He says, alcohol is the only way he can tolerate such evenings which are a far cry from the days when he used to utter Sant Gadge Maharaj's sayings[7] or epiphanies to Kaloo Bai[8] on the mountain top.
The basti abounds with drunks.

[4] Devotional song.

[5] A benevolent form of Vishnu.

[6] Harmonium.

[7] Sant Gadge Maharaj (1876–1956) was a holy man known for his care for the poor and helpless.

[8] The grove around the mountain-top temple of Kaleshwari Devi (Kaloo Bai) near Satara is renowned for its miraculous properties.

The high and mighty at Altamount[9] are drunk.
The hills of Mumbai are drunk.
The drunks do not realize that the Arabian Sea has seeped into their city.
The rubble has drowned. The cement has sunk. The drains are inundated.
All so quietly.
Mumbai is in a stupor.
As Bhagirathi Society said before she collapsed. Beware, Dada[10] Skyview. Remember what Makhtum Fakir Ali Paru[11] said: What the seas giveth, the seas taketh.
The next day, she collapsed. Just like her great-great-grandfather, the Flour Mill in Churchgate. Who was born in 1725. But drowned in the sea.
At that time, Bhagirathi's ancestor said: The Arabian Sea, is all I see.

End of Scene 11.

Scene 12.
Penultimate Scene.

Me: December 32nd.
I had seen nothing like this, before.
The sea had entered the city.
A fish called Matsya[12] tickles my feet.
A fish called Matsya had forewarned us about this. But who pays heed to a fish. Na?
Can you hear the silence?
No murmuring from the 56 languages and the 118 castes that inhabit these homes.
No one raises their voice.
Just sea-water and all that salt.
Sky View—Plot Number Two is like an island in the city. Marooned.
Manik stands upright.
So do He and She.
Hand in hand.
Ashraf's daughter, too.
Under the water tank. No one to kiss. For the first time in her tiny existence.

9 Altamount: An upmarket residential area of Mumbai. Bhagirathi Society and so on are different places in Mumbai.
10 A Marathi term to address an elder brother.
11 A Sufi Muslim saint (1372–1431).
12 A mythological fish, one of the avatars of Vishnu.

Ojasnath and Omkarnath[13] with their wife.
She has six bags of jalakhia.[14] One bag for lau khirsa, one for khaja.
Some makka manjee chatapatti, suji halwa, chattu bara.
It is the last supper.
Tembe Master is on the terrace. He is seated on the water tank. He plays the bhongli, the ceremonial drum of the Bhandaris[15] of Mumbai. He says:

In Samvat 1729, the Engrez[16] came from the Vilayat
In the favourable month of Jyesht to Mumbai
Lisbon gifts Mumbai to London as a dowry
And the Engrez prospered in this city of sin

Half of Mumbai's islands under the sea, at that time
This includes banks and mints and underworld crime
The flyovers, the factories, the flats, the colonies
Look now, how, the wheel has turned
The Arabian Sea is up to my knees

Silence.

Me: She tells He.
She: Marry me!
He: Er … OK.
Me: It is simple as that.
She: No dowry.
He: But naturally.
Me: I want to say, I wish the King of Portugal was as wise.
She: We sow sins. Punishment, we reap.
He: Our sins, multiply.
Me: The King of Portugal gifted the islands as dowry to King Charles II of England when he married Catherine of Braganza.
She: An island we were.

[13] Ojasnath and Omkarnath with their (shared) wife; Tembe Master: These are residents of Sky View—Plot Number Two, residents who stay in the building.

[14] Jalakhia, lau khirsa, khaja, makka manjee chatapatti, suji halwa, chattu bara: Various snacks, desserts, and breakfast items.

[15] A caste group in Mumbai.

[16] The English.

He: An island we return to.
Me: At Sky View—Plot Number Two. We, see the sea. She watches. She has not forgotten that sinful day on May 11th, 1661.

End of Scene 12.

Scene 13.
The 13th Scene at Sky View—Plot Number Two.

Me: December 33rd.
The Arabian Sea has risen to … to the sixth floor.
I feel the sea water in my cracks.
There are no waves. I feel a thud-thud-thud!!!
That is the 100-year-old Gulmohar. All three storeys of her.
She is not alone.
One lakh seventy two thousand buildings have sunk into this watery grave.
Automobiles and autorickshaws and elevators, pass by. All muted.
Strange as it may seem. Not a single human being.
It is like a silent film.
20 million Mumbaikars[17] and their city, drowned.
And not one whimper.
Two Arabian horses float by.
They look familiar.
It is the two horses that Jamsetjee Jejeebhoy[18] presented to Queen Victoria as a gift.
Each horse was worth thirty thousand rupees.
I feel a burpy belch in my intestines.
The Arabian Sea, she has risen to … to the seventh floor.
He and She can touch the sea.
It is icy.
The future is uncertain.
Nothing to say.
Everything is quiet.
Everything that has been fabricated since 1018 is under the water. From the copper plates of the Tagar ancestry in Thane to the stone inscriptions in the village Utan.
Ashraf's daughter says order lunch from McDonald's na?

[17] People of Mumbai.

[18] Sir Jamsetjee Jejeebhoy (1783–1859), merchant and philanthropist, was a great benefactor of Bombay (Mumbai).

Tembe Master hums Bhimsen Joshi.[19] He says, it is one way to survive.
Time ticks.
Drop by drop.
I feel weak.
I feel giddy.
My pipes have disintegrated.
My foundation, corroded.
How much longer can I stand, upright?
So much to do, so much to do.
I wanted to set up a committee who could monitor timely repairs that could be carried out on old structures which would help reduce number of dilapidated buildings that are listed before monsoon every year.
But not a single brother and sister, left.
Just me, and the sky.
I sigh.
One last time.
The sky sighs back at me.
At Sky View—Plot Number Two.
Tembe Master picks up the harmonium.
She hums.
He, the Unknown Office Bearer, applies Amrutanjam[20] on my back.
The sea water rises.
I sense my heartbeat stutter.
Manik scatters seeds on the floor.
Where are the butterflies which visit Sky View—Plot Number Two?
I wheeze, my circulation halts.
Just then, He and She spot one butterfly.
It is a rare orange-and-brown Red Spot
The butterfly lands.
Tembe Master plays the harmonium.
This is the end no?

FREEZE TABLEAU.
END OF SCENE 13.

END OF THE PLAY.
THE END OF MUMBAI CITY.

[19] Bhimsen Joshi (1922–2011) was a famous Indian vocalist.
[20] An aromatic balm for headaches and body pain.

Nine Reasons Why Playwrights Write Plays

Why nine?

Because of the Italian poet whose 15th-century manuscript *is carefully locked somewhere in this building.*

In the *Divine Comedy*, Virgil and Dante begin the journey into the underworld or the Nine Circles of Hell.

All playwrights make that journey into the Nine Circles of Hell.

Hell is not other people.

Hell is us.

Playwrights enter and re-enter *Hell*.

The words seek lucidity.

Mostly they lie.

As the extraordinary Georg Büchner[21] said in Darmstadt in July 1834: Whoever speaks the truth on this planet is hanged.

And so, truth must be hidden in a safe place.

Do not share truth with friends, family, loved ones.

You will suffer.

But you can share truth with audiences *only* as long as you can trust these audiences.

Because if you are caught uttering the truth, you will be taxed.

Direct tax—21 per cent.

Indirect tax—25 per cent.

Peace of mind tax—15 per cent.

Insomnia and barbiturate and badmaashi[22] tax—4 per cent.

Taxes for sundry diseases which include poverty—9 per cent.

Starvation and exploitation tax—6 per cent.

Paying obeisance to all kind of fool's tax—33 per cent.

Plus, nowadays there is Aadhaar.[23]

So, every single thought in your brain shall be linked to a UIDAI number; and taxed.

These are the Nine Circles of Hell.

There are other Circle of Hells.

[21] Georg Büchner (1813–1837) was a major German playwright.

[22] Naughty, villainous, badly behaved.

[23] Aadhaar is a 12-digit, unique identity number given to all Indian residents based on biometric and demographic data collected by the Unique Identification Authority of India (UIDAI).

I have created a tiny collection of 20 *one-liners* that I have overheard in the gent's cloakrooms *and* canteen area *and* greenrooms *and* backstage zone after a theatre show.

Before we stumble in the general direction of the *four-odd plays*, let me quickly share them with you. So for those of you who don't visit the theatre—often enough—you get a sense of the chit-chat.

1. You can understand a lot about the theatre if you comprehend it.
2. It's a serious sort of comedy, isn't it?
3. I hate plays that make me think! You tell me, am I supposed to watch the play or am I supposed to think?
4. I decided to direct the play when I read it. If I hadn't read the play, chances are I would not have directed it. (A well-known commercial director.)
5. I knew I was going to forget that line, so I didn't learn it.
6. Listen—if you can't imitate Mukta Barve,[24] then don't copy her.
7. My only problem with the theatre is the dialogues; everybody is talking all the time.
8. When a dialogue has double meaning, I don't know which meaning to follow.
9. Just when you think you know everything about the theatre, you're informed that 'Patta Baburao'[25] penned 16,000 lavanis.[26] Hmm. Sometimes, I feel, there's a bit too much of culture going around. And I can't digest it.
10. No one goes to see *Sahi Re Sahi*[27] since it's always House Full.
11. Children's plays are a very good thing because it gets the parents interested in the theatre.
12. Ultimately, every actor toes the line…
13. The lighting was great except for all that darkness.
14. If there were no actors, we would be speechless.
15. You should always go backstage after a show (good or bad) and say, 'Only you could have done it.'
16. Plays come and go, but debts accumulate!

[24] Mukta Barve is a popular Indian actress and producer.

[25] Patthe Bapurao (1868–1941) was a prolific poet-musician in the Maharashtrian musical theatre tradition.

[26] Lavanis ('beauties') are traditional dance-songs.

[27] A popular Marathi drama.

17. A good audience is usually thinking about something else!
18. The grandiloquent lines are magnifique, but I think it is the trifles that make a play. In fact the truth is, trifles make the sum of life.
19. After a particularly poor show, the ageing Tiwariji at Prithvi Theatre consoled the upcoming star by saying, look into the sky, even the sky is empty!
20. When despondency was at its worst, an actor believed he should die. The question was, should the actor die at home reading Sophocles;[28] or on the road reciting the lines from a Satish Alekar[29] play; or on the stage, revelling in Jon Fosse's silence?[30]

Jazz[31]

In 2014, St Stanislaus High School celebrated its sesquicentennial year. Seated in the St Peter's church on Hill Road, paying heed to the four-part harmony, I realized that, more than hockey, it was music that kindled a Stanislite's membranes. In the good old days it was an all-male chorus under the baton of Fr Irache and Fr Alieu, and the rich strains of the pipe organ in the choir loft.

At that time, I didn't realize it, but the organ belted out classics. The school with government support was plebeian. But the music was snobbish. Many years later, I realized that the church is a place where you can listen to music in the old-fashioned way. Today, with music being heard 'on the move' or 'on your headphones' this community sharing of music is fading away.

In a way, when I started writing *Jazz* (the musical) for Denzil Smith and his group Stagesmith, it was about reconnecting with the music from my school days. The research gave me the opportunity to relive the good old days.

[28] Sophocles (c. 496–c. 406 BC) was one of the greatest Athenian tragic dramatists.

[29] Satish Alekar is a Marathi playwright, actor, and theatre director.

[30] Jon Olav Fosse is a Norwegian writer and dramatist.

[31] *Jazz* (2008), like the plays *3 Sakina Manzil* (2004) and *Shakespeare and She* (2008), both of which are discussed later, is included in the volume of eight plays by Ramu Ramanathan, *3 Sakina Manzil and Other Plays*, edited by Lakshmi Chandra and published by Orient Blackswan in 2012.

Writing *Jazz* was easy. Since the ode to the contribution of Goan-Christian musicians to Bollywood music was a *salaam* to the Bandra[32] I knew, and the Bandra I loved.

The play traced the relationship between an olde worlde music arranger and his young sax student.

To quote from the play's production notes:

> When Hindi film music entered a period of rapid evolution during the Second World War, composers realised that the small groups they'd previously used could not effectively convey the drama unfolding on screen. So they formed large orchestras that ranged from dholaks[33] and sitars along with banks of violins, swathes of trumpets and a Hawaiian guitar or two. Since not many musicians from other communities knew how to play saxophones or clarinets, Goans came to form the bulk of the orchestras. Few Hindi film composers, most of whom were trained in the Hindustani classical tradition, knew how to score music for the new ensembles. That task was performed by a Goan 'arranger'.

Typically, the work proceeded thus. The producer would organize a 'sitting' (as the Goans came to call the *baithaks*)[34] at which the composer (most often a Hindu), the lyricist (usually an Urdu-speaking Muslim), and the arranger would flop down on comfortable cushions to listen to the director narrate the plot. When the director indicated the point at which a song was necessary, the composer would hum out a melody or pick it out on his harmonium. It was the arranger's task to note down these fragments, which the composer would later piece together into an entire song.

But even then, the composer would craft only the verse and the chorus. The arranger was responsible for fashioning the melodic bridges, for shaping the parts for individual instruments, and often even wrote the background music. The arranger wasn't merely a secretary. As I discovered while researching a previous essay, the Goans drew on their bicultural heritage to give Bollywood music its promiscuous charm, slipping in slivers of Dixieland stomp, Portuguese fados, Ellingtonesque doodles, cha cha cha, and Mozart and Bach themes.

[32] A neighbourhood in West Mumbai.

[33] The *dholak* is a South Asian, two-headed, hand-drum.

[34] A session or meeting.

Long before fusion music became fashionable, it was being performed every day in Bombay's film studios.

When I visited the St Stanislaus school church on a Sunday, two things happened: I flashed back in time. Also, I realized the church was built in 1853.

The Year 1853

1853 was the time Jyotiba Phule[35] had completed the first draft of his *Tritya Ratna*, one of the most modern plays of our times.

Phule penned the words 150 years ago, when the seven islands in this city were trying to rise above the seas. The play was performed when a steam engine crossed the mainland into VT station, carrying the tenets of democracy in its compartments.

That's how sanity prevailed in a little city, with a fortified fort, and a cluster of community homes, and the first of the cotton mills.

See how the dots have started to connect!

In the 1970s, I stayed in the LIC Colony, located opposite the Santacruz BEST[36] Depot. In those days, there was no paranoia and so, there was zero security at the depot gates. Therefore a lot of my time was spent playing 'bat-and-ball' in the Bus Depot. My cousins in Coimbatore climbed coconut trees. We climbed the double-decker bus.

My Ambu Athai,[37] who is dead, said to me on the same day as today Do you see the Western Ghats near Coimbatore and the Palakkad gap. It matches the gap in the central highlands of Madagascar from which it originated as a result of volcanic eruptions 88 million years ago.

Did you know that?

I said, I did not know. This city's history is much younger.

What I did know was this: Life was simple. Mumbai was a city of equals. A lot of my friends were children of Bhandaris[38] and Kolis and Kunbis; and Mahars and Mangs; and Scoundrel Iblis.[39]

[35] Jyotiba Phule (1827–1890) was a social activist, thinker, anti-caste reformer, and writer from Maharashtra.

[36] BEST stands for 'Bombay [now Brihanmumbai] Electric Supply & Transport', a giant civic transport and electricity provider in Mumbai.

[37] *Athai* means aunt in Tamil, so 'Aunty Ambu'.

[38] Bhandaris and so on are caste groups.

[39] Satan.

As a child I accompanied my friends to see a play performed for the LIC class IV union in the Community Centre in the LIC Colony. My first serious play was a *lok natya*[40] called *Ramnagari* by Ram Nagarkar,[41] who was also the *songadya*[42] in the superhit *lok natya*, *Vicha Majhi Poori Kara*, alongside the inscrutable Nilu Phule. The play begins, 'Saala, Hajjam, Ahe, Hajjam.'[43] It is a roadside altercation. Ram Nagarkar, the son of a barber, who is watching the entire episode, wonders: 'Why do people drag "our" *hajjam* profession into their petty fights?'

That's when I started to realize that in Mumbai theatre is language.

Also, I realized theatre is everywhere. Even today, there are more than 1,500 play performances in a month in four main languages, Hindi, English, Gujarati, and Marathi (and you can add Telegu, Kannada, and Konkani to this list). This beats the mono-lingual, mono-cultural theatre of New York or London or Berlin hands down. Plus, unlike the subsidized art of Delhi or government grants, the top Marathi and Gujarati plays net INR 2,50,000 at the box office. This is for a single show. All cash. No cheques.

Box office revenue was of INR 20 crores. This depleted to INR 15 crores after 8 November 2016 and half of that after the GST[44] Law was introduced in July 2017!

So much to say, so much to say.

So let's start in South-Central Bombay. This is the area from Khetwadi to Kamatipura: the epicentre of Bombay after the British royalty were gifted the island city by the Portuguese. The first thing to spring up was the theatre. There were thirty-five makeshift theatres which featured plays performed in English for the recreation of the British soldiers.

As old timers say about the theatre of Mumbai, it has to fulfil three conditions.

[40] Folk drama.

[41] Ram Nagarkar (d.1995) was a well-known Marathi actor and comedian.

[42] The jester or comic.

[43] Colloquial language/swearing: Hajjam is an ethnic group found in North India; they are barbers by profession.

[44] GST is Good and Services Tax, an indirect tax on the sale of goods and services.

1. It has to be close to a tram stop or railway station.
2. It has to be in proximity to a dingy bar.
3. It has to be located in a red light area.

Here I must share an anecdote I heard from Namdeo Dhasal.[45] I know it well. Because I heard it three times. Like all great writers. Namdeo Dhasal repeated himself. This Namdeo Dhasal anecdote has its mise en scène in the red light neighbourhood of Falkland Road and the Golpitha *chauraha*.[46]

These days it has the honorific title Patthe Bapurao Marg. Patthe Bapurao[47] is the doyen of *tamasha*.[48] Besides the 16,000 songs he composed, there is the legend about how he (a novice) participated in a *jugalbandi*[49] and defeated the opponent (a veteran) in a *sawaal-jawaab*.[50] A young and very pretty courtesan from the Mahar[51] community called Pawala was besotted by his singing and his poetry. The Brahmin Bapurao married the girl. On cue, the theatre performances were banned.

But the manager of the Bangdiwala theatre, a Mohammedan, ensured that 'the show must go on'.

He got the Brahmin–Mahar husband and wife to sit on the stage and charged two *annas* for the tickets. The audience watched the banned wedding on stage. The manager made more money at the box office from a staged wedding than from the actual show.

Namdeo Dhasal's mantra: a *theatrewallah* must *always* know how to beat the system.

3 Sakina Manzil

As I mentioned once before, one thing theatre enables us to do is to play hopscotch with time.

45 Namdeo Dhasal (1949–2014) was a Marathi poet, writer, and Dalit activist (in 1972, he was one of the founders of the Dalit Panthers).

46 Crossroads, intersection.

47 See footnote 25 earlier.

48 Traditional Marathi theatre, with lots of singing and dancing, often performed by local or travelling theatre groups.

49 Duet.

50 Call-and-response improvization, here competitive!

51 A low-caste (Dalit) community. Famous Mahars have included Namdeo Dhasal, mentioned here, and the great Dr Ambedkar.

It's time to flashback into *3 Sakina Manzil* territory.

To 1944.

In the sultry days of 1944, when there were no air-conditioners, there were theatres such as Baliwala Grand Theatre (Playhouse), wherein a play opened with a loud bang of exploding potash, whilst the curtain was being raised. And even as the audience went silent and attentive, occasional shouts from the vendors around the theatre percolated the auditorium: '*Pista-badam*!'[52] '*Chopdi*!'[53] '*Punkha*!'[54] '*Uthav jaldi*!'[55] and the incessant extolling of the ticket-seller: '*Khel abhi chalu hua*'.[56] For some of the performances in the Gothic-style theatres such as Victoria, Rippon, or Baliwala, the drama companies used to bring their own main curtain, which was operated by two men. Since the curtain pullers often dozed off, the cue to bring down the curtain was a shrill blast of a whistle. During one of the shows, the curtain pullers who were asleep were awakened by a shrill whistle, and so, they hurriedly brought down the curtain in the middle of the scene. It was only later that it was found out that the whistle was not blown by a prompter but by a BEST traffic conductor on the street.

I used this scene in *3 Sakina Manzil*.

The play was researched at the Asiatic Society. Subsequently, the play was performed at the Asiatic Society.

I plagiarized from reality. I borrowed from the city.

Whether *3 Sakina Manzil* rediscovered the magic of theatre, I don't know. Whether the play is a success or not, I don't know. Whether the play was understood, or misunderstood, I don't know. For me what mattered is, I had to write the play about the 1944 dock explosion which tore this city apart!

There was one other thing that *3 Sakina Manzil* taught me.

It is about *language*.

And how languages beget languages.

[52] Dried fruits (pistachios, almonds) for munching during the performance.

[53] Book, that is, the playtext being sold during the performance.

[54] A hand fan, to keep yourself cool.

[55] 'Come an' get 'em!'

[56] 'The performance has just begun!'

I met a Kutchi[57] businessman from Mandvi. At that time, I was struck by the multiple Kutchi dialects being used in the radius of the port area in Mumbai. Bhatia Kutchi, Memoni Kutchi, Khoja Kutchi, Lohana Kutchi, and Bania Kutchi. Each with regional variations. Then there were the Maplahs, the Jews, the Nagoris, the Marathas, the Mahars, the Mathadis, and the Kunbis.

That's when I started to realize that in Mumbai, theatre is language.

And this language is shifting.

Did you know, the biggest twenty-first-century crisis is that half of the 6,000 languages which the planet speaks will die?

Over 50 languages have only one speaker left.

If you are reading this, you must know, one language will vanish from this planet in the next month.

Never to be found again.

Simply because many languages have never been written down.

Many languages cannot be read.

They have never been.

This is a shame.

So many stories waiting to be told.

These languages are preserved through the theatre.

Theatre as a kind of living museum that preserves words.

That's why I love the theatre.

That's one of the reasons why I love theatre in this city.

Mumbai is a living museum of words.

Cotton 56 Polyester 84

There's also the simplicity of theatre in this city.

It springs up in the most unlikely of venues. From *maidans*[58] such as the Jambori Maidan which hosted the month-long Kamgar Fest (the oldest theatre festival in this city, established in 1939) to a cult play such as *Vastraharan* (see Chapter 22, 'Stories') whose 5,000 shows have been performed by millworkers from Lower Parel and

[57] Kutchis are people hailing from the Kachchh/Kutch Region of the western Indian state of Gujarat.

[58] An open urban space, often a park, used for meetings, sports, and so on.

Naigaon. In 'the good old days' of working-class solidarity, the plays were performed in the compound of the *chawls*[59] or in the Ganapati *mandals*.[60] The shows were mainly mythological productions, with artificial ornaments and gaudy costumes. The performances used to go on till the wee hours of the morning, and the audience contributed to a noble cause.

The working class and humble middle class provided a backbone to theatre in the city. Premanand Gajvi[61] was a BPT employee, Vinda Karandikar[62] taught English in a city college. Vijay Tendulkar[63] was a newspaper scribe. BEST employees and bank clerks enacted their plays. They were as important as cricketers and movie actors on the seven islands.[64] *Why?* Because they wove magic with words.

Perhaps the times (and the narratives) were easier. It was the playwright's theatre—and the pen was the *badshah*.[65] Then there was the director's theatre which introduced new forms, new ways of expressing content. And then there was the actor's theatre. Today, the times belong to the audience's theatre. The only problem is that we can't seem to get the audience into the auditorium. Or at least the right kind of audience.

This is what I told Meena Menon and Neera Adarkar.[66] As some of you may know, Meena and Neera penned a book: *One Hundred Years, One Hundred Voices: Oral History of Millworkers of Girangaon* (2004). Comrade Meena Menon wanted to organize readings from the book. I told her, Comrade, I would prefer to write a play. Fortunately, Sunil

[59] Working-class tenements as built, for example, for the millworkers in Mumbai.

[60] Temporary shrines to honour the much-loved god Ganapati (Ganesh), 'remover of obstacles'—the celebration in Mumbai of his birthday is one of the great popular festivals of India.

[61] Premanand Gavji is a Marathi poet, writer, and playwright; BPT stands for Bombay Port Trust.

[62] Vinda Karandikar (1918–2010) was a well-known Marathi writer, poet, critic, and translator.

[63] Vijay Tendulkar (1928–2008) was a playwright, writer for film and television, journalist, and social commentator.

[64] The 'seven islands' were the original islands that over many centuries came together to form the area of modern Mumbai.

[65] Great king, that is, 'the pen was king'.

[66] Meena Menon is a journalist; Neera Adarkar is an architect.

Shanbag[67] agreed to be part of the process. He was willing to direct the play. That's how *Cotton 56 Polyester 84* was staged.

My research began by attending court hearings in Room No. 56 of the high court (Justice Radhakrishnan's courtroom). The lawyers on either side were the *who's who* of India: Iqbal Chagla, Goolam Vahanvati, Arun Jaitley, Soli Sorabjee, Mukul Rohatgi, Abhishek Singhvi, and so on. No dearth of talent! Great lawyers. And even greater performers. The Bombay Environmental Action Group were the petitioners—and the four main individuals who had been working on this were Teesta Setalvad,[68] Gerson da Cunha,[69] Cyrus Guzdar,[70] and Debi Goel.

For me, it was like watching *Shantata! Court Chalu Ahe*[71] and *Stammheim—The Baader-Meinhof Gang on Trial*[72] in one go.

The High Court is a wonderful space for great drama. And the best thing is, it is free of cost. The *vaachika abhinaya*[73] is superb. And no one forgets their lines. It's in Room No. 56 of the high court that I rediscovered the magic of theatre.

As I saw it, the new world order has hypnotized an entire generation in Mumbai. This is what *Cotton 56 Polyester 84* tries to say.

Second Act

A playwright, any playwright, is the sum total of many plays.

There was a phase in my life when I watched plays non-stop.

Sometimes, the same play twice, thrice.

[67] Sunil Shanbag is an Indian theatre director, screenwriter, and film-maker.

[68] Teesta Setalvad is an Indian civil rights activist and journalist.

[69] Gerson da Cunha is an Indian stage and screen actor, social worker, and writer.

[70] Cyrus Guzdar and Debi Goel are public interest litigants.

[71] *Shantata! Court Chalu Ahe* (1968) is a successful play by Vijay Tendulkar about a group of teachers (and amateur actors) who stage a 'mock trial'—that goes wrong.

[72] *Stammheim—The Baader-Meinhof Gang on Trial* (1986) is a controversial film, written by Stefan Aust and directed by Reinhard Hauff, about the trial of members of the violent left-wing RAF group (the 'Baader-Meinhof Gang') in Stammheim Prison.

[73] *Abhinaya* is the art of expression in Indian aesthetics; *vaachika abhinaya*, one of its four elements, is the expression of speech.

And then in my brain, I would stage them again.

These plays would talk to each other.

Have a dialogue. Provide a cue. Do an encore.

I recall the first time, Cyrus Mistry's[74] *Doongaji House* talking to Naushil Mehta's[75] *Patro Mitro*. A Parsee building in Colaba[76] exchanging letters about Gujarati language, Gujarati literature, Gujarati culture, and above all, Vile Parle.

Then there was Uttam Gada's[77] *Maharathi* having a *guftagu*[78] with Shafaat Khan's[79] *Shobha Yatra* before *that* play was born at the August Kranti Maidan on the 50th anniversary of Indian Independence.

Meanwhile there was Jayant Pawar's[80] *Adhantar* which was very upset with Sai Paranjape's[81] *Sakhe Sejare* to *One Room Kitchen* to *Sambhoosanchya Chaalit* to *Batatyachi Chawl*. *Adhantar* argued with the others even though it was told to shut up. Since it was *not* as popular as the others.

Bhupen Khakhar's[82] *Mojila Manilal* told *Adhantar*, please don't be quiet. We plays do *not* have class, caste, creed. So *Mojila Manilal* and *Adhantar* went for a walk. They purchased *sev-mumbra*[83] and became best friends. Yes, ladies and gentlemen, Lalbaug[84] and Kalbadevi smoked *beedies* happily ever after.

In all this there was one play which did not talk to anyone.

Like Little Jack Horner, it sat in the corner.

It was Vijay Tendulkar's *Gidhade*!

Vultures.

Gidhadhe.

Horrid things.

[74] Cyrus Mistry is an Indian writer and playwright.

[75] Naushil Mehta is an Indian writer, director, and producer.

[76] Colaba and Vile Parle are districts in Mumbai.

[77] Uttam Gada is an Indian playwright and screenplay author.

[78] Quiet chat.

[79] Shafaat Khan is an Indian playwright, academic, and theatre director.

[80] Jawant Pawar is an Indian playwright and journalist.

[81] Sai Saranjape is an Indian film and theatre director, playwright, and screenwriter.

[82] Bhupen Khakhar (1934–2003) was a writer and playwright, though better known as a painter.

[83] A spicy Indian snack.

[84] Lalbaug and Kalbadevi are districts in Mumbai.

Vultures.

Gidhadhe.

Not nice, nor adorable.

Simply reprehensible.

Petty-minded beasts—squabbling and squawking at a stinking carcass.

Willing to attack each other over decomposing meat.

Vultures.

Gidhadhe.

Carrion eaters with beady twisted eyes

Undernourished, greedy, crooked beaks, often covered in blood and gore and guts and bloody eyeballs.

All so revolting.

Vultures.

Gidhadhe.

Most people would prefer to keep their distance from them.

But Tendulkar Saab didn't.

He cared for the vultures.

He placed them on the stage, in *our* living room.

The play was penned in 1961. It was finally staged in 1970.

The vultures were Ramakant and Umakant, with their lasciviousness and viciousness, plus their sister Manik's vulgar sensuality. Tendulkar made a link between vultures and the veneer of morality that prevailed in middle-class Maharashtra.

A warped saga of domestic violence; and how Manik copes with her desires and her family.

A bit like *Sakharam Binder* (another play that scowled in sullen silence).

A play due to which Tendulkar became officially associated with sensationalism, sex, and violence. Most of Maharashtra was stunned by the wanton display of illicit sex.

Today, Tendulkar's *Ghashiram Kotwal*[85] is an official text. So is Jayant Pawar's *Adhantar*. Likewise are *Mee Nathuram Godse Boltoy*[86] by Pradeep Dalvi and *Yada Kadachit* by Santosh Pawar.[87]

85 A political satire written in response to the rise of the Shiv Sena in Mumbai.

86 Dalvi's play, about the murderer of Mahatma Gandhi, has been highly controversial in India.

87 Santosh Pawar is a writer, actor, and director known for his comedies.

All taboo plays.

So? Has Mumbai been gentrified?

To find the answer.

You have to watch many more plays.

And then listen to *how* these plays *gossip* with each other.

In the middle of the night.

Because plays are creatures of the underworld; shadows of the low life.

And that's the best part about plays in this city.

Please note: This is not a nostalgia piece about the rollicking days of theatre. Last year, I judged the final round of a youth one-act play competition. Last week, the Loksatta one-act play competition concluded. In all, more than 350 groups from all over Maharashtra. The numbers are staggering.

They speak of Make in India.

We speak of Make in Mumbai.

Make in Mumbai is the one-act play.

One act suits the Mumbaiyya attitude. Short, to the point, and can be staged anywhere anytime.

This is one reason why Badal Sircar[88] and his one acts make him the most performed playwright among Mumbai's one-act theatrewallahs.

But the moment I cherished the most was during a Ram Lila[89] show at Azad Maidan! It was the Ashokavana[90] scene. The group decided that instead of a painted backdrop they would use a real tree. However, they decided to use the branch of a mango tree since a mango tree was available. This was placed above Sita-ma in Ravana's garden. Halfway through the scene the prop manager realized that the mango branch was 'not working'. So they added real mangoes to the branch. Even so, they felt the theatrical illusion was faulty. So they added all of Ravana's favourite fruits (bananas, grapes, apples, guavas, watermelons, and so on) onto the tree. Later the branch took on a life of its own; and assortments from a Coke can to a Centre Fresh wrapper were added. All this in the name of Lord Ravana.

And that's the magic of theatre in Mumbai. Always has been.

[88] Badal Sircar (1925–2011) was an influential Bengali playwright and theatre director.

[89] A popular folk drama performance of stories about Rama.

[90] Sita, Rama's wife, has been kidnapped by Ravana. She refuses to stay in his palace, preferring to sit in the garden under an Ashoka tree.

Shakespeare and She

The Epilogue!

I read *The Tempest* the other day.

Three insights:

1. The white colonizers arrive on an island. On that island lives Caliban. The white colonizers treat Caliban like a native and call Caliban's language vernacular. So Caliban learns *their* language.
2. Today, Caliban's speech out-dazzles the white colonizers'. He utters beautiful lines in the play. In fact Caliban utters the best lines in the play. Consider the cult Caliban line: 'You taught me language; and my profit on't is, I know how to curse.'
3. For me, Caliban is the ultimate mascot for Indian English writing.

On 16 February 2008, I opened a play at the Humara Shakespeare festival in Chennai called *Shakespeare and She*.

The play was part of a project with students in two architecture colleges and the IDC at IIT.[91]

The main motto of the workshop: the bard lives because his plays are the thing!

'Life is poorer without Shakespeare and we should meet him at a stage when we are ready for him.'

The thing is, while we have been seated (hunched over our laptops: blogging, Instagramming, Facebooking, and so on), Shakespeare's characters are roaming through the streets of Mumbai. For example: Shylock in Masjid Bunder. Romeo and Juliet opposite Ruia College. Henry IV getting off a rickshaw. Cleopatra at Vasai Koli market. And so on.

The plan is to explore the city—with a digital camera—and to find Shakespeare's characters (big, small, historical, irrelevant, tragic, comic, and so on). And create your own Shakespeare fable around that character!

So it's *simple*.

No getting intimidated by iambic pentameters or Thee, Thy, and Thou or complex plotlines or character motivations.

[91] The Industrial Design Centre at the Indian Institute of Technology Mumbai.

Just step out into Amchi Mumbai. Board your local train/BEST bus. Shoot the characters of apna Sheikh Saab. That's Sheikh-Spear!!!

The students shot thousands and thousands of photographs.

The Final Act!

I conclude with a story about how theatre transpires in this city.

An Actor on the Hot Tin Roof

Warren L. D'sylva is a young actor from Bandra. He bagged the best actor award at Thespo (a youth play competition) for his rendition of Hamm in Samuel Beckett's *Endgame*.

At the beginning of 2008, he wrote a play, *A Black Mujahid*, which was performed and directed as part of the Afro-American Film Festival at the American Centre.

A few days later, Warren received a phone call from an inspector at Chembur Police Station. The inspector had received a complaint about *A Black Mujahid*. Warren thought it was a practical joke till the inspector started to read out the synopsis of the play from his police file.

Warren's theatre group distributes a photocopy before each performance with information about the synopsis, cast, and so on. The inspector seemed to possess such a copy.

The inspector in his official baritone enquired about the performance: 'So, who is this Malcolm X?'

Warren explained, but the inspector lost interest.

Warren paused (dramatically), and said with a vague sort of finality: 'Malcolm X was a freedom fighter … kind of ….' The inspector had a ready riposte: 'If he is a freedom fighter, then why call him Mujahid?'

Then the inspector explained the reason for the call. Someone had watched the performance and was offended or, worse still, suspected Warren of preaching terrorism.

Summoned to the Police Station

Warren reached the police station. He was greeted (very warmly) by the inspector and his right-hand man (both in plain clothes). The police file was opened, the complaint was read out. It was 'this piece of paper which had some highly objectionable content written in it, please investigate'.

The Said Piece of Paper was the Synopsis of the Play

The inspector queried: 'If you say this play is about a black freedom fighter, why use a Muslim name—Mujahid?' Warren explained that Mejia is an Arabic term for a person who struggles. The police didn't believe the explanation. Warren requested for an internet connection. This seemed to excite the law enforcers.

'Yes, yes I have internet on my Toshiba laptop.'

In Search of a Mujahid

While Warren googled, the inspector was an eager spectator. He was amazed with *Wikipedia*. He read the meaning of Mujahid and explained it to the others.

He thought the complaint was a total waste of everyone's time. A printout of the *Wikipedia* link was filed along with Warren's statement.

But there was a hitch. They didn't know how to take a printout from the laptop. The inspector endearingly said: 'Beta, please do something.'

Warren realized the laptop wasn't networked to the printer. So Warren unleashed a pen drive and copy-pasted the Mujahid document onto a desktop computer. Everyone in the police station was most impressed.

They proceeded with the statement. *Chai* and *nashta*[92] was organized. The inspector started chit-chatting. Where did Warren study? St Xavier's. What did Warren study? English literature. Silence. 'Why not Marathi?' The inspector proceeded to describe his college days, the system of education, Nashik. He asked Warren about his *nataka* (drama) company. Warren told him, it's a bunch of friends. The inspector jotted down their names and addresses.

92 Tea and breakfast.

Malcolm X and Warren

Warren was probed about performance details; and for a brief history of Malcolm X. Warren gave him a longish lecture at the end of which, the inspector said, 'What you're saying is: "Malcolm X was a very good man."'

Some more tea was ordered. The conversation meandered from Toshiba laptops, to why Warren should not do a play with 'Mujahid' in the title, and how the inspector had attempted three papers in English literature.

By now, a four-page statement was readied. While signing it, Warren felt it would make for a very entertaining piece of theatre.

The inspector and his men thanked Warren. They waved goodbye. So did Warren.

Was it going to be the beginning of a beautiful friendship?

Viva Theatre.

Theatre Zindabad!

21

Speak Memory

PREMILA PAUL

A welcome trend in academia now is the enthusiastic crossing of borders; disciplines no longer respect boundaries. Literary texts top the required reading lists of courses on religion, history, and social sciences. Frontiers of literature also continue to widen and enthusiastically accommodate genres such as folk lyrics. All disciplines in humanities aim to sharpen the vision of their readers, create in them a sensitive awareness of the diversity of cultures/ethnicities and humanize their approach to life and people that will help restore dignity and humanity to the oppressed. If history offers valuable lessons for humanity to direct its future, in the words of Woody Guthrie, 'It's a folk singer's job to comfort disturbed people and to disturb comfortable people' (*AZ Quotes*, 'Woodie Cuthrie').

Journalists write history to a deadline; they record history in a hurry. In our 24/7 breaking news age, they record history in competition. Good journalists provide sources for historians. They provide first-hand, authentic data for the construction of history. History is thus available for both immediate and future consumption. Most writers are motivated by a strong desire and anxiety to record memory and preserve it for future generations. History, memoirs, biographies, autobiographies—all are inspired products of this desire and anxiety.

We all live in memory and in the memory tales of our families. The best books are memory-driven. If there is no memory, there is no history. Memory recasts, reconstructs, and reinterprets the past for the present and the future. Memory thus becomes a meaningful link and a vibrant interface between the past and the present. History itself is memory narrative. We have personal histories, public histories (oral and written), individual memory, and collective memory.

There is often selective representation or even misrepresentation in history. To use the Kashmiri poet Agha Shahid Ali's words in 'Farewell': 'My memory is again in the way of your history. [...] Your history gets in the way of my memory. [...] Your memory gets in the way of my memory. [...] My memory keeps getting in the way of your history' (2000, 7–9). There is also a concerted political effort to erase historical episodes so that collective memory does not percolate down to the next generation. The Jallianwalah Bagh massacre and Partition violence find eloquent expression because we have 'the Other'—the British or Pakistanis—to demonize. But the shocking collapse of our valued institutions of democracy and secularism are under-narrated. I want to focus on two shameful Indian historical episodes: the Emergency of 26 June 1975 to 18 January 1977, and the more localized anti-Sikh pogrom of 1984. These two are purely home-made, Made in India atrocities, and we have no one else to blame for them.

For illustration, I have chosen three literary texts—visual and print—by journalists who have turned to writing fiction or screenplays. Journalists have the closest encounter with current events. Deeply affected by the assault on humanity, some journalists go beyond mere reporting and choose artistic modes to express human trauma and also expose the state machinery's betrayal of its citizens.

The ruthless imposition of Emergency by the state leading to utter denial of freedom is deliberately kept out of history textbooks in India. It feels easier and safer to study the history of the distant past. The young post-Emergency generation may not understand the irony of suspending democracy to save democracy. In the words of Shashi Tharoor (1996), 'The world's largest democracy spent 22 months as the world's largest banana republic.'

During this turbulent period, some dared to express their resistance through art with deft subversive techniques. There was also the secret circulation of Emergency literature. Many writers were imprisoned and silenced. As press censorship was in force, some print media editors dared to mock oppression itself by publishing blank pages as eloquent editorials.

When the Emergency was lifted, anger and frustration poured out to form a sub-genre of Emergency literature, mainly in regional languages. In English, Nayantara Sahgal, Salman Rushdie, and Shashi Tharoor have also dealt with this theme in their works. However, Rohinton Mistry's *A Fine Balance* (1996) is the most striking narration of the Emergency horror. It is not always an external enemy that destroys peace, rips the democratic/secular fabric, or robs you of your freedom. Some journalists-turned-creative writers have attempted to exorcize their haunting fear through art. Based on real-life events, their literary works seek reassurance of faith and stability in the sacred institutions of democracy and the judiciary; they attempt to reclaim the rights of all citizens.

Democracy is on the decline, constantly getting redefined, its very spirit stifled in different parts of India. So it is crucial that we should recall, remember, recount, record, and narrate these memories to the next generation, to the next and the next, so that the ugly events remain in the past and not invade the present. Narrating memory is a life-affirming exercise, an ethical responsibility.

The haunting story of the disappearance of Rajan, a lively student of the Regional Engineering College (REC), Calicut, was published by the journalist Jayachandran Nair. In 1989, it was made into a disturbing political film, *Piravi*, by Shaji Karun. The disappearance of Rajan jolted the student community in the 1970s. The film about a father's pathetic search for his son (called Raghu in the film) and the vulnerability/helplessness of people in an oppressive system connected with the audience instantly. The film was a sweeping success.

The 80-year-old father, a retired teacher, returns home to despair after the last bus each night, to resume his walk of hope, his bus and boat ride, in the morning. His days begin with hope and determination and end in sheer despair. The viewers accompany him, heavy-hearted, knowing well that it will be a repeat experience of the day before, the day before that, and the day before that. The eyes of actor

Premji convey hope and agony in alternation. Lightning, thunder, and rain heighten the utter helplessness of the family. The lush greenery that he trudges through each day is in contrast to the parched emotions of the family.

A newspaper report of Raghu's arrest brings relief and the father clings to prayers and hope: his son is in jail, not gone, not dead. The sister, Malati, is aware that jail can keep a lie locked up, can keep truth locked up, leaving those outside clinging on to a lie as the truth. The Home Minister had once received assistance for his education from Raghu's father. That raises the father's expectations. But the minister helps only in sustaining the lie. The violent story has just one action: waiting; and just four characters: the father, the mother, the sister, and the boatman. The fifth character is kept off-screen, but his looming absence owns the screen. His absence is the very atmosphere; the futility of waiting is the lingering awareness.

The film has heart-wrenching moments. The mother goes insane with pain. For her, every entrant to the house is either Raghu or a messenger from Raghu. In the final scene, the father, who is holding on desperately to hope and prayers, slips and falls. The boatman, who ferries him day after day, extends his hand and helps him up. Delirious with grief, the father sees Raghu in the boatman. The rain-soaked village dampens and darkness descends. The father breaks into laughter, laughter of relief, laughter of triumph, and the viewers are left crying. The unseen presence of Raghu enhances the contemporary and universal appeal of the film. *Piravi* won 4 national awards and 31 awards around the world.

We recall another film, *Missing* (1982), by Costa Gavras, based on the book *The Execution of Charles Horman: An American Sacrifice* by Thomas Hauser. It is also based on a well-documented, true story: of the disappearance of a politically aware, Harvard-educated journalist during the military coup sponsored by the United States of America (USA) to replace President Salvador Allende in Chile. In the novel, the film, and in real life, after a determined search and legal efforts for seven long months, the journalist's wife and father manage to recover his body. Missing is an agonizing reality; absence becomes a fact of life; fear of missing becomes a state of mind. Some families such as Rajan's are fated to live without knowing the end. Condemned to an endless search, they shuttle between hope and despair. Their grief has no closure.

Memory narratives are important. We should continue to narrate these stories so that we do not have to live them again in reality. What was Rajan's offence? Rajan was a talented singer and a strong champion of the underprivileged and the dispossessed. As the Home Minister entered the venue of a college function during the Emergency, Rajan was singing a film song that seemed to make fun of those in power. Did Rajan aim the song at the Minister? Did he mean it? Did he time it for the Minister's entry? Did he deserve custodial torture and death? Did the family deserve such mental agony and irreparable loss? Is such state brutality justified?

The incident rocked the Kerala Assembly and finally the Home Minister was forced to resign. The father had a tough where-there-is-a-will-there-is-a-way attitude. But he painfully realized that where there was a law, there was always a loophole. He had to wait till the Emergency was lifted to file a case against the government. Professor T.V. Eachara Varier's first-hand account, *Memories of a Father*, which includes a photo of his young son Rajan, was published in 2004 by the Asian Human Rights Commission in Hong Kong.

Journalist C.P. Surendran was inspired to write his first novel, *An Iron Harvest*, based on Rajan's death and T.V. Eachara Warrier's fight for justice and to restore his son's honour. Rajan stands for many students who have disappeared and who were struck down in their youthful idealism. *An Iron Harvest* is dedicated 'to those who died believing and to those who survived their belief'.

Journalist turned novelist K.R. Meera's *The Gospel of Yudas* is another powerful memory narrative. It deals with post-Emergency trauma and the haunting fear of a return of the horror. The novel unsettles and jolts the reader out of complacency.

The Gospel of Yudas depicts a riverside Kerala village caught in an 'Emergency state of mind' four decades after the Emergency was lifted. A retired policeman who once revelled in prison ruthlessness is now imprisoned within his own body, crippled by Parkinson's disease. His fifteen-year-old daughter Prema carries the burden of familial guilt. Her obsessive allegiance to the Naxal ideology that her father had vowed to root out puts her on a relentless pursuit of Yudas, the broken Naxalite. Her attraction to Yudas is purely guilt-driven. Yudas cannot accept her love as he is obsessed with the guilt of betrayal. One burdened soul pursues another burdened soul.

Prema's love represents the call and challenge of life, but Yudas's loyalty is to the dead. He remains closer to corpses, dredging the brutalized bodies, including that of his beloved Sunanda, out of the river and gorges.

There is no instance in the novel of Yudas saving a dying or drowning person. It is invariably a bloated, disfigured cadaver that he surfaces with. Yudas had once refused to teach Prema how to swim, an act of and attempt at survival. Rejection of life is reiterated. Yudas had called out Sunanda's name in delirious pain, and he had not really betrayed the woman whom he loved the most. But the stoic Sunanda, the leader of the movement, could remain tight-lipped even during brutal interrogation. The Naxalite slogans that Yudas shouts as he plunges and surfaces are dismissed by people as the screams of a disoriented man. But Prema's chanting of 'Naxalbari Zindabad' is more an invocation of love and admission of familial guilt. With the river as her guide and route, Prema tracks Yudas down each time he goes missing. She calls him by his real name Das (meaning 'devotee') but he eludes her grasp each time to claim his identity as 'Yudas', the archetypal betrayer, a failed Naxalite and a failed lover. Romance is a luxury for those who live and die for ideology.

Prema eventually jumps into the water to dredge out the pregnant Sangeeta, Sunanda's niece, again an instance of the promise of life cut short. Is that Prema's act of expiation? An atonement of familial guilt? Is Yudas fated to remain the archetypal betrayer? Is his repeated immersion a baptism of sorts? Can he ever become a Das again? 'Let's run away. The world needs us. Our love. Sacrifice. Our blood ...' urges Prema (2016, 19). But he has no desire to respond to the call of redemption. Does Prema's idealism become a reality in death? In offering her life to save Sangeeta, Prema seems to romanticize the ultimate approval of Yudas and her commitment to Naxal ideology. But termination of life seals all possibilities of romance, love, or even living for a cause. What does *The Gospel of Yudas* teach? Every life, well- or ill-lived, offers its lessons. A teenager near the old torture camp asks, 'Didn't all that happen a very long time ago? It's all over! Could we just stop talking about it?' But a wise old man responds, 'You have to keep talking about them or such times will come back. Remind ourselves, and everyone, to talk about them—all the time' (2016, 108). The novel is a riveting and rewarding read.

Memory narratives matter. They help us endure pain, embolden us to seek answers, empower us to demand justice, and help us empathize with the victims. There are many roads to empathy. What is important is to *act* on that empathy.

Civil disobedience as promoted by Gandhi, Thoreau, Martin Luther King Jr, and Nelson Mandela claims the right to defy and disobey unjust/immoral laws (and face the consequences). Rosa Parks in black American history 'sat down' in the bus so that her fellow blacks could stand up and stand tall. Getting rid of the so-called 'enemy', inconvenient to the regime in power, is not uncommon in India, and the people who carry this out sometimes become highly decorated police officers.

When an individual shows inner courage and has the capability to oppose the big power gods, the social institutions and the state connive to enforce social barriers and establish hierarchy with brute force, to render that individual powerless—as seen in the treatment of the marginalized in Arundhati Roy's *The God of Small Things*. And the stories of Mahasweta Devi[1] illustrate how the custodians of the law crush dissent and gun down individuals who dare to defy them. Rape is used as a tool to subdue and suppress daring women. To use the words of James Baldwin ([1976] 2011): 'That victim who is able to articulate the situation of the victim has ceased to be a victim: he, or she, has become a threat' (115).

India has a history of riots. Every decade has been marked by an outbreak of violence. The 1984 violence against the Sikhs in the aftermath of Indira Gandhi's assassination by her bodyguards is an under-recorded piece of post-Independence Indian history. It is also under-represented in literature. After 33 long years, on persistent demand, the Wall of Truth inaugurated in the Rakab Ganj Gurdwara complex in New Delhi on 15 January 2017 sought to commemorate the 1984 carnage in which more than 3,000 Sikhs (and also non-Sikhs who tried to save the victims) were killed. We need to remember that it was not exactly a riot but targeted killing—selective killing of an easily identifiable denominational minority.

[1] Mahasweta Devi (1926–2016) was a Bengali writer and social–political activist.

Still under the shock of betrayal by the trusted bodyguards and forced into a political position that he never craved, Rajiv Gandhi had to face hundreds of microphones thrust into his face to capture every sound bite that issued from him. Just hours, barely a day, after the assassination of his mother, the media demanded an explanation from him for the violence that his party loyalists indulged in. The inexperienced leader gave an unfortunate response: 'When a big tree falls … the ground beneath it is bound to shake.'

Rajiv Gandhi's statement about 'the big tree' smacks of thoughtlessness, insensitivity, and irresponsibility. It inspired an IAS[2] officer, N.S. Madhavan, to write a story entitled 'Vanmarangal Veezhumpol' ('When Big Trees Fall'). This powerful story forms the basis of an amazing film, *Kaya Taran* ('Chrysalis'). The screenplay and direction are by Sashi Kumar (see Chapter 23, 'Where *Is* the Mind without Fear?'), winner of many prestigious best/eminent journalist awards. *Kaya Taran* (which earned him the G. Aravindan Best Debutant Film-Maker award, 2004) is a very sensitive depiction of the crisis of identity in a multicultural society. The film condemns the callous apathy of the state machinery, which amounted to complicity in the killing of Sikhs. Considering the enormity of the massacre, it is surprising that there are so few books or films on this subject. *Kaya Taran* is an exceptionally sensitive memory narrative, which stresses the need to deal with the past in order to come to terms with the present.

Sashi Kumar was a media correspondent in Bahrain in 1984 and had heard harrowing reports of the carnage from his Sikh friends. The horror stories had remained in his consciousness and continued to pain him. The 2002 Godhra violence brought back to him memories of the anti-Sikh carnage. Both these events are mere symptoms of the challenge of retaining and nurturing one's identity in a plural society. When we cry we do not see things clearly. When we are too close to a traumatic event, our perception can be distorted. Processed by time and memory, Sashi Kumar telescopes these two events of two different decades to contextualize the deep-seated prejudices. Despite assurances of equality enshrined in the Indian Constitution, and the lip-service paid to diversity and plurality, these events emphasize majoritarian intolerance and the vulnerability of minorities. When

2 Indian Administrative Service.

genocidal tendencies erupt, it takes very little for the unruly elements to unleash mob frenzy. This latent volatility makes fear the dominant emotion among the minorities. Fear can seep down to the next generation and the next.

Sashi Kumar shows a high level of human sensitivity and cultural awareness. Sikhism is a religion that reconciles two different faiths. Sikhs, who have for long enjoyed the reputation of being security *providers*, had to go into hiding. Even Bishen Singh Bedi, the former captain of the Indian cricket team, had to flee to safety with fellow Sikhs. The fleeing of these symbols of patriotism and courage has done great damage to the collective image and collective psyche of the Sikh community. No literary text or film has so effectively addressed the complex issue of identity crisis as *Kaya Taran*.

The film focuses too on the rich human potential for love and harmony. Feeble, cloistered Carmelite nuns, who live to recite rosaries, spring to action and demonstrate Christian compassion. The home for aged nuns in Meerut becomes a warm refuge for a Sikh mother and her young son, Preet, who climb over the high compound wall and escape as the rest of their family is butchered. The inner space of the nunnery is foregrounded as a site of history. The child victim, Preet, livens up the nunnery, adds joy to the chosen life of denials, adds colour to the nuns' black and white robes.

During the 1984 violence against the Sikhs, some people of other faiths—Hindus, Muslims, and Christians—rose in protest against the carnage and the police apathy, and risked their lives to save the Sikhs. One such real-life hero is the Church of North India's former Delhi Bishop, Rev. Maqbul Caleb, the author of *Count Your Blessings*. He dared the violent mob and literally turned both his home and church into shelters for the hounded Sikhs. Much-loved and respected by people of all religious affiliations in Delhi and Dalhousie, he passed away in 2016. His death was mourned and his funeral attended by people of different faiths, particularly Sikhs. A live coverage of the hounding of the Sikhs and the role played by Rev. Caleb in Delhi are part of a documentary, *Riding the Tiger*, directed by Michael Singh.

When the Sikh mother and child are hiding inside, the perpetrators keep a watchful eye on the nunnery as they know that they couldn't have gone far. Sister Agatha, the administrator and caregiver of the nunnery, decides that she has to act if she is to save them, and save them she must. The only way the nuns can facilitate the escape of the mother and son is by destroying the identifiable markers of their religious identity. A traumatic scene follows. Preet wails when his hair is forcibly cut, the hair that he has had from his very origin in his mother's womb. For his mother, putting on a nun's habit to pass as a nun is a comparatively simpler way to safety. She is adult enough to understand the desperate need for them to fake their identity. Preet also has to fake death, in a desperate attempt to live. He is forced to undertake the bumpy ride out in a coffin. The trauma is mitigated in the film with a surrealistic dance of nun-like figures with long flowing hair around a Christ-like figure emerging from a coffin. The scene has suggestions of Mary Magdalene and religious conversion. Preet is reborn from the coffin as a non-Sikh. The question remains: is it possible for him to shed an intricate part of himself, to go turbanless and be at peace with himself?

The adult Preet's experience of suffocation in an elevator when the power fails is a reminder of his ride to safety in the coffin. Is the confined pupa (chrysalis) stage one of suffocation or of security? Is the coming out as butterfly, flapping wings, an experience of release and freedom? Is this a process of regeneration? By raising such questions, the film emphasizes the importance of nurturing one's own identity in a multicultural society.

Eighteen years later, Preet, now a journalist, returns to the same nunnery on a memory trail, commissioned to write a story on conversion after the 2002 massacre in Gujarat. His interaction with Sister Agatha is a liberating experience as it reconnects him with his troubled past and helps him come to terms with his memory and reclaim his real identity. His to-shave-or-not-to-shave stare at the mirror in the morning is significant. Preet washes off the lather to retain his two-day old stubble. He returns to his identity and freedom on his own terms, no longer tormented. Preet is turbaned and is at peace with himself. The man who goes to write a story on conversion returns converted. *Kaya Taran* includes self-reflexivity about journalism while dealing with the majoritarian violence of the 1980s and 1990s against minority communities. Journalists who had covered the Trilokpuri massacre of the Sikhs in real life play themselves in the film, which greatly enhances its impact.

Though *Kaya Taran* centres on violence, it steers clear of direct depiction of it. It is communicated to the viewers through the effective use of light and sound and also through the expression of fear by those in the nunnery. There are visual moments and musical moments that can leave us all silent and reflective.

The purpose of a memory narrative is not to encourage victims to look back in anger or provoke bitterness, but to seek answers and tap love and acceptance from humanity. It is important to find common ground for hope. We are handcuffed to history. In the words of Maya Angelou,[3]

> History, despite its wrenching pain,
> Cannot be unlived, and if faced with courage,
> Need not be lived again.

Memory narratives remind us of the terrible blunders of history and help us to learn life's lessons from them. Because, as Santayana teaches us, 'Those who cannot remember the past are condemned to repeat it' ([1905–6] 2017, 92).

The print and visual texts that I have referred to continue to offer valuable lessons for India today. They teach us to question individual attitudes and institutional policies. Is India rising? Is India shining? Should alleviation of poverty and communal harmony not be our primary concern in the aspirational policy? Should we only talk about development and corporate tax?

Fringe elements have the potential to trigger diet politics (see Chapter 17, 'Caste on the Plate') or caste politics in order to oppress, destroy differences, and hegemonize. It is the duty of the state to put down riots and to offer protection to *all* its citizens. The Emergency may be over but not the Emergency's highhandedness and police excesses: 'custodial deaths' and 'encounter deaths' continue to happen, making the sinister abbreviations CD and ED part of police lingo and human rights lingo.

The 2017 New Year calendars took political centre stage for more than one reason. The Jammu & Kashmir Bank claimed that it showcased successful Kashmiri youth on its calendar in order to spread the message of social upliftment. The APDP (Association of Parents

[3] From her poem 'On the Pulse of Morning', which she recited at the 1993 Presidential Inauguration of Bill Clinton.

of Disappeared Persons) reacted by bringing out a different calendar, featuring just 12 young people to represent the 7,000 and more persons missing since 1989, and demanding immediate governmental action. This conflict of calendars signifies a conflict of perspectives, a conflict of messages, and a conflict of political positions. Time moves on, and we flip page after page in our calendars. But the human predicament remains the same. The days of missing children are not over, even in the capital city. Young students are brutally silenced. Parents continue their search in agony.

Can history be healed? Is tragedy to be watched when enacted, recorded, and forgotten in the name of forgiveness? The Anglican Rector of Liverpool, Canon Nicholas Frayling, has a meaningful response to this question:

> I used to think the answer was straightforward. The way to deal with the pain of history was to forgive and forget. The trouble is, forgive and forget does not work because it is untrue to human psychology and it is bad theology as well. The only way to deal with pain and resentment is not to forgive and forget, but to remember and repent or, more realistically, remember and change. (2000)

You cannot and should not deny but accept reality. There is a Jewish saying that is quite appropriate here:

> Deliverance comes through memory. Forgiveness is only possible through memory. And he who suppresses, he who forgets, lengthens our imprisonment. (Quoted in Stubley 2008, 221)

It is in the darkest moments that we should seek light through memory. History has its lessons. Memory narratives matter. They are a call for justice; they make a demand to restore honour to the victims.

Memory narratives matter. To quote Shashi Deshpande's lines from *Small Remedies* (2000):

> Memory, capricious and unreliable though it is, ultimately carries its own truth within it. As long as there is memory, there's always the possibility of retrieval, as long as there is memory, loss is never total. (324)

Memory should narrate itself, as it is a definite step towards healing. Memory narratives are a wake-up call to remember and reset our moral compass. They are a call to establish a where-the-mind-is-without-fear space for us and for others. Memory narratives are thus agents of change.

22

Stories

HILDA DAVID

I was driving with J in an Uber. She is in her mid-forties. Her husband is a Shetty.[1] Two sons. The elder son works for an IT firm. She drops him off to work and then surges forth to conquer the roads. She was Hindu. Now she is not. She said to me, one big reason is how they look at lower castes. And the other? I ask her. She replies, 'How they see women.'

That's why these Hindus say Kaliyuga[2] is here. Since the lower castes and women have a voice.

J, who believes in the religion of humanity, says there are only two-and-a-half castes. The man caste, the woman caste, and transgender.

She drops me off for a show.

Curiously enough, the show I was about to see was *The Gentlemen's Club*.[3]

[1] The Shettys are a community, originally a warrior caste group from Karnataka, now largely urbanized and often found in Mumbai.

[2] The 'final age', one of discord and spiritual degeneration.

[3] *The Gentlemen's Club* (original title, *Tape: The King of Drag)*, written by Vikram Phukan and devised by the theatre group The Patchworks Ensemble, opened in Mumbai in 2015.

It's about a gender switch.

Someone told me this is the theatre theme of the season. In total, eleven plays about gender. Men playing women. And women playing men.

Also solo plays.

Why? I am asked.

I guess because it is always the solo voices that have a story to tell.

The Solo Voice of Ara

One such solo voice was that of Krishnaji Howlaji Ara (6 April 1914–30 June 1985). Born in Bolarum near Hyderabad, he had a darkish complexion, below-par looks, and an unimpressive persona. He was a bachelor and he painted sumptuous female nudes.

I met an art historian and he narrated the saga of this painter.

Ara's mother died when he was three years old and his father remarried. Ara's father was a cleaner. Ara escaped from his witch of a stepmother at the age of seven.

Ara worked for a European lady as a houseboy. His passion and talent for painting were noticed by the European lady who purchased watercolours and paper for him so that he could draw and paint during his spare time. That's how the small boy got appreciation and encouragement.

Ara worked with an Englishman, C.C. Gulilan, in 1930. Like his father, he earned his living through car cleaning.

Ara participated in the Indian freedom movement. He was part of Mahatma Gandhi's Salt Satyagraha, the famous Salt March of 1930, and was jailed. C.C. Gulilan felt sorry for him and Ara was released from prison after five months.

Ara cleaned cars at Yokohoma Corporation, a Japanese company, for a monthly salary of INR 18. The staff quarters were located at Walkeshwar within the premises of the company, where Ara was given a small room to use.

World War II commenced, Pearl Harbour was bombed by Japan, and the owner of Ara's company disappeared after this attack. Ara stayed in his staff quarters in Walkeshwar. This room remained his residence and studio till his dying day.

Ara's paintings grabbed the attention of Rudy von Leyden, an art critic from *The Times of India*. Through Leyden, Ara became acquainted with painters and artists in Mumbai.

Ara did not attend school. He had no formal training in art.

Ara's nudes were bold and brutal. His stepmother had ill-treated him and tortured him. The hate and the angst are evident in his nudes.

Ashish Balram Nagpal exhibited the paintings after Ara's death in 1991. Most of them were alleged to be fake. Rage and outrage!

Ara became famous as a painter, but died in extreme penury.

This is the story of art in this country.

The Tale of Vastraharan

There is another story, too. It's a bit more cheerful.

There is a play called *Vastraharan*. This is a play I love and relish. It has notched up 5,000 shows. And each time the play has stunned audiences with its rustic Malvani[4] and half-cracked style.

Vastraharan. The play is about a play within a play that almost doesn't happen (remember the climax in Kundan Shah's film *Jaane Bhi Do Yaaron*?). It's Malvani, it's *lok natya*,[5] and in spite of being rooted within the tradition of the Mahabharata, it's cutting-edge contemporary. In fact, with Machindra Kambli's deliberate style of misdirection, it is able to move outside the usual Marathi middle-class drawing room and language. There's nothing snobbish or smug about it; nor clumsy-preachy.

This was perhaps the reason why, in spite of the thousands of shows, the play never morphed into one of those 'classic productions' that could nationally cash in on its fame and glory, as lesser productions did during that time.

Which is a pity.

One big reason for the lack of official recognition for *Vastraharan* seems to be this: the play is immensely enjoyable. Critics say it lacks gravitas. I disagree. I think it's a delightful satire of a nationally constructed notion of tradition which has been shoved down our throats.

[4] A dialect of Konkani, with influences from Marathi, which is often used for newspaper articles and plays.

[5] Folk drama.

It has hilarious peccadilloes which are spot on, even prescient, and its call for a real organic memory of the Mahabharata is a superb antidote to anyone suffering through the excesses of 'taking one's culture too seriously'.

The play was penned in 1962 by a young Gangaram Gavankar, the 'class *vidushak*' (class clown) at the J.J. School of Art, who submitted his play to Damu Kenkre. These were the 20-odd pages of *Aaj Kaay Nataka Hovacha Naay*, which was penned in the college canteen. Kenkre kept the handwritten script in his college locker. A few days later the script was lost!

Gavankar re-wrote the play from memory. He did this four times. Each time that the gods tried to banish the play's script from the planet, Gavankar the playwright recreated it.

When you ask Gavankar, how so, he says: 'I have grown up on Dashavtari[6] folk theatre, which is performed by simple village folks during festivals such as Hanuman Jayanti, Ram Navami, and so on. I recall how the local actors would add unintentional humour.'

Consider this: Narad Muni delivers a long-winded dialogue without a hitch. On cue, his co-star aka Lord Vishnu nods his head in appreciation saying, '*Kya baat hein Bhagya* [the name of the actor playing Narad] you have learnt your lines well!' To which Narad Muni replies, in Malvani, 'Easier said than done. Do you know I sent my wife and kids packing off to her maternal home so that I could learn my lines with total concentration?' And following this interlude, the actors resume their divine roles yet again!

This play written in Malvani had absolutely no takers. Yet, five decades later, *Vastraharan* has staged its 5,000th show.

The plot is simple. With apologies to Ved Vyasa,[7] the play opens with Dushasana 'missing'. The actor's wife has threatened him with dire consequences if he does Draupadi's *vastraharan* (disrobing): she will walk out of the home with the children. So who is going to disrobe Draupadi's saree at the Kauravas' party?

The play is episodic and a comic tour de force whose humour, of observation and incident, explodes at every moment. Of course it

6 Connected with the ten avatars of Vishnu.

7 A sage and scribe to whom the authorship of the Mahabharata is traditionally ascribed.

helped to have Machindra Kambli, who played Tatya Sarpanch. And, on cue, to have Pu La Deshpande endorse the play as one of the finest examples of a farce; it catapulted the Bhadrakali production to a box office bestseller.

Note to self: *I think we are born each day, because every day has a story to tell and we are the stories we live. In the absence of stories, plays can suffice.*

Curiously enough, at the same theatre, Bhadrakali Productions' *Sangit Devbabhli* (*Thorn Tree: The Musical*), written and directed by Prajakt Deshmukh, is also the talk of the town.

It is a play about two unhappy women. Rukmani aka Lakhubai (the housemaid) works in the house of saint-poet Tukaram's wife, Avali (she with the angry, bitter tongue). The two actors, Shubhangi Sadavarte (Avali) and Manasi Joshi (Lakhubai), sing with aplomb. They and the orchestra deliver the music, by Anand Oak, with finesse.

Performed by two young actresses, the play reminds me of my favourite passage in literature in Dostoyevsky's *Brothers Karamazov*. Ivan (the brooding atheist) has a hallucinated encounter with a shabby aristocratic devil, who refutes his complex atheism.

Granted, Prajakt Deshmukh is no Fyodor Dostoyevsky!

Even today, three out of five Indians are rural peasants.

So, are they poor, uneducated, superstitious, and illiterate? Or are they 'the real people'?

In most towns, the way of life has hardly changed in the past hundred years. D.B. Mokashi[8] celebrates this in *Palkhi* and *Anandovari*, and Deshmukh celebrates it in *Sangit Devbhabhli*.

Everyone knows everyone, everyone sports the same clothes, everyone's hair is cut in the same way, everyone eats from the same food bowl, everyone sleeps in the same room. But contrariwise there are also toilets in the open air, high death rates due to waterborne diseases, spitting into a person's eye to get rid of a sty, feeding children mouth to mouth or calming baby boys by stroking their penis.

The two women play out their parts until the lesson is learnt and Lakhubai aka Rukmini returns to her husband.

[8] A Marathi novelist and short story writer of the immediate post-Independence generation.

And as you exit the hushed auditorium, you realize that the overall life statistics have not improved and we remain a malnourished lot.

The Myth of Vitthal

Then there is the myth of Vitthal.[9] How does one negotiate it? That evening I came across a small palimpsest about Dr B.R. Ambedkar.[10]

In 1929, Ambedkar presided over a meeting at Trymbak. There was talk of building a memorial in the name of Chokhamela.[11] Ambedkar was not enamoured by Chokhamela since he found him willing to accept the status quo. Ambedkar said that rather than building a memorial, one should remove the blot of untouchability.

His words were:

> The appearance of Tulsi leaves around your neck will not relieve you from the clutches of money lenders. … You will not get salaries at the end of the month because you make pilgrimages to Pandharpur. (Quoted in Conway 2017, 7)

I am told that Ambedkar's family members were followers of the Kabir and Ramananda Bhakti and Yalkot sects. For instance, his wife wanted to make a pilgrimage to some of these places.

Ambedkar would not allow her to because he knew she would not be allowed into the temple. So he consoled his wife and family members, saying,

> What of that Pandharpur which prevents its devotees from seeing the image of God? By our own virtuous life, selfless service and spotless sacrifice in the cause of downtrodden humanity we would create another Pandharpuri. (Quoted in Conway 2017, 8)

[9] The temple of Vitthal (a form of Krishna or Vishnu) at Pandharpur is the most heavily visited temple in Maharashtra.

[10] Dr B.R. Ambedkar (1891–1956): Inspirational Dalit leader and principal architect of the Indian Constitution, a major figure in modern Indian history.

[11] A fourteenth-century saint from Maharashtra. As a member of the 'low-caste' Mahar community, Chokhamela was forbidden access to the Pandharpur temple—as was Dr Ambedkar, also a Mahar, in the twentieth century.

Note to self: *Is such a rationalist view tenable in this day and age?*

Answer: *A friend says, 'But of course! Look at Gopal Ganesh Agarkar, an uncompromising secular rationalist; an agnostic and one who believed in the life here and now.' Historian Aravind Ganachari calls Agarkar* dev na mannara dev manoos *(the godly man who did not believe in God). Ganachari sincerely believes that a secular rationalist approach to today's problems is the only solution. Unfortunately, the reality is that Agarkar, while revered by intellectuals, remains the least followed among the pantheon of Marathi leaders.*

But Why ...

Science brings me to Michael Frayn's *Copenhagen*. This text has recently been directed by Sharad Bhutadia in Marathi. It was staged by his team from Kolhapur and they managed to ensure that the piece was uncontaminated. In this day and age of TV aesthetics, that must have been tough.

The first line ('But why?') is extraordinary. When I first saw the play in London, I was so jealous of Michael Frayn. It is a stroke of genius! The line is on a par with the opening line of *Hamlet*: 'Who's there?' But unlike *Hamlet*'s opening line, that 'But why?' *is* the play, to my mind. It says everything ...

So why *did* Werner Heisenberg come to Copenhagen?

Niels Bohr was a great scientist and a man of huge culture. Why was he fearful of the Gestapo and what they could achieve?

The play is also about the friendship between Bohr and Heisenberg. Was it a genuine friendship? Was it one-sided, or was there friendship on both sides? Was it a professional friendship, or manipulative? Did it get destroyed forever on the night of the meeting?

But why?

A problem with the text is that it is based on Thomas Powers's book, *Heisenberg's War*. Powers was a science journalist, but many historians of science say he was an unreliable one. The play is therefore based on shaky ground, since Powers totally absolves Heisenberg of all his fascist Gestapo connections.

Like in all great texts, there is a postscript.

The play edition I have has a postscript by Frayn. There is also a post-postscript. Both are helpful. Especially in the case of the two letters released by the respective families. The Bohr letter was written and re-written (philosopher that he was, he dithered for years) before he sent it. As for the Heisenberg letter, it was written to his wife Elisabeth while Heisenberg went to Copenhagen. Again, historians say both letters are PR missiles, but they reveal a lot. Interestingly, Heisenberg's letter was never posted because he was afraid of the Gestapo.

Note to self: *The great plays have postscripts which haunt you ever after.*

The Glass Menagerie

I read the Tennessee Williams biography by John Lahr. It's a tragic tale about the transformation of the great American playwright into the *rakshasa*[12] he became as he aged.

It's true, the more precocious you are, more ungraceful is your fall.

And so, for me, watching bohemian poet-cum-brother-cum-son Tom in Rage's production of *The Glass Menagerie* was interesting, especially since I knew that when he (Tom aka Tennessee Williams) grows up, he will die alone in a hotel room, aged 71. His biographer John Lahr has hinted that Tennessee Williams's death was deliberate, since he was filled with despair at the loss of his art, but it may just have been a banal accident.

I flashed back to Chicago, a year before I was born. This is where the play opened after World War II (with twenty-four curtain calls on opening night, it is said).

Most people feel that *The Glass Menagerie* is Amanda's play. But I have always thought this was Tom's play. Alas, Tom, the anti-hero of sorts, was Tennessee Williams's anti-fascist critique of white orthodox American society.

It is all very confusing. Because today, in Trump's United States of America (USA), the tables have turned. The white Catholic Amanda has won.

Tom is irrelevant/insignificant and fading away like an old black and white photograph.

[12] Demon.

Note to self: *I walk home with a sigh for Tom, Tennessee Williams, and even the USA. The loudest sigh is reserved for us. RIP.*

Hai Rui Dismissed from Office

The Kisan Long March of 2018 began its trudge on 6 March from Nashik and entered Mumbai on 12 March. The anniversary of the Salt March. The dots are joining as you can see: Ara and even Frayn's 'But why?'

In 2018, more than one lakh[13] farmers had protested in Nashik. The 180 kilometre, six-day march started after the government did not fulfil its promises. On 12 March, a written agreement conceding to the demands was sought. The government had six months to deliver.

I recalled a play and decided to read it. It was a Chinese play penned by Wu Han for the Peking Opera in 1959–60. It was called *Hai Rui Dismissed from Office*. He revised it several times before the final version of 1961 (*Wikipedia*: 'Hai Rui Dismissed from Office').

In the play, Hai Rui speaks up for the peasants:

> You pay lip service to the principle / that the people are the roots of the state / But officials still oppress the masses / while pretending to be virtuous men / They act wildly as tigers / and deceive the emperor / If your conscience bothers you / you know no peace by day or night.

But that's not why I recall the play. It was the role played by Yao Wenyuan in relation to the play, soon to become a member of the notorious Gang of Four.[14]

Yao Wenyuan fancied himself as Balzac to Mao's Napoleon, wielding his 'golden' pen to smite the bourgeois intellectuals and 'right deviationists' who might get in Mao's way. When the *Hai Rui* play was staged, Yao Wenyuan wrote the most brutal theatre review of all time.

He checked himself into a sanatorium, pretending to be ill, in order to write his 10,000 words of diatribe against the play—the review was so tedious that the *Beijing People's Daily* published it as a piece

[13] A lakh is a unit in the Indian numbering system equal to 100,000.

[14] A group of prominent Chinese Communist Party officials who were deeply involved in the notorious so-called Cultural Revolution of 1966–76.

of 'Academic Research'. Like the play, there were many drafts of the review—ten is the most often-quoted number—three of which Mao wrote himself. The core argument, however, was Yao's: 'If we do not clean up, it will harm the people's cause.'

The play review, published in 1965, unleashed a great purge.

That's why theatrewallahs like me believe that play reviews are dangerous things (poor attempt at a joke).

More articles followed in the Chinese newspapers and journals attacking public figures in the name of party purity. From January 1967, factories, banks, and power plants were seized nationwide, while the Red Guards and the army sought out, terrorized, or simply killed anyone who agreed with the play and disagreed with the criticism. Yao was in charge of propaganda: so the hate-filled articles, the staged 'free debates', and the 'big-character' posters and banners and cartoons can to some extent be traced back to him. Thousands died. Wu Han died in prison in 1969.

Cut to the 21st century: Yao Wenyuan, the last of the Gang of Four, died on 23 December 2005, aged seventy-four.

In China, Chairman Mao is long gone. Others now determine the path that China should take.

But the play has been restored and is studied; and the playwright has a statue in his honour.

Note to self: *Don't despair. Sometimes the walls are the publishers of the poor.*

Chaka Darpan and *Malharaoche Nataka*

As the playwright Ramu Ramanathan once told me, every Indian citizen who sees a play should be aware of *Chaka Darpan* and *Malharaoche Nataka*.

This is our history.

But why?

The Dramatic Performances Act came into existence in 1876. Two plays *Chaka Darpan* (in Bengali) and *Malharraoche Nataka* (in Marathi) were silenced. And ever since, this Act has been used in a deadly combination with Sections 124A (sedition), 153A (incitement to communal disharmony), and 144 (joining unlawful assembly) of the Indian Penal Code. Many such laws should be reframed in Independent India.

Our babus take pride in continuing the colonial legacy of repression. Which is why that beast called freedom of expression is pretty much a sham.

Or is it?

23

Where *Is* the Mind without Fear?

The Paul Linder Love Endowment Lecture, 2017*

SASHI KUMAR

Thank you for that very hearty welcome—an overly generous introduction. It is indeed a pleasure to be back at The American College after about a decade, although the sombreness of the decade is underlined by the absence of the person we are celebrating today. Distinguished faculty, alumni, students, guests, and friends: when Dr Nair and Dr Premila Paul invited me to speak to you again, to be in this college again, I had no hesitation in accepting because of the virtual presence of Dr Love, the warmth of a presence I have cherished.

Although my interaction with him has been brief and not continuous, the warmth of the presence becomes even more significant at a time when warmth, when an atmosphere of love, of bonding, of fraternity, of

* This is a slightly abridged version of the lecture given by Sashi Kumar on 14 September 2017, in the Paul Linder Love Endowment Lecture Series at the Study Centre for Indian Literature in English and Translation (SCILET) at The American College, Madurai, India. We are grateful for permission to print Sashi Kumar's lecture.

solidarity are under dire threat.[1] Dr Nair said we are here to celebrate Dr Love. Indeed, we should celebrate Dr Love, because there is little to celebrate these days and it is only on campuses, in crucibles of learning and thinking where the mind is, hopefully, still without fear, that one can celebrate intellectuals, humane personalities such as Dr Love. It was mentioned here that one of his abiding principles was that there should be disagreement, there should be debate, diversity of views, and pluralism, all of which are under threat. It is only again in the protected environment of the university, in the make-believe world, if you like, of the university, that one can assume that there is a freewheeling atmosphere of interaction, debate, pluralism, disagreement, and diversity.

The world out there is increasingly strange. It is increasingly intimidating. It is increasingly despairing—and dismaying. The world out there is not the world we recognize. It is not the world we deserve. Seventy years after Independence, if we must think again and again before we say anything, if we must worry about what we will appear to be seen as when we do or say something, if we must look over our shoulder to make sure we are not being targeted physically or metaphorically … what has that independence brought us? What is that independence worth?

Many years before that historic occasion when we gained Independence, the poet laureate sang:

> Where the mind is without fear and the head is held high;
> Where knowledge is free;
> Where the world has not been broken up into fragments;
> By narrow domestic walls;
> Where words come out from the depth of truth;
> Where tireless striving stretches its arms towards perfection;
> Where the clear stream of reason has not lost its way;
> Into the dreary desert sand of dead habit;
> Where the mind is led forward by thee;

[1] In his introductory words before the lecture, Professor R.P. Nair said, 'Paul Love has always been described as a man who was the embodiment of love, compassion, and also courage. He was a unique person, a very rare blend of compassion and courage. These are the qualities that we do need in India today.' The speaker, too, moves from the outstanding qualities of Paul Love to the precarious situation in which India now finds itself.

Into ever-widening thought and action;
Into that heaven of freedom, My Father, let my country awake![2]

We have heard the flip side of that poem here by one of your scholars[3]

At midnight on 14–15 August 1947, our first Prime Minister of India, Jawaharlal Nehru, inaugurated us into a new chapter of freedom with words written in letters of gold that are etched in our minds:

> Long years ago, we made a tryst with destiny, and now the time comes when we shall redeem our pledge, not wholly or in full measure, but very substantially. At the stroke of the midnight hour, when the world sleeps, India will awake to life and freedom. A moment comes, which comes but rarely in history, when we step out from the old to the new, when an age ends, and when the soul of a nation long suppressed, finds utterance. It is fitting that at this solemn moment we take the pledge of dedication to the service of India, and her people, and to the still larger cause of humanity.

And he continued:

> The ambition of the greatest man of our generation has been to wipe 'every tear from every eye'. That may be beyond us, but so long as there are tears and suffering, so long our work will not be over.

Have we, we need to ask ourselves, now stepped out from the old to the new? *Is* it a nation whose soul has been liberated? *Has* the ambition of the greatest man of our times, Gandhiji, come anywhere near to being fulfilled? To wiping 'every tear from every eye'?

We are in a very defining moment—in all the negative sense of the word 'defining'. Because the values that our freedom fighters, the pioneers of our constitution, stood for are being challenged on a daily basis: our values of pluralism and secularism. The very preamble of our Constitution is being challenged, contested, even ridiculed, on a daily basis. The preamble of the Indian Constitution says that we

[2] Rabindranath Tagore's famous Bengali poem, here in his own English translation, may have been written as early as 1900. The English version was published in 1912, in *Gitanjali*.

[3] Sanjukta Dasgupta's modern update of the poem, included in this book (Chapter 8, 'A Failed Dream'), was read out just before Mr Kumar's speech.

are a sovereign socialist secular democratic republic. All of these are important. Sovereign ... socialist ... secular ... democratic ... republic. What we have instead is a very strong contestation of these entirely liberal values, these plural values, which have been the cornerstone of our belief in democracy. Today, therefore, the big question before us is: 'Is there a mind without fear?' Or: 'Where *is* that mind without fear?'

Economically, of course, it has made no difference. Seventy years after Independence we continue to be embattled economically. We remain a society where the poor, the marginalized, continue to live by and large outside the visibility of our collective consciousness. They are marginalized not just in absolute physical terms but also in terms of the representation they get in the media. When we speak about dramatic growth stories of our GDP, it is of course rendered ridiculous by the fact that all that growth hasn't trickled down to this marginal section, which is both substantive and substantial in our country.

Socially, we are caste-bound; identity politics rides roughshod over us. We live in narrow silos, as it were, in a world broken down by narrow domestic walls, as Tagore said, where we are overly aware of our caste identities, our religious identities, our ethnic identities, our subnational identities, and where we live in these 'silos' literally and yet call ourselves a nation.

Our value systems have changed dramatically. We find it ridiculous that we should be doing anything for the other, for the poorer sections. In television debates, you will find anchors who are aghast when someone says we should give a subsidy to the poor. The anchor immediately asks, 'Did you really say *subsidy*?' As if 'subsidy' were a dirty word—a vulgar word, like 'terrorism'. So we have moved into a so-called globalized, liberalized jargon which is meant to unite mankind in the global sphere but has actually created more and more narrow casting. We are now more and more narrowly cast in our minds, in our mental mindsets.

Religiously, what was once a plural (shall we say) regime is increasingly becoming one where the hegemony of the majority is being established. The Constitution of India is secular in its ambition: it gives all citizens of India the right to practise their own religion, to profess their own religion, and to propagate their own religion. But today we find that there is, although it is not stated, almost a move, a subterranean move, towards what one could call a Hindutva state. And therefore the difference, if any, between Pakistan, a theistic state, and India is becoming very, very narrow and very notional. Because that was what once distinguished us. We are moving from a landscape of religious differentiation, of pluralism, to one of homogenized religion. And because Hinduism as a religion, as Mr Nair hinted in his introductory remarks,[4] does not lend itself to that homogeneity, because Hinduism has traditionally been a syncretic faith—Hinduism is not homogeneous, and does not lend itself to fundamentalism, because there is no text—all hell is now let loose.

No efforts have been spared to create and foist a false fundamental character onto this religion, which is why today we are told that there can be only one Ramayana, not a hundred. If you say 'a hundred Ramayanas' it is sacrilege. Because a hundred Ramayanas will not give you that one single fundamental text. And therefore the very nature of a religion is being distorted in order to create a false homogeneity, a preponderance of the majority, a control by the majority, which goes against the very grain of that religion.

The forces of Hindutva are certainly a threat to other religions. Islam primarily, Christianity, Judaism, all the other religions that we have, Sikhism perhaps too, but even more than that the forces of Hindutva are a threat to Hinduism itself. And it is not that these forces are really religious in the spiritual sense of the term. What we have here is the use of religion to mobilize the masses towards a political agenda … a political agenda which is very different from understanding, experiencing, and living religion in its spiritual dimension. So you have this subversion of religion from within even in Hinduism, and that is not Hinduism! Hinduism will not lend itself to that, and I have faith in the larger logic and the larger legacy, the larger heritage, the larger momentum of Hinduism, which will sooner or later defy this challange and throw it out!

India cannot be a Hindutva state. And Hinduism is not a Hindutva state any more than Islam is the Islamic state. That is a distortion of Islam, by those proponents who commit all their gory acts in the name of their so-called Islamic state. We see a similar trend happening in

[4] In his remarks, Professor Nair said, 'You cannot be a Hindu fundamentalist because there is nothing fundamentalistic about Hinduism. It doesn't have a foundation, it doesn't have a founder, it doesn't have a founding text.'

terms of the understanding of the majoritarian religion state, where there is a process of Othering … you Other the other, that which is different.

This is therefore an era of proto-fascism. It is not full-blown fascism. If it were full-blown fascism, we wouldn't be able to have this meeting, but the first few steps towards that have been taken. And it is in the nature of fascism not to have normalcy, not to have communal harmony, in society. It is in the nature of fascism to have a society that is always in a state of flux, of agitation, of turbulence. That was the nature of the ultra-fascist known as Hitler ('In normalcy a nothing, in chaos a titan'). And that is the nature of fascism.

If you look at what has been happening over the last few years, you find this engineered flux in society, this engineered instability, this polarization and communal division. In order for the spectre of proto-fascism to rise, we are socially, economically, and religiously in the realm of fear, uncertainty, and trepidation.

The Constitution of India is a great document. There are very few documents of such an exhaustive nature, because it had to take account of the multifarious requirements and demands, the various strands of society, in the dynamic that is India. And it is a tribute to the foresight of the framers of our Constitution, particularly Dr Ambedkar, who piloted it, that it is inclusive, comprehensive, and exhaustive. It has taken care of almost all possible eventualities.

Recently we had a very significant Supreme Court judgement, unanimously delivered by the bench, on the Right to Privacy as a Fundamental Right. But there are two articles in that Fundamental Rights chapter which are of even more importance. They are important at all times, but even more important today. One is Article 19 1A of the Constitution, Freedom of Speech and Expression. And the other is Article 21, which is an even more basic existential right: Protection of Life and Personal Liberty.

These two cornerstones, shall we say essential aspects, of our Constitution are being challenged on a daily basis. Where is the right to free speech, and where is the right to life? Because free speech now endangers your life. Is that what we deserve after 70 years of Independence? Free speech can be countered by even freer speech. Free speech can be countered by rude speech, if you like. If you don't like someone, troll them! That only shows your character. But if you send a motorcyclist with a helmet and a home-made pistol to challenge free speech, that is a very unequal battle. And that is what is happening now. Not once, not twice, but repeatedly.

There is no freedom of expression. There is no freedom to live.

So the question arises: What do these clauses mean? Are they worth the paper they are written on? We are in a dangerous situation in which this sacred document called the Constitution of India is being made a mockery of. It is being ridiculed. Free speech is now very dangerous, as we have seen recently in the instance of Gauri Lankesh. As I wrote in *Frontline*, whoever killed her killed her many times. They killed her physically. Not satisfied with that, they continued to kill her by killing her character, by assassinating her role, by being vicious, by spewing poison on the internet against her. And yet they continue to be enraged because, with all of that, her stature is still rising.

You kill a person and that person refuses to die—what do you do? You kill a person and that person grows even bigger than when she was alive—what do you do? And you thought you had perfected the art of killing! Because the ideas that she stood for, the ideas that Pansare (Chapter 14, 'Here Is a Country …') stood for, the ideas that Kalburgi (Chapter 15, 'The Spark in Their Words') stood for—of humanity, of fellow feeling, of reaching out to the poor and the marginalized, to the oppressed, and to the Dalits, and of countering unreason with reason and blind belief with science—such ideas make these people see red. So there is a kind of victory even in what is a physical killing, and there is abject defeat for *them* because that killing has only made it worse for them—because the ideas have suddenly grown manifold. The spirit of Gauri Lankesh is suddenly looming before them, and they don't know how to kill ideas. They haven't constructed a home-made pistol for that yet.

We are in a situation where our Constitution—the very cornerstone of our liberty—is what is at stake. And these matters are universal: our Constitution, the Universal Declaration of Human Rights, these are the principles by which you live in a modern society. You cannot be an exceptionalist with a philosophy or religion or ideology that says you are a law unto yourself and that *this* is the way to do it. Yet, whoever strays from their mark is to be punished or killed or taught a lesson. This is, I think, the essential dilemma and this fear is becoming overwhelming. But simultaneously I think that the voices against it are also gaining in strength—which is what the proponents of fear, the merchants of death, the retail traders in fear who unleash the street gangs are unable to combat.

This is The American College, so allow me to quote the resonant second sentence of the [United States] Declaration of Independence of 1776:

> We hold these truths to be self-evident, that all men are created equal, that they are endowed by their Creator with certain inalienable Rights, that among these are Life, Liberty and the pursuit of Happiness. (*Wikipedia*: 'United States Declaration of Independence')

Pursuit of happiness and not pursuit of fear, or sadness, or dread, or greed. That is what is sought to be denied. And then there is the fear of and by the media. I'd be remiss in my duty as a media practitioner if I didn't point out the key and culpable role played by a good section of the Indian media in feeding into this vicious atmosphere. Not in challenging it, or countering it, but in feeding into it. In capitulating before these regressive forces, in celebrating that regression and in adding to this whole environment of fear, dismay, depression, and sullenness that has overcome us.

You look at channel after channel after channel—they have stopped giving you news. They are telling you what to do. Short of saying 'Sit, stand, go eat and come back', they tell you everything else. And that is a pathetic situation to find yourself in, 70 years after Independence. The media are supposed to represent reality. They are supposed to describe the world to you, not to prescribe what you should be doing. The media are supposed to reflect what is happening, not set an agenda and pursue it and pretend that *that* is what is happening. You cannot create news. You can only report news. That is the cardinal principle of the media. But increasingly the media are manufacturing news and manufacturing consent for the establishment, for these regressive forces. So they are playing a pathetic role in the current situation. And the bigger the media, the worse the problem is.

So what are we to do? I think a good section of society is already aware of this. But it takes time for the silent majority in a country to act, to move against what they see as pernicious, as being against the essential values that they live for, but when they *do* move, the tipping point is reached very soon. And then this entire edifice, this entire make-believe of a homogenized state, of a hegemony of one religion, of the majoritarianism of one creed, will collapse. I am already beginning to see that difference in small but perceptible ways. Which is a tribute to the resilience of the Indian people, who will not be cowed.

It is true that the people of this country decided to give a new dispensation, a new ideology, a chance. Because the earlier government, I refer here of course to the last Congress government, was corrupt. And corrupt to an exponential degree. It is also true that the problems that we are facing today did not come to us overnight. This whole communalization of society, this whole pandering to what I call the saffron vote bank, was actually initiated by the Congress regime, and paradoxically under the prime ministership of a modern young man such as Rajiv Gandhi. It was during his time that the media were for the first time desecularized, by putting the epic *Ramayana* on prime-time TV on Doordarshan in the 1980s.

Now, there is nothing wrong with celebrating your epics, your cultural heritage. Absolutely nothing wrong! But when you use it again for the singular political purpose of mobilizing the masses for your elections, making them an electorate, seeing them as a vote bank, there is injustice both to the epic and, in the process of what you are doing, to democracy. It is a matter of record that Rajiv Gandhi called a film-maker named Ramanand Sagar, who is a box office film-maker who has made big films, and told him that he wanted *Ramayana* telecast on Doordarshan prime time: fifty-plus episodes on Sundays. Many of you were probably too young (or not even born) to remember this. But when that serial was telecast, the entire city, every city in India, came to a halt. There would be no traffic on the roads. And before the serial began, they would garland the television frame and do poojas[5]—which is fine.

What is *not* fine is the version of the Ramayana that was chosen. Which was the Tulsi Ramayana. As the scholar Romila Thapar has demonstrated, this is the Ramayana, or a version of the Ramayana, that was a response to a perceived Muslim invasion of India in the thirteenth century. So you choose a particular version of the Ramayana that has a combative element in it, and you exaggerate the combative element and convert a pacific, beneficent, munificent god-figure such as Rama into one that is aggressive, an invader, a ruthless warrior.

[5] Offer prayers.

If you look at the calendar art in Hindu homes in south India or elsewhere before the *Ramayana* serial became such a big hit, the standard calendar art depiction of Rama is as a god-figure standing pacifically with Sita by his side, Hanuman at his feet, and Laxman on one side, and blessing the world—which is indeed the pacific manner in which most gods who can be depicted are shown—you'll find that it is a recurring motif. But in the Doordarshan version, you have a Rama who is conquering, who is unleashing his arrow, or rather putting an arrow to his bow to unleash it and conquer the world. That iconic shift is significant because thereby you have not only desecularized the media, you have also done tremendous damage to the image of Rama as a pacific god. I am giving this as an example just to show how this has been worked. It has not happened overnight. The Congress regime sowed the wind and we today under the Bharatiya Janata Party (BJP) regime are reaping the whirlwind.

We are trying to 'fundamentalize' a religion which is fighting tooth and nail *against* being fundamentalized, because it is not in its nature to be fundamental. And therefore it is so that the biggest insult that the Hindutva forces are handing out is less to the minority religions than to the majority religion of the country, which is Hinduism. This is an insult which a Hindu, someone who is religiously or spiritually or philosophically a Hindu, should be really angry about, very, very upset. And I think that he or she is now beginning to get upset about it.

In ever so many ways, we have been seeing this whole process of homogenization going on before our eyes.

We have been seeing science replaced by mythology. We are told that the existence of god figures with animal traits proves that we had cosmetic surgery in Vedic times! (Although by that token, the Greeks must have been way ahead in terms of cosmetic surgery, because they had mythological creatures that were half lion, half human, or half goat, half man, or even triple beasts …) Is that an argument? I can understand these things being dealt with on the level of folklore, or on a metaphorical level, but this is now the stuff of papers at science congresses!

'Where the mind is without fear', the poet sang, 'and the head is held high, where knowledge is free.' But knowledge is not free. Knowledge is unfree. Knowledge is coming to realize that it must subscribe to a regime of unfreedom. So even knowledge is being marshalled. It is being requisitioned to this petty cause of homogenizing society, our culture, and therefore our politics. It should be a matter of dire concern for universities, for the crucibles of excellence and learning, of scientific dispute, and debate, that the current thinking in the corridors of power is that you cannot have that kind of debate and discussion, and that this is the way it should go. That science is to be used for religion; it is to be a handmaiden of religion, blind faith, and mythology.

This can have tremendous consequences for future generations. We are not talking about a temporary vitiation of all these values. This can have a huge impact a decade or two down the line. Institutions of excellence are being converted to mouthpieces of this ideology, of this kind of blinkered philosophy. And a man of the stature of A.K. Ramanujan was pilloried for speaking about a hundred Ramayanas, when we actually have a thousand.

It is important for this whole approach to stigmatize the Other. It is not enough to say: 'You don't belong to us.' Because you don't belong to us, we have to tar you with black paint. Sorry, that is the way it goes. This is the kind of majoritarianism, the excessive majoritarianism, that we have seen. And however they may try to control it, after a point they can't, because the street elements, the lumpen elements, have gotten out of hand. So you live with fear in the cultural sphere of censorship. Not so much formal censorship, or pre-censorship of cinema. The censor board, and the ridiculous things done until recently under the former chief of the censor board, are laughable. But the censor board is only a token body now. Whether the film you make will run in a theatre or not depends not on whether you get the censor certificate but on whether the street gangs will allow you to release the film and will allow viewers to come and see it. They will parse it, they will scrutinize it for anything that they see as damaging to your faith. So there is no validity even for pre-censorship.

We can notionally claim that there is no pre-censorship in other forms of the media, in print, in the press, on television, or online. There is only post-censorship, or post-consequence shall we say. If you say something silly that is defamatory or something that hurts someone's sensibilities or something that is seditious, you can be hauled up. But there, you do not have pre-censorship, you have what could be called pre-emptive censorship. Pre-emptive censorship, whereby the practitioners, the people who are involved as journalists or as media people, have begun to think about whether what they say or write or do on the internet, or in print, or on television, will upset so-and-so. So you are now constantly looking over your shoulder.

Where is freedom of expression in such a situation? And you are, whether you like it or not, beginning to say what they want and what they want to hear. And not what they *should* hear. This is the way, consensually, that the so-called media ecology is evolving. I think, therefore, that it is important, since most of you assembled here are young and it is your future that is more at stake than ours, that you should be interrogating these things, you should be analysing them.

I am not suggesting that you should go out onto the streets and start demonstrating, but that you should start filtering, you should start critically examining whether what I am saying is true or wrong, whether what you are seeing around you is a shift in terms of our trajectory of democracy. Is it beneficial or is it dangerous to our way of acquiring knowledge? Is the information that we are awash with through television, through the internet, through the cybersphere, of any use to us if it is not giving us the ability to draw a distinction between information and knowledge? Is that knowledge that, cutting through the clutter of information, you arrive at empowering? Is it transformative in nature? Will it make a difference to your lives and the lives of the majority of people around you?

This is your bounden duty as citizens, as young citizens of this country. Because it is *your* country, *your* society, it is *your* culture, it is *your* future.

We are taught on a daily basis what nationalism is. Isn't that an insult? Seventy years after Independence to be told that these are the ways to be nationalistic? You shall do this, or that, or the other. Who is telling us this? Those who are telling us this are those who were hiding under their cots during the Independence struggle. They would not have even participated in the Independence struggle. Those who are telling us this are those who wrote craven letters of apology to the British. Those who are telling us this are those who would not hoist the national flag in their party headquarters until the 1970s. They would only hoist their party flag. And *they* are telling us, *they* are teaching us, what nationalism is? Isn't it an insult when they tell an Indian citizen that he or she is or isn't a nationalist, and that it is for *them* to decide? And to be told, through the media: 'If you say this, you are anti-national—go to Pakistan!'

At the drop of a hat, you are now told to go to Pakistan. It has become so repetitive that it is laughable (as if the Pakistan Tourism Board were paying them a commission)! How can you treat your people like that? How can you ask any Indian, 'Are you a nationalist?' when your own track record is so pathetic.

Nationalism, as Benedict Anderson has told us, is all about *imagined* communities (1983). On a given day, if all of us are reading the newspaper, that is an imagined community, because we are all thinking about and discussing the same thing. We may not be exaggeratedly nationalistic—and I don't think it is important to be. It is important to be patriotic and every Indian who was born in this country and is an Indian citizen *is* patriotic and doesn't have to be taught patriotism. 'Breathes there the man with soul so dead', sang the poet:[6]

Breathes there the man with soul so dead,
Who never to himself hath said,
'This is my own, my native land!'
Whose heart hath ne'er within him burn'd
As home his footsteps he hath turn'd
From wandering on a foreign strand?
If such there breathe, go, mark him well;
For him no Minstrel raptures swell;
High though his titles, proud his name,
Boundless his wealth as wish can claim;
Despite those titles, power, and pelf,
The wretch, concentred all in self,
Living, shall forfeit fair renown,
And, doubly dying, shall go down
To the vile dust, from whence he sprung,
Unwept, unhonour'd, and unsung.

That is patriotism, and none of these people who are advocates or champions of 'nationalism' would pass the patriotism test. Because

[6] Sir Walter Scott (1771–1832). The poem is 'Patriotism 1: Innominatus' (in *The Oxford Book of English Verse*, 1939 edition, 640).

they slunk away when it mattered. They would not lend their shoulders to the Independence struggle when it mattered. They rode pillion on the JP[7] movement and claimed that they were martyrs of the Emergency.[8]

So this is the nature of the conspiracy against this wonderful land called India. This is the nature of the conspiracy against this wonderful religion called Hinduism. This is the nature of the conspiracy against the plural values we have cherished, the conspiracy against our heritage, against the struggle that gave us that birthed Independence for which hundreds of thousands of our people gave their lives. And now they appropriate those icons. They have appropriated Gandhiji and are quick to take offence if you as much as suggest: 'Wasn't it one of you who killed Gandhi?' Because Gandhi is too deeply entrenched in the psyche of the people and you cannot yet (I say *yet*) dispense with him as you are now trying assiduously to dispense with Nehru or some of the other leaders of the Independence movement. But even as you pretend to be, shall we say, holding the tail end of the legacy of Gandhi, you quietly resurrect Godse[9] (who killed the Mahatma) and give that man cult status.

This is hypocrisy. It is not just a conspiracy, it is a conspiracy of hypocrisy. I am sorry if I am sounding so passionate about this, because this really does affect the elemental nature of what we are as Indians. This is actually an assault on our identity, far more than Aadhaar[10] cards are an assault on our privacy.

I am not surprised that the two come in tandem, through both Congress and BJP governments, to steal your identity. The biggest theft of identity that is taking place is by these instruments that are

[7] An incoherent populist protest movement inspired by Jayaprakash Narayan (1902–1979).

[8] A twenty-one–month period (June 1975 till March 1977) of dictatorial direct rule by Prime Minister Indira Gandhi in which she could rule by decree, suspend elections, and curtail civil rights.

[9] Nathuram Godse (1910–1949) on 30 January 1948, murdered Gandhi in the garden of the Birla House in New Delhi. A fervent Hindu nationalist, Godse had been a member of the right-wing, paramilitary Rashtriya Swayamsevak Sangh (RSS).

[10] Aadhaar is a twelve-digit, unique identity number given to all Indian residents and based on biometric and demographic data collected by the Unique Identification Authority of India (UIDAI).

laying bare your personal lives, your personal record, things that should be private. What does it matter if the Supreme Court then rules that privacy is a fundamental right? And so you see the contradiction between what the highest court of the land says and what the executive is doing. You see the contradiction between what the Constitution says and what, in the separation of powers, one arm of that separation, the executive, and another, the legislature, are sometimes doing.

You see also how the media are colluding in this. Nevertheless, there are, of course, some exceptional people in the media who are putting across the other side, which is how we know the way things are going. I am not broad-brushing or tarring the media. They have played a great role in bringing some of the terrible things that are going on around us to light.

Finally, I don't want you all going out of here with heads hanging and thoroughly dismayed and sullen and feeling hopeless about the future. I can sense that the resilience of India has been touched; its pride and dignity. However slowly that will gather momentum, I can see the process is in its beginning, in its nascent stages. SCILET is a literary institution, and so I keep quoting poetry! Therefore, as the poet Arthur Hugh Clough[11] (1819–1861) said:

> Say not the struggle naught availeth,
> The labour and the wounds are vain,
> The enemy faints not, nor faileth,
> And as things have been they remain.
>
> If hopes were dupes, fears may be liars;[12]
> It may be, in yon smoke conceal'd,
> Your comrades chase e'en now the fliers,
> And, but for you, possess the field.[13]
>
> For while the tired waves, vainly breaking,
> Seem here no painful inch to gain,

[11] 'Say not the Struggle Naught availeth,' in the *Oxford Book of English Verse*, 898.

[12] At this point, the speaker interjected, 'There is still that hope that fears may be liars. So let's prove those fears liars!'

[13] 'So *you* have to be involved!'

Far back, through creeks and inlets making,
Comes silent, flooding in, the main.

And not by eastern windows only,
When daylight comes, comes in the light;
In front the sun climbs slow, how slowly!
But westward, look, the land is bright!

If you look towards the horizon in the east during sunrise you will find that the east, where the sun is rising, is still dark because the sun hasn't risen yet. But if you per chance turn 180 degrees and look the opposite way, you'll find that it is already lit. So that is the nature of the hope that I see before us. And I am sure that very soon that light will fall.

On that hope, and thanking you again for this opportunity, I ask you to think through your lives—to think through the context in which you are living your lives—because these really are very significant and very decisive moments. This is a decisive phase in our history.

Thank you very much.

BIBLIOGRAPHY

Association of College & Research Libraries (ACRL). n.d. 'ACRL Framework for Information Literacy Sandbox—A Platform and Repository for Sharing Framework Materials'. Available at: http://sandbox.acrl.org (accessed 21 July 2020).

Adler, Nancy. 1997. *International Dimensions of Organizational Behavior*. Cincinnati, OH : ITP.

Akhtar, Shabbir. 1989. *Be Careful with Muhammed! The Salman Rushdie Affair*. London: Bellow Publishing.

Allcott, H., and M. Gentzkow. 2017. 'Social Media and Fake News in the 2016 Election'. In *Journal of Economic Perspectives* 31(2), 211–36.

Alvarez, A. 1959. 'London Letter'. In *Partisan Review* 26(2), 286.

Ambedkar, B.R. (1948) 2017. *The Untouchables: Who Were They and Why They Became Untouchables*. New Delhi: Kalpaz Publications.

American Library Association (ALA). 1989. 'Presidential Committee on Information Literacy'. Webpage no longer available at time of writing.

———. 2015. 'Framework for Information Literacy for Higher Education'. Chicago, IL: Association of College & Research Libraries. Available at: http://www.ala.org/acrl/standards/ilframework (accessed 21 July 2020).

Amis, Kingsley. 1978. 'Introduction'. In *The New Oxford Book of English Light Verse*. Edited by K. Amis. Oxford: Oxford University Press, viii–xix.

———. 1984a. 'Frightfully Good, Old Betjeman'. In *The Observer*, 20 May.

———. 1984b. 'My Friend John'. In *Daily Mirror*, 21 May.

Anderson, Benedict. 1983. *Imagined Communities: Reflections on the Origin and Spread of Nationalism*. London & New York: Verso.

Angelou, Maya. n.d. 'On the Pulse of Morning'. In *PoemHunter.com*. Available at: https://www.poemhunter.com/poem/on-the-pulse-of-morning-2/ (accessed 21 July 2020).

Anonymous (Joe Klein). 1996. *Primary Colors: A Novel of Politics*. New York: Random House.

Appadurai, Arjun. 1988. 'How to Make a National Cuisine: Cookbooks in Contemporary India'. In *Comparative Studies in Society and History* January, 30(1), 3–24.

Appignanesi, Lisa, and Sara Maitland. 1989. *The Rushdie File*. London: Collins.

AZ Quotes. n.d. 'Woody Guthrie Quotes'. Available at: www.azquotes.com/author/6039-Woody_Guthrie (accessed 21 July 2020).

Baldwin, James. (1976) 2011. *The Devil Finds Work: An Essay*. New York: Vintage Books.

Baruah, Sukrita, and Abishek Angad. 2018. 'Dadri Lynching: No Question of Returning Home, Just Hope Case Moves Quickly, Says Akhlaq's Kin'. In *The Indian Express*, 28 September. Available at: https://indianexpress.com/article/india/dadri-lynching-home-just-hope-case-akhlaq-kin-5377441/ (accessed 21 July 2020).

Basava. 1984. *Lord of the Meeting Rivers, The: Devotional Poems of Basavanna*. Translated by Kamil V. Zvelebil. New Delhi: Motilal Banarsidass–UNESCO.

———. n.d. *Basava Vachananjali: An Anthology of the Vachanas of Basavanna*. Available at: http://www.taralabalu.org/vachana_flipbook/ (accessed 21 July 2020).

Basham, A.L. (1954) 1980. *The Wonder That Was India* (in two volumes). London: Sidgwick & Jackson.

Bassett, Tony. 1984. 'Betjeman the People's Poet Dies'. In *Sunday People*, 20 May.

BBC News. 2017. 'Poland Asked to Explain Naked Nazi Gas Chamber Video'. In *BBC News*, 30 November. Available at: http://www.bbc.com/news/world-europe-42178470 (accessed 21 July 2020).

———. 2018. 'Buffalo Bottoms Prove Too Much for Iranian TV Censors'. 5 September. Available at: http://www.bbc.com/news/blogs-news-fromelse-where-45421865 (accessed 21 July 2020).

———. 2019. 'Indian Scientists Dismiss Einstein Theories'. 7 January. Available at: https://www.bbc.com/news/world-asia-india-46778879 (accessed 9 July 2020).

Beard, Henry, and Christopher Cerf. 1992. *The Official Politically Correct Dictionary and Handbook*. New York: Villard.

Beauman, Nicola. 1993. *Morgan: A Biography of E.M. Forster*. London: Hodder & Stoughton.

Beckett, Samuel. (1952) 1956. *Waiting for Godot*. English version. London: Faber & Faber.

———. (1986) 2006. *Krapp's Last Tape*. Originally published in 1958. In *Krapp's Last Tape and Other Shorter Plays*. London: Faber & Faber, 213–23.

Bennett, Alan. 1978. *The Old Country*. London: Faber & Faber.

Berger, John, Sven Blomberg, Chris Fox, Michael Dibb, and Richard Hollis. 1972. *Ways of Seeing: Based on the BBC Television Series with John Berger*. London/Harmondsworth, Middx.: BBC/Penguin.

Berners-Lee, T. 2010. 'Long Live the Web: A Call for Continued Open Standards and Neutrality'. In *Scientific American*, 1 December. Available at: https://www.scientificamerican.com/article/long-live-the-web/ (accessed 21 July 2020).

Betjeman, John. 1931. *Mount Zion*. London: Culcross Press.

———. 1937. *Continual Dew: A Little Book of Bourgeois Verse*. London: John Murray.

———. (1958) 1984. *John Betjeman's Collected Poems*. Compiled and with an Introduction by the Earl of Birkenhead. Fourth edition. London: Guild Publishing.

———. 1994. *Letters*: Vol. 1, *1926 to 1951*. Edited by Candida Lycett Green. London: Methuen.

Bhardwaj, Ananya. 2017. 'Muslim Boy Stabbed to Death on Train after Argument Turns into Religious Slurs'. In *Hindustan Times*, 27 June. Available at: https://www.hindustantimes.com/india-news/man-stabbed-to-death-2-injured-on-mathura-train-after-fight-with-passengers-for-allegedly-carrying-beef/story-BiJyILYlUloErWASvKQ51M.html (accessed 21 July 2020).

Biswas, Soutik. 2018. 'The Myth of the Indian Vegetarian Nation'. In *BBC News*, 4 April. Available at: http://www.bbc.com/news/world-asia-india-43581122 (accessed 21 July 2020).

Bosmajian, Haig. 2006. *Burning Books*. Jefferson, NC, & London: McFarland.

BRICS. 2015. 'Building Respect on the Internet by Combating Hate Speech. Nationale Studie Deutschland'. Available at: http://www.bricks-project.eu/wp/wp-content/uploads/2016/03/National_Study_Germany_German.pdf (accessed 21 July 2020).

Brown, Dennis. 1999. *John Betjeman*. Tavistock, Devon: Northcote House/British Council.

Brown, Mark. 2017. 'Royal Academy Prepares for the Great Spectacle'. In *The Guardian*, 6 July, 11.

BT Archives. Photograph Library. Ref: E7351.

Bulmer-Thomas, Ivor. 1985. 'Obituary: Sir John Betjeman 1906–1984'. In *Transactions of Ancient Monuments Society* 29, 218.

Caleb, Maqbul. 2006. *Count Your Blessings: The Autobiography of Maqbul Caleb, Bishop*. Dalhousie, HP: Maqbul Caleb.

Carr, N. 2008. 'Is Google Making Us Stupid?' In *The Atlantic*. Available at: https://www.theatlantic.com/magazine/archive/2008/07/is-google-making-us-stupid/306868/ (accessed 21 July 2020).

Case, D.O., and L.M. Given. 2016. *Looking for Information: A Survey of Research on Information Seeking, Needs, and Behaviour*. Bingley, West Yorkshire: Emerald Group Publishing.

Casson, Hugh. 1984. 'John Betjeman (Obituary)'. In *The Architectural Review* 176(1050).

Cavafy, C.P. 1961. *The Complete Poems of Cavafy*. Translated by Rae Dalven, with an Introduction by W.H. Auden. London: The Hogarth Press.

Chesterton, G.K. 1928. 'Our Note Book'. In *Illustrated London News*, 5 May, 780.

Churchill, Randolph. 1931. 'Review'. In *The Architectural Review* December, 70, 184.

Conway, Christopher. 2017. '"I Am the Mahar of Your Mahars": Cokhmel, the Modern Dalit Movement, and the Dalit Christian Theology'. In *The Apollonian* 4(1–2), 5–26.

Costello, M., J. Hawdon, and T.N. Ratliff. 2017. 'Confronting Online Extremism: The Effect of Self-Help, Collective Efficacy, and Guardianship on Being a Target for Hate Speech'. In *Social Science Computer Review* 35(5), 587–605.

Council of Europe. 1997. Recommendation (97)20 of the CoE, 30 October. Available at: https://rm.coe.int/1680505d5b (accessed 21 July 2020).

Courtney, C.R. 2017. 'Proposed German Legislation Threatens Broad Internet Censorship'. In *Committee to Protect Journalists*. Available at: https://cpj.org/blog/2017/04/proposed-german-legislation-threatens-broad-intern.php (accessed 21 July 2020).

Cunningham, Valentine. 1988. *British Writers of the Thirties*. Oxford: Oxford University Press.

Curtis, Anthony. 1984. 'Obituary: Sir John Betjeman'. In *Financial Times*, 21 May.

Dale, Peter N. 1986. *The Myth of Japanese Uniqueness*. London and Sydney/Oxford: Croom Helm/The Nissan Institute for Japanese Studies.

Dante Alighieri. 1986. *The Divine Comedy: Paradiso* (completed 1320). Translated by Allen Mandelbaum. New York: Bantam, 1986.

David, Hilda, and Francis Jarman, eds. 2017. *India Diversity*. Noida, India: Om Books International.

'Declaration of the Rights of Man—1789'. In *The Avalon Project: Documents in Law, History and Diplomacy*. Yale Law School, Lillian Goldman Law Library. Available at: http://avalon.law.yale.edu/18th_century/rightsof.asp (accessed 21 July 2020).

Delaney, Frank. 1984. 'Endpiece'. In *The Listener*, 24 May.

Delaney, Helen. 2010. 'Martin Creed, Work No. 227: The Lights Going On and Off, 2000'. In *Tate*, May. Available at: http://www.tate.org.uk/art/artworks/creed-work-no-227-the-lights-going-on-and-off-t13868 (accessed 21 July 2020).

Demetz, Peter. (1970) 1972. *Postwar German Literature: A Critical Introduction*. New York: Schocken.

Deshpande, Shashi. 2000. *Small Remedies*. New Delhi: Viking Penguin.

Diakopoulos, N. 2015. 'How Uber Surge Pricing Really Works'. In *Washington Post Wonkblog*, 17 April. Available at: https://www.washingtonpost.com/news/wonk/wp/2015/04/17/how-uber-surge-pricing-really-works/ (accessed 21 July 2020).

———. 2016. 'Accountability in Algorithmic Decision Making'. In *Communications of the ACM* 59(2), 56–62.

Doniger, Wendy. 2018. *Beyond Dharma: Dissent in the Ancient Indian Sciences of Sex and Politics*. New Delhi: Speaking Tiger.

Dostoyevsky, Fyodor. (1880) 1993. *The Brothers Karamazov*. Translated by David MacDuff. London: Penguin Books.

Drabble, Margaret, and Jenny Stringer, eds. 1987. *Oxford Companion to English Literature*. 1987. Oxford: Oxford University Press.

Driberg, Tom. 1931. 'Review'. In *Daily Express*, 12 November.

Eco, Umberto. (1980) 1989. *The Name of the Rose*. Translated by William Weaver. London: Picador.

Eliot, T.S. 1915. 'The Love Song of J. Alfred Prufrock'. In *Bartleby.com: Great Books Online*. Available at: http://www.bartleby.com/198/1.html (accessed 21 July 2020).

Ellis, Samantha. 2004. '*Pygmalion*'s Opening Night in London, 11 April 1914'. In *The Guardian*, 14 February. Available at: https://www.theguardian.com/stage/2004/feb/11/theatre (accessed 21 July 2020).

Ellis-Petersen, Hannah. 2015. 'Tracey Emin's Messy Bed Goes on Display at Tate for First Time in 15 Years'. In *The Guardian*, 30 March. Available at: https://www.theguardian.com/uk-news/2015/mar/30/tracey-emins-messy-bed-displayed-tate-britain-first-time-in-15-years (accessed 21 July 2020).

Epstein, R., and R.E. Robertson. 2015. 'The Search Engine Manipulation Effect (SEME) and Its Possible Impact on the Outcomes of Elections'. In *Proceedings of the National Academy of Sciences* 112(33), E4512–21.

European Commission. 2017. 'Antitrust Commission Fines Google €2.42 Billion for Abusing Dominance as Search Engine'. 27 June. Available at: http://ec.europa.eu/malta/news/antitrust-commission-fines-google-%E2%82%AC242-billion-abusing-dominance-search-engine_en (accessed 21 July 2020).

Evening Standard. 1984. 'Betjeman'. 21 May, leader page.

Fellion, Matthew, and Katherine Inglis. 2017. *Censored: A Literary History of Subversion and Control*. London: The British Library.

Finn, Peter, and Petra Couvée. (2014) 2015. *The Zhivago Affair: The Kremlin, the CIA, and the Battle over a Forbidden Book*. New York: Vintage Books.

Fishkin, R. 2017. 'The State of Searcher Behaviour Revealed through 23 Remarkable Statistics'. Available at: https://moz.com/blog/state-of-searcher-behaviour-revealed (accessed 21 July 2020).

Forsa Institute. 2016. *Ethik im Netz: Hate Speech*. Available at: https://www.medienanstalt-nrw.de/fileadmin/user_upload/lfm-nrw/Service/Veranstaltungen_und_Preise/Medienversammlung/2016/EthikimNetz_Hate_Speech-PP.pdf (accessed 10 October 2020).

Forster, E.M. (1908) 1988. *A Room with a View*. London: Guild Publishing.

———. (1971) 1987. *Maurice*. London: Guild Publishing.

———. (1972) 1979. 'The Purple Envelope'. In *The Life to Come and Other Stories*. Harmondsworth, Middx.: Penguin, 64–83.

Frayling, Nicholas. 2000. 'An English Repentance'. In *The Guardian*. 11 March. Available at: https://www.theguardian.com/uk/2000/mar/11/northernireland.comment (accessed 21 July 2020).

Frayn, Michael. 2003. *Copenhagen*. Student edition. London: Methuen.

Fuller, Roy. 1984. 'The Poet'. In *The Sunday Times*, 20 May.

Furbank, P.N. (1977) 1978. *E.M. Forster: A Life*. Originally published in two parts, 1977, 1978. New York and London: Harcourt Brace Jovanovich.

Gierow, H. 2017. 'Netzwerkdurchsetzungsgesetz verstößt gegen Menschenrechte'. In *Golem.de*, 9 June. Available at: https://www.golem.de/news/zensur-netzwerkdurchsetzungsgesetz-verstoesst-gegen-menschenrechte-1706-128290.html (accessed 21 July 2020).

Glancey, Jonathan. 1984. 'John Betjeman: Poet of Place'. In *The Architectural Review* 175(1048).

Goldberg, S.L. 1962. *Joyce*. Edinburgh and London: Oliver & Boyd.

Goodman, B., and S. Flaxman. 2016. 'European Union Regulations on Algorithmic Decision-Making and a "Right to Explanation"'. In *arXiv preprint*, arXiv:1606.08813. Available at: https://arxiv.org/pdf/1606.08813.pdf (accessed 21 July 2020).

Gracie, Carrie. 2012. 'Qin Shi Huang: The Ruthless Emperor Who Burned Books'. In *BBC News*, 15 October. Available at: http://www. bbc.com/news/magazine-19922863 (accessed 21 July 2020).

Gramsden, K.W. 1962. *E.M. Forster*. Edinburgh and London: Oliver & Boyd.

Greene, Graham. 1950. *The Third Man*. London: Heinemann.

———. 1955. *The Quiet American*. London: Heinemann.

———. 1960. *A Burnt-out Case*. London: Heinemann.

Grigson, Geoffrey. 1984. *Recollections*. London: Chatto & Windus.

Guinn, Jeff, and Douglas Perry. 2005. *The Sixteenth Minute: Life in the Aftermath of Fame*. New York: Tarcher.

Hall, Edward T. 1959. *The Silent Language*. New York: Doubleday.

Hankins, Justine. 2005. 'Flogging a Dead Horse'. In *The Guardian*, 15 January. Available at: https://www.theguardian.com/lifeandstyle/2005/jan/15/weekend.justinehankins (accessed 21 July 2020).

Harrison Studio. n.d. 'Portable Fish Farm: Survival Piece #3, 1971'. In *The Harrison Studio*. Available at: http://theharrisonstudio.net/portable-fish-farm-survival-piece-3-1971 (accessed 21 July 2020).

Hastings, J., ed. 1913. *Encyclopaedia of Religion and Ethics*. Edinburgh: T. & T. Clark.

Haucap, J., and U. Heimeshoff. 2014. 'Google, Facebook, Amazon, eBay: Is the Internet Driving Competition or Market Monopolisation?' In *International Economics and Economic Policy* 11(1-2), 49–61.

Hauser, Thomas. 1978. *The Execution of Charles Horman; An American Sacrifice*. New York: Harcourt Brace Jovanovich.

Hawdon, J., A. Oksanen, and P. Räsänen. 2017. 'Exposure to Online Hate in Four Nations: A Cross-National Consideration'. In *Deviant Behaviour* 38(3), 254–66.

Heilbut, Anthony. 1996. *Thomas Mann: Eros and Literature*. New York: Knopf.

Heine, Heinrich. (1823) 2013. *Almansor: Eine Tragödie*. Berlin: Michael Holzinger (CreateSpace).

Heneghan, Tom. 2004. 'Low Profile for German Koran Challenger'. From: *Reuters*, 11 November. Archived on the Wayback Machine Internet Archive. Available at: https://web.archive.org/web/20070107195840/http://www.tiscali.co.uk:80/cgi-bin/news/newswire.cgi/news/reuters/2004/11/11/world/lowprofileforgermankoranchallenger.html&template=/news/templates/newswire/news_story_reuters.html (accessed 21 July 2020).

Hewson, David. 1984. 'Memories of Betjeman Are Summoned by Bells'. In *The Times*, 30 June.

High Commissioner for Human Rights, Office of the. 2017. 'Mandate of the Special Rapporteur on the Promotion and Protection of the Right to Freedom of Opinion and Expression'. Available at: http://www.ohchr.org/

Documents/Issues/Opinion/Legislation/OL-DEU-1-2017.pdf (accessed 21 July 2020).

Hillier, Bevis. 1984. 'Betjeman's Way with the English Everyday'. In *The Arts Guardian*, 19 May.

———. 1988. *Young Betjeman*. London: John Murray.

Hyde, H. Montgomery, ed. 1990. *The* Lady Chatterley's Lover *Trial*. London: The Bodley Head.

I Keep Vigil of Rudra: The Vachanas. 2010. Translated by H.S. Shivaprakash. New Delhi: Penguin.

Ingrams, Richard, ed. 1971. *The Life and Times of Private Eye, 1961–1971*. Harmondsworth, Middx.: Penguin.

———. 1984. 'Poet of England'. In *The Spectator*, 26 May.

Isasi, A.C., and A.G. Juanatey. 2016. 'Hate Speech in Social Media: A State-of-the-Art Review'. Available at: http://ajuntament.barcelona.cat/bcnvsodi/wp-content/uploads/2017/01/Informe_discurso-del-odio_ENG.pdf (accessed 21 July 2020).

Jarman, Francis. 2014–15. 'Writing as Resistance?' In *American College Journal of English Language and Literature (ACJELL)* 3, 21–30.

Jenkins, Roy. (1987) 2012. *Stanley Baldwin*. London: Bloomsbury.

Jha, D.N. 2009. *The Myth of the Holy Cow.* Originally published in India in 2001 as *Holy Cow*. Delhi: Navayana Publishing.

Johnson, Samuel. (1755) 1785. *A Dictionary of the English Language*. Sixth edition. London: J., F. & C. Rivington, et al. Available at: https://archive.org/details/dictionaryofengl01johnuoft (accessed 21 July 2020).

'Joseph Beuys—Sculptor'. Available at: https://josephbeuys.wordpress.com/about/ (accessed 21 July 2020).

Josipovici, Gabriel. 1977. *The Lessons of Modernism*. London: Macmillan, 1977.

Joyce, James. (1916) 2000. *A Portrait of the Artist as a Young Man*. London: Penguin.

Jubany, O., and M. Roiha. 2016. 'Backgrounds, Experiences and Responses to Online Hate Speech: A Comparative Cross-Country Analysis'. *PRISM Project*. Available at: http://www.unicri.it/special_topics/hate_crimes/Backgrounds_Experiences_and_Responses_to_Online_Hate_Speech_A_Comparative_Cross-Country_Analysis.pdf (accessed 21 July 2020).

Julius, Anthony. 2002. *Transgressions: The Offences of Art*. London: Thames & Hudson.

Kahneman, D. 2011. *Thinking, Fast and Slow.* New York: Macmillan.

Kaiman, J. 2013. 'Tiananmen Square Online Searches Censored by Chinese Authorities'. In *The Guardian,* 4 June. Available at: https://www.theguardian.com/world/2013/jun/04/tiananmen-square-online-search-censored (accessed 21 July 2020).

Kalburgi, M.M. 2003. *The Fall of Kalyana: A Play*. Translated by Basavaraj Naicker. Bangalore: Basava Samithi.

———. 2010. *Marga*, I. Bangalore: Sapna Book House.

Kanavi, Shivanand. 2015. 'Prof. M.M. Kalburgi, a Tireless Researcher'. Published first on the author's blog and then in *Outlook*, 31 August. Available at: https://www.outlookindia.com/website/story/prof-mm-kalburgi-a-tireless-researcher/295207 (accessed 21 July 2020).

Karkare, Aakash. 2016. 'Why an Ex-Journalist Chose to Document His Dalit Culture in a Food Book'. In *Scroll.in*, 15 November. Available at: https://scroll.in/magazine/820140/why-an-ex-journalist-chose-to-document-his-dalit-culture-in-a-food-book (accessed 21 July 2020).

Karnad, Raghu. 2015. 'Murder in the Academy; M.M. Kalburgi's Dangerous Literary Studies'. In *The Wire*, 30 August. Available at: https://thewire.in/9597/yesterday-basavanna-today-kalburgi/ (accessed 21 July 2020).

Kashyap, Aruni. 2013. *The House with a Thousand Stories*. New Delhi: Viking Penguin.

Knobloch-Westerwick, S., B.K. Johnson, and A. Westerwick. 2015. 'Confirmation Bias in Online Searches: Impacts of Selective Exposure before an Election on Political Attitude Strength and Shifts'. In *Journal of Computer-Mediated Communication* 20(2), 171–87.

Komaromi, Anne. n.d. *About Samizdat*. University of Toronto Libraries. Available at: http://samizdat.library.utoronto.ca/content/about-samizdat (accessed 21 July 2020).

Krantijyoti Savitribai Phule Women's Studies Centre. 2009. *Isn't This Plate Indian? Dalit Histories and Memories of Food*. Pune: University of Pune.

Kriyavin Tarkalat Tamil Akarati (Dictionary of Contemporary Tamil). 1992. Edited by P.R. Subramanian et al. Chennai: Crea-A.

Lahr, John. 2014. *Tennessee Williams: Mad Pilgrimage of the Flesh*. New York: W.W. Norton.

Larkin, Philip. 1971. 'Introduction'. In *John Betjeman's Collected Poems*. Boston, MA: Houghton Mifflin.

———. 1984. 'Betjeman, from Obscurity to TV stardom'. In *The Daily Telegraph*, 21 May.

Lawrence, D.H. (1915) 2011. *The Rainbow*. London: Vintage Classics.

———. (1923) 2016. *Kangaroo*. CreateSpace Independent Publishing Platform.

———. (1928) 2007. *Lady Chatterley's Lover*. Ware, Herts.: Wordsworth.

———. 1996. *The Selected Letters of D.H. Lawrence*. Edited by James T. Boulton. Cambridge: Cambridge UP, 1996.

Lee, Newton. 2016. 'To Google or Not to Google'. In *Google It: Total Information Awareness*. Edited by N. Lee. New York: Springer, 3–52.

Leiner, B.M., V.G. Cerf, D.D. Clark, R.E. Kahn, L. Kleinrock, D.C. Lynch, J. Postel, L.G. Roberts, and S. Wolff. 2009. 'A Brief History of the Internet'. In *ACM SIGCOMM Computer Communication Review* 39(5), 22–31.

Lewandowski, D. 2008. 'Search Engine User Behaviour: How Can Users Be Guided to Quality Content?' In *Information Services & Use* 28(3–4), 261–8.

Lincoln, Abraham. n.d. 'Letter to Henry L. Pierce and Others'. In *Abraham Lincoln Online: Speeches & Writings*. Available at: http://www.abrahamlincolnonline.org/lincoln/speeches/speeches.htm (accessed 21 July 2020).

Linder, Douglas O. n.d. 'Testimony of Oscar Wilde'. In *Famous Trials*. Available: http://law2.umkc.edu/faculty/projects/ftrials/wilde/Crimwilde.html (accessed 21 July 2020).

Lord, Graham. 1984. 'Just a Simple Epitaph'. In *Sunday Express*, 20 May.

Los Angeles Times, The. 1984. 'Betjeman Obituary', 21 May, 14.

Machiavelli, Niccolò. (1532) 1974. *The Prince*. Translated by George Bull. Harmondsworth, Middx.: Penguin.

MacLeish, Archibald. (1926) 1985. 'Ars Poetica'. In *Archibald MacLeish: Collected Poems, 1917–1982*, 106–7. Boston, MA: Houghton Mifflin.

Madhavan, N.S. 1993. 'Vanmarangal Veezhumpol' ('When Big Trees Fall'). In *Higuitta*. Kottayam, KL: DC Books, 1993.

———. 1998. 'When a Big Tree Falls'. Translated by K.M. Krishnan. In *Indian Literature*, 183, January–February 41(1), 48–58.

Mandela, Nelson. (1994) 1995. *Long Walk to Freedom*. London: Abacus.

Mandelstam, Nadezhda. (1970) 1999. *Hope against Hope*. Translated by Max Hayward. New York: Random House.

Mann, Klaus. (1936) 1995. *Mephisto*. Translated by Robin Smyth. New York: Penguin.

Marzorati, Gerald. 1989. 'Salman Rushdie: Fiction's Embattled Infidel'. In *The New York Times*, 29 January, section 6, 24.

Menon, Meena, and Meera Adarkar. 2004. *One Hundred Years, One Humdred Voices: The Millworkers of Girangaon—An Oral History*. Calcutta: Seagull Books.

Meera, K.R. 2016. *The Gospel of Yudas*. Gurgaon: Penguin Books India.

Metzger, M.J., and A.J. Flanagin. 2013. 'Credibility and Trust of Information in Online Environments: The Use of Cognitive Heuristics'. In *Journal of Pragmatics* 59(Pt B), 210–20.

Mill, John Stuart. (1859) 2002. *On Liberty*. New York: Dover.

———. 1862. 'The Contest in America'. Project Gutenberg eBook, reprinted from *Fraser's Magazine*, February. Available at: http://www.gutenberg.org/files/5123/old/2004-02-conam10h.htm (accessed 21 July 2020).

Milner, Catherine. 2002. 'The Tate Values Excrement More Highly Than Gold'. In *The Telegraph*, 30 June. Available at: http://www.telegraph.co.uk/news/uknews/1398798/The-Tate-values-excrement-more-highly-than-gold.html (accessed 21 July 2020).

Mistry, Rohinton. 1996. *A Fine Balance*. London: Faber & Faber.

Mokashi, D.B. (1964) 1987. *Palkhi: An Indian Pilgrimage*. Translated by Philip C. Engblom and Eleanor Zelliot. Albany, NY: State University of New York Press.

Moncel, Count du. 1882. *The Telephone, the Microphone and the Phonograph*, authorized translation. London: Keegan Paul, Trench & Co.

Mondal, M., L.A. Silva, and F. Benevenuto. 2017. 'A Measurement Study of Hate Speech in Social Media'. In *HT '17: Proceedings of the 28th ACM Conference on Hypertext and Social Media*, Prague, Czech Republic, 4–7 July, 85–94.

Monteith, S., and T. Glenn. 2016. 'Automated Decision-Making and Big Data: Concerns for People with Mental Illness'. In *Current Psychiatry Reports* 18(12), 112.

Moore, M. 2016. *Tech Giants and Civic Power*. London: Centre for the Study of Media, Communication and Power, King's College, University of London.

Mukherjee, Deep. 2019. 'How Pehlu Khan Lynching Case Fell: Family Blames "Poor" Probe'. In *The Indian Express*, 15 August. Available at: https://indianexpress.com/article/india/how-pehlu-khan-alwar-lynching-case-fell-family-blames-poor-probe-5906288/ (accessed 21 July 2020).

Murdoch, Iris. (1992) 2003. *Metaphysics as a Guide to Morals*. London: Vintage.

Murugan, Perumal. 2014. *One Part Woman*. Translated by Aniruddhan Vasudevan from the original *Madhurobhagan* published in 2010. London: Penguin.

Nabokov, Vladimir. 1955. *Lolita*. Paris: Olympia Press.

Narayan, Nayantara. 2015. 'Kalburgi's Scholarship Got Him into Trouble with Lingayats, and with Hindutva Forces Too'. In *Scroll*, 31 August.

Nayak, N. Dinesh. 2015. 'Kannada Writer Was at the Centre of Controversies'. In *The Hindu*, 31 August. Available at: http://www.thehindu.com/news/kannada-writer-was-at-the-centre-of-controversies/article7597511.ece (accessed 21 July 2020).

New Statesman and Nation. 1931. 'Brevities on Books'. 5 December.

NDTV. 2018. 'Editors Guild Condemns Government Order on Fake News: Full Statement'. In *NDTV*, 3 April. Available at: https://www.ndtv.com/india-news/editors-guild-condemns-government-order-on-fake-news-full-statement-1832384 (accessed 21 July 2020).

Nietzsche, Friedrich. (1879–80) 1913. *Human, All-Too-Human: A Book for Free Spirits: Part Two*. Translated by Paul V. Cohn. New York: The MacMillan Company.

Noelle-Neumann, E. 1974. 'The Spiral of Silence—A Theory of Public Opinion'. In *Journal of Communication* 24(2), 43–51.

O'Brien, Edna. (2012) 2013. *Country Girl*. London: Faber & Faber.

O'Neil, C. 2017. *Weapons of Math Destruction: How Big Data Increases Inequality and Threatens Democracy*. New York: Broadway Books.

Onions, C.T., ed. 1996. *Oxford Dictionary of English Etymology*. With the assistance of G.W.S. Friedrichsen and R.W. Burchfield. Oxford: Oxford University Press.

Online Tamil Poetry. 2018. 'Kurunthokai-157'. 21 March. Available at: https://oldtamilpoetry.com/2018/03/21/kurunthokai-157/ (accessed 21 July 2020).

Ovid (Publius Ovidius Naso). 2003. *Tristia: Book Two*. Translated by A. S. Kline. Available at: http://www.poetryintranslation.com/PITBR/Latin/OvidTristiaBkTwo.htm (accessed 21 July 2020).

Page, Norman. 1987. *E.M. Forster*. Houndmills, Hants.: Macmillan.

Pandey, Neelam. 2018. 'After Darwin, MoS of HRD Targets Newton'. In *Hindustan Times*, 28 February, 1.

Parekh, Bhikhu. 1989a. 'The Holy Text and the Moral Void'. In *New Statesman and Society*, 22 March.

———. 1989b. 'Rushdie and the British Press'. In *Social Studies Review*, November, 44.

Patnaik, Prabhat. 1993. 'The Fascism of Our Times'. In *Social Scientist*, 21(3–4), 69–77.

Patole, Shahu. 2015. *Anna He Apoornabrahma*. Aurangabad: Janshakti Vachak Chalval.

Pawar, Daya. 2015. *Baluta*. Translated by Jerry Pinto. Delhi: Speaking Tiger.

Pawar, Urmila. 2015. *Weave of Life: A Dalit Woman's Memoirs*. Translated by Maya Pandit. Kolkata: Bhatkal & Sen.

Pawel, Ernst. (1984) 1992. *The Nightmare of Reason: A Life of Franz Kafka*. New York: Farrar, Straus & Giroux.

Piper, John. 1984. 'The Man'. In *The Sunday Times*, 20 May.

Piper, Myfanwy. 1984. 'The Game of Social Comment'. In *The Times*, 30 October.

Plato. 1956. *Great Dialogues of Plato*. Translated by W.H.D. Rouse. New York: Mentor.

Popper, Karl. 1945. *The Open Society and Its Enemies*. London: Routledge & Kegan Paul.

Primo. 2017. 'Peer-Reviewed Instructional Materials Online Database'. Available at: http://primodb.org (accessed 21 July 2020).

Pryce-Jones, Alan. 1931. 'Review'. In *The London Mercury*, December, 202.

Quiller-Couch, Sir Arthur, ed. (1900) 1939. *Oxford Book of English Verse 1250-1918*. New edition. Oxford: Oxford University Press.

Ramanathan, Ramu. 2012. *3 Sakina Manzil and Other Plays*. Edited by Lakshmi Chandra. Hyderabad: Orient Blackswan.

Ramm, Benjamin. 2017. 'The Writers Who Defied Soviet Censors'. In *BBC News*, 24 July. Available at: http://www.bbc.com/culture/story/20170724-the-writers-who-defied-soviet-censors (accessed 21 July 2020).

Réage, Pauline. (1954) 2013. *The Story of O*. Translated by Sabine d'Estree. New York: Ballantine.

Rees-Mogg, William. 1967. 'Who Breaks a Butterfly on a Wheel?' In *The Times*, 1 July, a scan of the editorial is available on *It's Only Rock'n Roll [sic]: The Rolling Stones Fan Club*. Available at: https://www.iorr.org/talk/read.php?1,1755802,1756208 (accessed 21 July 2020).

Reips, U.D., and U. Matzat. 2016. 'New Internet Myths: No Truth in a Postfactual World?' In *International Journal of Internet Science* 11(1), 1–7.

Ros, Amanda McKittrick. 1933. *Fumes of Formation*. Belfast: Carswell & Son.

Ross, Alan. 1984. 'Magical Material'. In *The Times Literary Supplement*, 9 November.

Roy, Arundhati. 1997. *The God of Small Things*. London: Flamingo.

Rushdie, Salman. (1988) 1989. *The Satanic Verses*. London: Viking Penguin.

———. 1989. 'Between God and Devil'. In *The Bookseller*, 31 March, 1151.

———. (2002) 2003. *Step across This Line: Collected Non-fiction 1992–2002*. London: Vintage.

Sacks, Harvey, Emanuel A. Schegloff, and Gail Jefferson. 1974. 'A Simplest Systematics for the Organization of Turn-Taking for Conversation'. In *Language* 50(4), 696–735.

Sahgal, Nayantara. 2015. 'The Unmaking of India: Why Writer Nayantara Sahgal Is Returning Her Sahitya Akademi Award'. In *Scroll.in*, 6 October. Available at: https://scroll.in/article/760247/the-unmaking-of-india-why-writer-nayantara-sahgal-is-returning-her-sahitya-akademi-award (accessed 21 July 2020).

Santayana, George. (1905–6) 2017. *The Life of Reason*. CreateSpace Independent Publishing Platform.

Satchidanandan, K. 2015. 'They Feared His Words: A Tribute to M.M. Kalburgi'. In *Indian Cultural Forum*, 21 October. Available at: http://indianculturalforum.in/2015/10/21/a-tribute-to-m-m-kalburgi/ (accessed 21 July 2020).

Schegloff, Emanuel A., and Harvey Sacks. 1973. 'Opening Up Closings'. In *Semiotica* 8(4), 289–327.

Shahid Ali, Agha. 2000. 'Farewell'. In *The Country without a Post Office: Poems 1991–1995*. New Delhi: Ravi Dayal.

Shelley, Percy Bysshe. 1840. 'A Defence of Poetry'. In *Essays, Letters from Abroad, Translations and Fragments*, Vol. 1. Edited by Mrs Shelley. London: Edward Moxon, 1–57.

Shirky, C. 2008. *Here Comes Everybody: The Power of Organising without Organisations*. London: Penguin.

Shklovsky, Viktor. (1917) 2017. 'Art as Technique'. Translated by Lee T. Lemon and Marion J. Reis. In *Literary Theory: An Anthology*, 3rd edition. Edited by Julie Rivkin and Michael Ryan. Chichester, West Sussex: John Wiley & Sons, 8–14.

Shneiderman, B. 2016. 'Opinion: The Dangers of Faulty, Biased, or Malicious Algorithms Requires Independent Oversight'. In *Proceedings of the National Academy of Sciences of the United States of America* 29 November, 113(48), 538–40.

Silverman, C. 2016. 'This Analysis Shows How Viral Fake Election News Stories Outperformed Real News on Facebook'. In *Buzzfeed.com*, 16 November. Available at: https://www.buzzfeed.com/craigsilverman/viral-fake-election-news-outperformed-real-news-on-facebook (accessed 21 July 2020).

Sjeklocha, Paul, and Igor Mead. 1967. *Unofficial Art in the Soviet Union*. Berkeley and Los Angeles: University of California Press.

Smith, David, and Lauren Gambino. 2017. 'Republican Fears Mount after Trump's White House Cull'. In *The Observer*, 30 July.

Speaking of Siva. 1973 Edited and translated by A.K. Ramanujan. Harmondsworth, Middx.: Penguin.

Speed, E., and R. Mannion. 2017. 'The Rise of Post-Truth Populism in Pluralist Liberal Democracies: Challenges for Health Policy'. In *International Journal of Health Policy and Management* 6(5), 249–51.

St John-Stevas, Norman. 1984. 'John Betjeman—This Most English of Poets'. In *Sunday Express*, 20 May.

Stamp, Gavin. 1984. 'John Betjeman'. In *The Spectator*, 26 May.

Stern, Ulrike. 2001. 'Verbrannt und verboten: Erich Kästner und das Berlin der Nazizeit'. In *Das literarische Berlin im 20. Jahrhundert*. Edited by Silvio Vietta. Stuttgart: Reclam, 119–33.

Stubley, Eleanor V., ed. 2008. *Compositional Crossroads: Music, McGill, Montreal*. Montreal, QC, and Kingston, ON: McGill-Queens UP, 221.

Sunday Times, The. 2004. 'I Could Have Done That! But I Didn't'. 24 October. Available at: https://www.thetimes.co.uk/article/i-could-have-done-that-but-i-didnt-923vldbtjff (accessed 21 July 2020).

Surendran, C.P. 2006. *An Iron Harvest*, New Delhi: IndiaInk.

Sutherland, John. (1982) 1983. *Offensive Literature: Decensorship in Britan, 1960–1982*. Totowa, NJ: Barnes & Noble.

Tagore, Rabindranath. n.d. *Gitanjali*, 35 (Tagore's own translation). In *Poetry Foundation*. Available at: https://www.poetryfoundation.org/poems/45668/gitanjali-35 (accessed 21 July 2020).

Tate. n.d. 'Carl Andre, "Equivalent VIII", 1966'. Available at: http://www.tate.org.uk/art/artworks/andre-equivalent-viii-t01534 (accessed 21 July 2020).

Taylor, Brandon. 2014. 'Picasso and the Psychoanalysts'. In *Ugliness: The Non-Beautiful in Art and Theory*. Edited by Andrei Pop and Mechtild Widrich. London & New York: I.B. Tauris, 49–68.

Tendulkar, Vijay. 2003. *Collected Plays*. New Delhi: Oxford University Press.

Times, The. 1984a. 'Betjeman Buried at His Favourite Cornish Church'. 23 May.

———. 1984b. 'Betjeman Obituary'. 21 May, 14.

———. 1984c. 'Landmarks of a Campaigning Poet Laureate'. In *The Times*, 21 May.

———. 1984d. 'True Laureate'. 21 May.

Tharoor, Shashi. 1996. 'Mixing Pain with Hope'. In *India Today*, 15 March 1996.

Thucydides. 1954. *The Peloponnesian War*. Translated by Rex Warner. Harmondsworth, Middx.: Penguin.

Todd, Bella. 2016. 'Marianne Faithfull Talks Heroin, The Rolling Stones and 60s London'. In *Time Out*, 1 February. Available at: https://www.timeout.com/london/music/marianne-faithfull-interview (accessed 21 July 2020).

Toronto Globe and Mail. 1984. 'Betjeman Obituary'. 21 May, 37.

Torres, Louis, and Michelle Marder Kamhi. 2000. *What Art Is: The Esthetic Theory of Ayn Rand*. Chicago & La Salle, IL: Open Court.

Trilling, Lionel. 1972. *Sincerity and Authenticity*. Cambridge, MA: Harvard University Press.

Tusiani, Joseph. (1960) 1961. 'Introduction'. In *The Complete Poems of Michelangelo*. Translated by J. Tusiani. London: Peter Owen.

United Nations Human Rights. (1948) n.d. 'Universal Declaration of Human Rights'. Available at: https://www.ohchr.org/EN/UDHR/Documents/UDHR_Translations/eng.pdf (accessed 21 July 2020).

Valmiki, Omprakash. 2009. *Joothan*. Delhi: Radhakrishan Prakashan.

van Gulik, R.H. (1961) 1974. *Sexual Life in Ancient China*. Leiden: E.J. Brill.

Varier, T.V. Eachara. 2004. *Memories of a Father*. Translated by Neelan. Hong Kong: Asian Human Rights Commission.

Visaji, Vikram. 2016. 'M.M. Kalburgi, the Tireless Scholar and Fearless Critic'. In *Words Matter: Writings against Silence*. Edited by K. Satchidanandan. New Delhi: Viking Penguin, 71–9.

Vishal, Anoothi. 2016. *Mrs. L.C.'s Table: Stories about Kayasth Food and Culture*. Gurgaon, Haryana: Hachette India.

Vlachos, Helen. 1970. *House Arrest*. London: André Deutsch.

Wain, John. 1961. 'John Betjeman'. In *The Observer Review*.

'Walter'. 2017. *My Secret Life*, 11 volumes. Edited by S.F. Renarde and S.F. Leather. London: Treefrog Publishing.

Warraq, Ibn. (2004) 2010. 'Apostasy, Human Rights, Religion, and Belief: New Threats to Freedom of Opinion and Expression. In his *Virgins? What Virgins? and Other Essays*. Amherst, NY: Prometheus Books, 321–9.

———. (2009) 2010. 'On Becoming English'. In his *Virgins? What Virgins? and Other Essays*. 15–36.

Washington Post, The. 1984. 'Betjeman Obituary'. 20 May, C10.

Waugh, Auberon. 1984. 'Is Trifle Sufficient?' In *The Spectator*, 26 May.

Werner, Christoph. 2019. *Lifting the Iron Curtain: Tales of a Bygone Country*. Hamburg: tredition.

White, Andrew. 1965. *Thomas Mann*. Edinburgh and London: Oliver & Boyd.

White, R.W. 2016. *Interactions with Search Systems*. New York: Cambridge University Press.

White, R.W., and E. Horvitz. 2009. 'Cyberchondria: Studies of the Escalation of Medical Concerns in Web Search'. In *ACM Transactions on Information Systems (TOIS)* 27(4), 23.

Whur, Cornelius. 1845. *Gratitude's Offering*. Norwich: Jarrold & Sons.

Wikipedia. n.d. 'Aathichoodi'. Available at: https://en.wikipedia.org/wiki/Aathichoodi (accessed 21 July 2020).

———. n.d. 'Alexandr Solzhenitsyn'. Available at: https://en.wikipedia.org/wiki/Aleksandr_Solzhenitsyn (accessed 21 July 2020).

———. n.d. 'Anne Desclos'. Available at: https://en.wikipedia.org/wiki/Anne_Desclos (accessed 21 July 2020).

———. n.d. 'Artist's Shit'. Available at: https://en.wikipedia.org/wiki/Artist%27s_Shit (accessed 21 July 2020).

———. n.d. 'Bücherverbrennung 1933 in Deutschland'. Available at: https://de.wikipedia.org/wiki/B%C3%BCcherverbrennung_1933_in_Deutschland#Die_verfolgten_Autoren (accessed 21 July 2020).

———. n.d. 'Erich Kästner'. Available at: https://de.wikipedia.org/wiki/Erich_K%C3%A4stner#Berlin_1933.E2.80.931945 (accessed 21 July 2020).

———. n.d. 'Gauri Lankesh'. Available at: https://en.wikipedia.org/wiki/Gauri_Lankesh (accessed 21 July 2020).

———. n.d. 'Generation Snowflake'. Available at: https://en.wikipedia.org/wiki/Generation_Snowflake (accessed 21 July 2020).

———. n.d. 'Günter Brus'. English and German versions. Available at: https://en.wikipedia.org/wiki/G%C3%BCnter_Brus (accessed 21 July 2020).

———. n.d. 'Hai Rui Dismissed from Office'. Available at: https://en.wikipedia.org/wiki/Hai_Rui_Dismissed_from_Office (accessed 21 July 2020).

———. n.d. 'Helen Vlachos'. Available at: https://en.wikipedia.org/wiki/Helen_Vlachos (accessed 21 July 2020).

———. n.d. 'Kenneth Tynan'. Available at: https://en.wikipedia.org/wiki/Kenneth_Tynan (accessed 21 July 2020).

———. n.d. 'List of Cognitive Biases'. Available at: https://en.wikipedia.org/wiki/List_of_cognitive_biases (accessed 21 July 2020).

———. n.d. 'Mikis Theodorakis'. Available at: https://en.wikipedia.org/wiki/Mikis_Theodorakis#cite_note-47 (accessed 21 July 2020).

———. n.d. 'United States Declaration of Independence' (1776). Available at: https://en.wikipedia.org/wiki/United_States_Declaration_of_Indepe-ndence (accessed 21 July 2020).

Williams, I. 2017. 'China's Internet Crackdown Is Another Step toward "Digital Totalitarian State"'. In *NBC News*, 6 September. Available at: https://www.nbcnews.com/news/china/china-s-internet-crackdown-another-step-toward-digital-totalitarian-state-n798001 (accessed 21 July 2020).

Williams, Tennessee. 1999. *The Glass Menagerie* (first performed 1944, first published 1945). New York: New Directions.

Wineburg, S., S. Grew, J. Breakstone, and T. Ortega. 2016. 'Evaluating Information: The Cornerstone of Civic Online Reasoning'. *Stanford Digital Repository*. Available at: http://purl.stanford.edu/fv751yt5934 (accessed 21 July 2020)

Wittgenstein, Ludwig. (1953) 2009. *Philosophical Investigations*. Translated by G.E.M. Anscombe, P.M.S. Hacker, and Joachim Schulte. Chichester: Wiley-Blackwell.

Wolfsfeld, G., E. Segev, and T. Sheafer. 2013. 'Social Media and the Arab Spring: Politics Comes First'. In *The International Journal of Press/Politics* 18(2), 115–37.

Zhong, Z., T. Wang, and M. Huang. 2017. 'Does the Great Fire Wall Cause Self-Censorship? The Effects of Perceived Internet Regulation and the Justification of Regulation'. In *Internet Research* 27(4), 974–90.

INDEX

Editors and Contributors

Editors

Hilda David is an Associate Professor of English at the Symbiosis College of Arts and Commerce in Pune, India. A novelist, stage director, and teacher, she also coordinates the Centre for Liberal Arts at Symbiosis, where she teaches advanced creative writing. She has been a consultant to the Norwegian Ministry of Foreign Affairs and coordinated and organized the Ibsen Festivals in Pune and Delhi. Dr David was chosen by the English-Speaking Union to represent India at the Shakespeare Workshop in London, UK, in 2008. Her works have been translated into Hindi, Urdu, and Kannada. She is the co-editor, with Francis Jarman, of *India Diversity* (2017).

Francis Jarman taught English, comparative cultural studies, and intercultural communication at Hildesheim University, Germany, until his retirement in 2013. Dr Jarman has taught and lectured in Egypt, Thailand, and Japan as well as at nineteen European universities in fourteen different countries, been a Scholar in Residence at Symbiosis International University, Pune, and a Visiting Professor at The American College, Madurai, India. He is a novelist, playwright, and classical numismatist, and the co-editor, with Hilda David, of

India Diversity (2017). His most recent novel is *Cold from Your Breath* (2019).

Contributors

Jane Dryhurst Beckerman grew up in England and in Wales, completed her degree in English literature in Bangor, and taught in London while she worked on a PhD on poets of the 1930s for several years at Cambridge, UK. She then returned to Wales, taught, learned Welsh, obtained an MA in Welsh History, and completed her latest publication, a history of the ancient 'cursing well' on her property.

Jürgen Beneke was, until his retirement, Professor of Applied Linguistics at the University of Hildesheim in Germany. Dr Beneke founded the Intercultural Competence Centre of the Rhineland-Palatinate and is the author of numerous monographs on intercultural topics. He has been a consultant to major industrial enterprises, international airlines, and the armed forces on questions of internationalization and intercultural management, specializing in rhetoric and communication, knowledge management, intercultural communication, intercultural management and organizational development, and language teaching in vocational education.

Sanjukta Dasgupta is a poet, short story writer, critic, and translator, as well as Professor of English (and former Head of English and Dean of the Faculty of Arts) at the University of Calcutta, India. Dr Dasgupta's research interests include postcolonial theory and texts, colonial and postcolonial women's writing, migration and diaspora studies, literature and film, women and/in Indian films, translation studies, and creative writing.

Joachim Griesbaum was born in Lahr in the Black Forest, Germany, in 1971. He obtained his doctorate in information science in 2006 from the University of Konstanz and joined the University of Hildesheim in 2008. Professor Griesbaum's research interests include information behaviour, social media, e-learning, knowledge management, and online marketing.

Githa Hariharan is a distinguished writer and commentator. Her first novel, *The Thousand Faces of Night* (1993), was awarded the Commonwealth Writers' Prize, and this and other works of fiction and non-fiction by her have been translated into several languages. In 1995, she challenged the Hindu Minority and Guardianship Act as being discriminatory against women. The landmark case, *Githa Hariharan and Another v Reserve Bank of India and Another*, led to a Supreme Court judgement in 1999 on guardianship. She is also a Founder Member of the Indian Writers Forum (www.indiancultural-forum.in). For more on her work, see www.githahariharan.com.

Aruni Kashyap, a poet, novelist (*The House with a Thousand Stories*, 2013), and translator, writes in both Assamese and English and teaches creative writing at the University of Georgia in the United States of America. His poems presented in this volume are a stark reminder of the many (not only in India) whose voices are not heard or are heard too late. As Kashyap himself says in a *Tribune* interview, 'I am a political writer. I am interested in the many ways in which human rights intersect with literature and storytelling. My fiction is shaped by Assamese politics, aesthetics, and literary traditions—both oral and textual. I use these to write about fundamental aspects of contemporary Indian reality that have been ignored by Indian English fiction for a long time.'

Peer Khan is a discreet penname used by this writer only for poetry. Khan is presently working on a sequence of sonnets reflecting the diversity of India, its cultural, spiritual, and linguistic richness, and its social complexity.

Sashi Kumar is a writer, academic, film director, and media personality. He founded India's first regional satellite TV channel, *Asianet*, and founded and chairs the Media Development Foundation, a public trust that set up and runs the Asian College of Journalism in Chennai, India, of which he is currently the Chairman.

M. Mohankumar was a member of the Indian Administrative Service (IAS) and retired as Chief Secretary to the Government of Kerala. He has published eight volumes of poetry and a collection of short stories.

Perumal Murugan is the author of novels, poems, and short stories, a university teacher (Professor at Government Arts College, Attur, Tamil Nadu, India), and scholar. He is widely regarded as the outstanding writer of his generation in Tamil. His novel *One Part Woman* (2010) caused a storm of outrage among caste and Hindu religious groups, culminating in the local authorites bullying him into issuing an apology and agreeing to withdraw all copies of the book; he announced that he was going to give up writing. But in July 2016 the Madras High Court ruled strongly in the author's favour, dismissing the case against *One Part Woman*, and directed the state to offer artists and writers better protection when they came under attack.

Kingshuk Nag is one of India's pre-eminent journalists. Since 1993, he has worked for *The Times of India* as its Business News Chief, based in Delhi and Bangalore, in which role he brought business news to the front page in the wake of economic liberalization, and then as Resident Editor from 2000 in Ahmedabad and from 2005 to 2016 in Hyderabad, India. In his Ahmedabad post, Nag was witness to the Bhuj earthquake, the installation of Narendra Modi as Chief Minister, and the violent events of 2002. He received the Prem Bhatia Award for Outstanding Political Reporting & Analyses of the Year in 2002 for his 'courageous reporting of [the] Gujarat riots'. Among his publications are biographies of Netaji Subhas Chandra Bose, Atal Bihari Vajpayee, and Narendra Modi.

Dipti Nagpaul-D'Souza is Assistant Editor—Features at *The Indian Express*. She started out as a film journalist and soon began to explore society through the prism of cinema. Today, she writes on socio-political issues, discriminatory practices in gender and caste, as well as about Mumbai—the city that has been her home and muse for over a decade. She is a recipient of the prestigious Ramnath Goenka Excellence in Journalism Award (2011) and was also chosen for the Asia Journalism Fellowship programme in 2016.

Manjula Padmanabhan is an author, playwright, and cartoonist.

Bhikhu Parekh, born in 1935 in Gujarat, is an eminent political scientist. He studied at the University of Bombay, India, and the London

School of Economics and Political Science, UK, where he received his PhD in 1966, before going on to build a distinguished academic career in Britain and India. Between 1981 and 1984 he was Vice Chancellor of the Maharaja Sayajirao University of Baroda, Gujarat, India. He served on the Commission for Racial Equality (CRE) and was chairman of the Commission on the Future of Multi-Ethnic Britain, whose findings (2000) are widely known as the 'Parekh Report'. Since 2000, Professor Parekh has sat, as Lord Parekh, as a member of the upper house of the British Parliament, the House of Lords.

Premila Paul until her retirement taught literature in English at The American College, Madurai, India, and has published on Indian literature and gender issues. Currently Associate Director of the renowned Study Centre for Indian Literature in English and Translation (SCILET), Dr Paul is one of its three founding members.

Jerry Pinto is a Goa-born, Mumbai-based, prize-winning Indian writer of poetry, prose, and children's fiction in English, as well as a journalist.

Ramu Ramanathan is a playwright, director, and editor based in Mumbai, India, a city that he both loves and loathes. He admits: 'I have perhaps penned more plays than I should have,' and when asked about the publication of a volume of eight of them, he joked that he had no idea what the book would achieve, except that it might increase the number of PhD theses on Indian English theatre.

R. Raj Rao is a poet, playwright, novelist, academic, critic, and biographer. Dr Rao was formerly Professor of English and Head of the English Department at Pune University, India, and is a well-known gay rights activist. His latest book is *Criminal Love? Queer Theory, Culture, and Politics in India* (2017).

Nayantara Sahgal is a distinguished writer, feminist, and political commentator. By virtue of the family to which she belongs she was ideally placed to observe the birth and development of the Indian nation. Her father died in prison during the Independence struggle, her mother had a dazzling diplomatic career as ambassador to (among others) the Soviet Union, the USA, the United Kingdom (UK), and the United Nations, and her uncle, Jawaharlal Nehru, was the first Prime Minister of India. Despite her membership of the Nehru family, her independent critical sense led to a serious falling out with her cousin Indira Gandhi as her government became increasingly autocratic. Nayantara Sahgal was associated with the founding of the People's Union for Civil Liberties (PUCL), and served as its Vice-President in the 1980s. Her published works include ten novels, a collection of short stories, memoirs, and collections of letters. Among her distinctions are the Sahitya Akademi Award, the Sinclair Prize, the Commonwealth Writers' Prize, and an Honorary Doctorate of Letters from the University of Leeds, UK. She has held Fellowships at the Bunting Institute of Radcliffe College, University of Massachusetts; the Woodrow Wilson International Center for Scholars, Washington DC; and the National Humanities Center, North Carolina, and in 1990 she was elected to the American Academy of Arts and Sciences, Cambridge, USA.

Christoph Werner is a German novelist who was born and raised in the German Democratic Republic, that is, in communist East Germany. Before his retirement, he taught at various universities in East and West Germany, working in the fields of technical English, translation, and English teacher training. Among Dr Werner's publications are a volume of short stories and four novels, the most recent being *Paulus Luther* (2015), which was published in the USA in 2017 titled *Shadows of My Father: The Memoirs of Martin Luther's Son*. Christoph Werner lives in Weimar, Germany.